Political Transition and Development Imperatives in India

Political Transition and Development Imperatives in India

Editors

Ranabir Samaddar
Suhit K. Sen

Routledge
Taylor & Francis Group
LONDON NEW YORK NEW DELHI

First published 2012 in India
by Routledge
912 Tolstoy House, 15–17 Tolstoy Marg, Connaught Place, New Delhi 110 001

Simultaneously published in the UK
by Routledge
2 Park Square, Milton Park, Abingdon, OX14 4RN

Routledge is an imprint of the Taylor & Francis Group, an informa business

© 2012 Mahanirban Calcutta Research Group

Typeset by
Star Compugraphics Private Limited
5, CSC, Near City Apartments
Vasundhara Enclave
Delhi 110 096

Printed and bound in India by
Avantika Printers Private Limited
194/2, Ramesh Market, Garhi, East of Kailash,
New Delhi 110 065

British Library Cataloguing-in-Publication Data
A catalogue record of this book is available from the British Library

ISBN: 978-0-415-52289-2

This book is printed on ECF environment-friendly paper manufactured from unconventional and other raw materials sourced from sustainable and identified sources.

Contents

Acknowledgements

With two companion volumes on the present history of governance in India, Calcutta Research Group (CRG) completes almost a decade-long study of some of the specific features of post-colonial democracy, particularly in India. In course of these years we have picked up themes of autonomy, justice, and governance. Our work began with investigation into the role and function of autonomy in Indian democracy. This was followed by research on popular perceptions of social justice, law and its limits in delivering justice, and the ways in which marginalities have produced demands for justice. Now, in the two volumes (*Political Transition and Development Imperatives in India* and *New Subjects and New Governance in India*) we shift our focus to the specifics of post-colonial governance, the developmental paradigm of governance, and its interface with popular claims, rights, and justice. Autonomy, justice, and governance — these are three of the fundamental areas of democratic theory and research which, we felt, have been neglected in traditional historico–political studies of democracy. In this sense these are different from the usual studies of civil society, elections, parliament, bureaucracy, and social capacity for democratic function that crowd the field of democratic studies. These are also different from studies of individualism, liberty, and freedom. But hopefully, together these volumes will throw new light on some of the less discussed aspect of Indian democracy.

These researches were carried out all through in a dialogic manner. A large number of people — scholars and non-scholars — participated in workshops, dialogues, and meetings held in different parts of the country. Several institutions collaborated with the CRG. Besides the dialogues and workshops, the research drew inspiration from the wide-ranging discussion in the Third Critical Studies Conference (Kolkata, 2009) held on the theme 'Empires, States, and Migration', and the two symposia on 'Bio-politics, Development, and Governance' (Kolkata, 2010).

The contributors to the two volumes are indebted to each other as much as to the discussants and other participants in the dialogues. Our collective thanks are, in particular, to Itty Abraham,

S. Anandhi, Sahana Basavapatna, Sibaji Pratim Basu, Sudeep Basu, Parthasarathi Banerjee, Paula Banerjee, Pradip Kumar Bose, Subhas Ranjan Chakraborty, Sabyasachi Basu Ray Chaudhury, Dwaipayan Bhattachrya, Indira Chowdhury, Bidhan Kanti Das, Samir Kumar Das, Rajarshi Dasgupta, Vivek Dhareshwar, Pallab Kumar Goswami, Ruchira Goswami, Suresh K.C., R. Limbadri, Manabi Majumdar, Deepak Kumar Mishra, Bishnu Mohapatra, Amites Mukherjee, Dulali Nag, Arun Kumar Patnaik, Pradip Phanjoubam, Prasanta Ray, and G. Krishna Reddy.

The Ford Foundation supported the research and dialogue programme on governance. It also supported the past two programmes on autonomy and social justice. Our thanks to Stephen Solnick, Representative of the Ford Foundation in India, and in particular to Bishnu Mohapatra, Programme Executive, Ford Foundation, who gave us advice and interesting ideas all through the three research programmes.

Without the members of the CRG team none of these would, of course, have been possible. We take this opportunity to thank each and every member of the CRG team and the CRG network, especially Sutirtha Bedajna and Mithilesh Kumar, who contributed substantially to the production of the book.

The assistance of the Ford Foundation in publication of the volume is hereby acknowledged. The views expressed, however, are not necessarily those of the Ford Foundation.

Introduction

Ranabir Samaddar and Suhit K. Sen

This volume of articles seeks to explore what we are designating the first transition in India. It collectively seeks to explore, however, not just the transition from colonial to constitutional rule in the country but also the configurations of power and legitimacies that emerged in constitutional India, with an eye particularly on the developmentalist structures and paradigms that both provided the context for the transition and the establishment of the post-colonial state and proved central to the project. In this context a raft of ideas are interrogated — important among them are the idea of liberal constitutionalism itself, the spaces it provides for rights and claims, the assumptions it makes about citizenship and its appurtenant duties, the assumptions it further makes about what it can, or has to, become in the particular (exceptional?) context of India, and so on.

It is important to note at the outset — and this will become clearer both in the course of this Introduction as well as the volume — that any enquiry into governance and the structures of government has to begin with the issue of this first transition and that of development. From a historical perspective, those who managed the transition from the colonial to a constitutional regime had to deal with one pre-eminent problem: how to acquire legitimacy for the new state. This legitimacy could not be derived in any unproblematic way from the legitimacy of the Congress as the bearer of the nationalist movement mainly because in its transition from a movement to a ruling party the Congress had to now dispense with all kinds of claims that actually ran against the idea that the state was the supremely legitimate and superordinate fount of sovereignty and legitimate political power. Some of the arguments that had to be engaged with and negated in the course of crafting the state came from the Gandhian ideological strand and some from populist, rank-and-file ideas of a more direct form of participatory democracy. At the heart of what became the project of creating the legitimacy of the state, as will become clearer, was the idea of development. The questions we have posed must, therefore, be posed in this context.

These questions are posed in some of the articles, most starkly the final one by Ratan Khasnabis, in the context of the political economy of India. That is to say, this volume seeks to situate particular questions in the more general frame of how society, power, and the economy were reconfigured during and since the first transition, if at all they were. This entails, of course, thinking about, implicitly or explicitly, whether there was any fundamental transformation in the balance of power in politics, society, and the economy in the process of the transition, and if there was, what its lineaments were.

From whichever disciplinary vantage the question of transition is viewed, one question has to be addressed, and it has been in a number of ways; a multitude of judgments have been delivered. This question concerns the issue of continuity and change, to use a well-worn phrase. In other words, how much and what subsisted of the colonial regime, especially of government and governance, through the transition, into the constitutional order. In one very real sense, this question is something of a red herring because it cannot be answered with any simplistic reference, for instance, to the similitude between the Government of India Act of 1935 and the constitution of independent India, or, for instance, to the continuities in the bureaucratic structures through which both colonial and constitutional India were governed. We would certainly argue, emphatically, that the meanings of legality and constitutionalism changed fundamentally as India traversed the distance between colonial and constitutional rule, not least because there was one fundamental change: the meanings of law and governance itself were radically transfigured as the meanings of sovereignty and legitimacy themselves changed and intruded into the political life of the 'nation', even though there is no easy way in which these transformations can be read. Meanings of most of the foundational ideas of the new nation-state were protean and fundamental concepts were always open to multiple interpretations and manipulations through complex processes of contestations and conflicts as, especially, the articles by Ranabir Samaddar, Benjamin Zachariah, Suhit K. Sen, and Kalpana Kannabiran attempt to demonstrate.

We shall return to the question of the transition later. What a number of the articles in this volume also seek to do is to locate within the configurations of the emerging state what the limits of rights were and what citizenship meant in the context of the ideological aspirations of the political managers of the new state. Like the question of transition, these are not untroubled problems. We could well begin with an important proposition made by Zachariah. It is not our intention to recapitulate the article here. We would do well, however, to consider the Indian state's project of first defining what the nation itself was or should have been or was going to become and, therefore, what citizenship itself could be or could be limited to being. One of the non-negotiable tenets of the Nehruvian elite state managers was that India would not be a 'confessional' state and, therefore, neither was its own identity or the identities of its citizens to be derived from ascriptive locations or kinships, imagined or otherwise. Quite on the contrary, these identities were to conform to some universal, liberal-humanistic template. Nehru's ideas, of course, were perhaps too complex to be reduced to this formula. Nevertheless, this seems to be an admissible statement about state ideology in the first flush of independence. This ideological project was, however, difficult to execute precisely because it thinned down the idea of identity to the extent that barely any vestige of an identity remained. It was difficult to imagine within this ideological frame what being Indian would or could mean and how that was different from being, say, an Eskimo in Alaska or a Polynesian in Hawaii. So the big problem was how the identity of Indianness could be fleshed out.

One of the important ways in which this fleshing out was attempted was through the construction of a kind of civic nationalism, to which the idea of development was central. We shall come to the problems implicit in this project in a bit. For the moment, however, we need to take note of the way in which both the ideas of civic nationalism and development were pitched. What is common to both is a kind of paternalist language in which the sovereign subject/citizen relationship was incessantly reiterated, at least by implication. Thus the voice of the political and 'modernising' social elite can clearly be heard enjoining and not infrequently hectoring the 'masses' about proper social conduct, both in the statute books, especially the constitution,

and in quotidian social and political life. The burden of this admonitory advice was that the masses must forsake the medieval/
feudal remnants and the detritus of tradition from their collective and individual, public and private lives and embrace the
values of 'modernity'. What was to be gained from modernity's
embrace was development. It was implicit in the arguments of
the elite state managers that material development would both
be the payoff and would in turn increasingly help in the fitness
of time to make the nation and its citizens more modern, less
tied to the vexing communitarian (communal) identities of the
medieval past. It went without saying, of course, that what development meant and how it was to be disseminated would be
decided in some rarefied social and political and spheres. The largely illiterate and unsophisticated masses would have no role to
play in shaping the discourses or forms of development or how it
was to be propagated. In other words, they were to be its passive
recipients and beneficiaries. This deeply problematic idea has
been noted in diverse spheres in the articles contained in this
volume — for instance, those by Zachariah, Kalpana Kannabiran,
and Swarna Rajagopal — and elsewhere. Here, we refer not to development in its strictly economic sense but in the broader sense
of modernist progress. The foregoing is not necessarily a critique
of modernity or its claims to universality or a celebration of what
we may unsatisfactorily designate pre-modern. It is merely to set
the stage to a critique of the Indian elite's statist project in the
transition from colonial to constitutional rule. Before embarking
on that, it is to be noted that the foundations of this statist project was underpinned, as Samaddar discusses at length, by a
juridico-political discourse that celebrated the sovereignty and
puissance of the state. It was only by establishing the legal sovereignty of the state that, we may say, democracy and the regime
of rights and claims could be established. The basis of this claim,
too, was the universalism of modernity. There is an additional
element to the critique of the overweening claims of the state.
Zachariah forcefully points to the conflation of nation and
state in his discussion of civic nationalism as the alternative to
confessional nationalism. We may well argue, with Zachariah,
that civic nationalism and developmentalism were the principal ideological manoeuvres through which this conflation was
sought to be consummated to both overcome the problem of
identity and to aggrandise the claims of the state over the citizen

and establish it at the commanding heights of the polity as well as the economy, as Samaddar notes as well. We may also note that this led to the establishment of a state-led political system that has been increasingly exposed as formally representative without being participatory.

Before going into the details of the critique of the transition, however, we must take note, somewhat by way of digression, of one of the articles in this volume that seems to go against the grain of some of the arguments outlined above. Ashutosh Kumar shows, in his study of election manifestos and campaigns, a curious gap between the perceptions of political parties and voters. Kumar points to two interrelated phenomena. First, that in the liberalisation era of the 1990s and beyond, while the electorate seemed to be deeply suspicious of the new policy predicated on the establishment of an economy that would be increasingly market-driven, with its concomitant widening of economic and social disparities, the two main political parties, the BJP and the Congress, persisted in their manifestos in extolling liberalisation and the market. Kumar also shows, however, that when political parties, more or less across the spectrum, hit the trail, they did not campaign principally on the basis of any economic or development agenda at all, whether of the 'socialist' or 'market' variety. What they did was seek to mobilise on the basis of the politics of precisely those communitarian and communal identities that the Nehruvian elites had so vociferously decried. Is this, then, an obvious contradiction? Clearly, it is not. It is a reflection of two problems with the project of modernisation on which the post-independence elite had embarked. The first, of course, was that it comprehended dimly, if at all, the true relationship between state and society, which arose all too often from misapprehensions about the character of both. In other words, the 'constructors' of both the nation and the state trusted too uncritically the power of law to remodel society in their image. This arose, second, out of an inability to grasp the idea of democracy as something more than a merely formal and juridical construct, which led to incomplete apprehensions about the political relationship between 'leaders' and the 'masses' and how it was embedded in the political economy of the post-independence regime. Sen's article tries to explore, in a limited context, the wide disparities in ideas about sovereignty and legitimacy and power between Congress leaders and party workers in the immediate aftermath of the transfer of power.

As Zachariah points out in his article in this volume, and others have elsewhere, the problem with constructing a nation-state on a system of legitimation that invoked a civic nationalism at the heart of which was some kind of developmentalism was not merely that it established a paternalist relationship between the elite political managers of the state and the 'masses', the *tabula rasa* on which the development story was to be written. Perhaps more crucial was the problem that in the so-called Nehruvian socialist model of a mixed economy in which the state would hold the commanding heights, which was no variant of socialism at all in the first place but rather a state-enabled variant of arrested capitalist development as Khasnabis points out, the people or 'masses', whose development was purportedly the agenda-setting desideratum, were being asked to make inordinate sacrifices in the present, which in rhetorical terms would be rewarded in some form of afterlife. We would not like to push this metaphor too far. The principal problem with this demand, as hindsight so tragically reminds us, is that the future never really arrived as it has the habit of not conveniently doing. Instead, disparities widened and deprivation intensified, until the age of liberalisation and globalisation buried the fictions of socialism and launched a full-blown capitalist, market-driven economy whose managers did not feel any need even for one fleeting moment to be apologetic about either disparity or deprivation. It is that later trajectory that Khasnabis and Kumar, for instance, document in the fields of the polity and economy.

Rajagopalan and Kannabiran provide us with a different dimension to this story. Rajagopalan's discussion of state policy with regard to female infanticide (and to a lesser extent foeticide) draws attention again to the state–citizen (or state–society) disjuncture that we have been discussing. Her narrative reminds us that even the better meaning interventions of state managers to impose certain normative — liberal — codes on citizens fail not only because of a gap in understanding but also because the presumptions from which these interventions flow often tend to reinforce precisely those presumptions from which the 'problems' themselves flow. In this case, state actions tended to reinforce those frames of reference within which female infanticide was justified. That it often ended up penalising mothers guilty of killing their daughters, who were in many senses victims themselves, without addressing fundamental issues, is another part of the story. Kannabiran demonstrates in detail in her discussion of disability and state policy in relation to it, in the context of constitutional law, how liberal jurisprudence can itself become one of the foundational barriers to liberty. We may add that this may well be one of the intrinsic characteristics of the liberal, constitutional project itself. Kannabiran does end on an optimistic note though, pointing out that the enshrinement of rights in the constitution can itself provide the means of surmounting these barriers.

We think there is one inescapable question, signposted earlier in the Introduction, this and its companion volume raise, and that is: What is the relation between the first transition and the second? Is there a logical connection? We would like to argue, especially in the context of the articles by Khasnabis and Kumar, that there is an ineluctable connection. Let us return to the first transition. It has now become clear, if it had not been clear enough in the first place in the 1950s and 1960s, that there was a massive failure of state action in the Nehru–Indira period not measured by objectives imposed upon these regimes from outside their paradigm, but judged by the objectives stated by the regimes themselves. These failures were across the board — in the sphere of the economy, that is, the failure to address the problem of poverty and disparity; in the sphere of the political system, for instance, the failure to guarantee constitutional provisions regarding freedoms, liberties, and equality before the law; and in the sphere of society, say, the failure to provide the conditions for that modernity and civic, associational citizenship, and nationalism that was at the heart of the 'Nehruvian' project. We would like to highlight, by way of exemplification, one aspect of this failure that we have not referred to make the connection.

One of the conditions, one would have thought, for realising the modernist, liberal project enshrined in the constitution and extolled by the Nehruvian elite would have been the creation of the conditions for its realisation. Surely, the elite would not have thought that a society that was still deeply steeped in tradition and by and large unacquainted with the liberal constitutional, one may even say lawyerly, ethos would rapidly embrace the Nehruvian vision. The lack of both a political and governance underpinning to the modernising ambitions of the post-colonial ruling class was, in fact, to be exposed in multiple ways several decades down the line with what is now understood to be the broadening and deepening of electoral participation beginning with the plebiscitary initiatives of the early Indira Gandhi period and helped on in no uncertain fashion by the entry into the political arena of regional 'backward caste' groups, especially in the post-Mandal period. It would be very easy to overstate this case, as has often been done in both academic and other literature. While it can hardly be argued that either of these eras marked a fundamental break from the immediate post-independence period or pointed India in the direction of a political system and culture that by incorporating into them large doses of vernacular styles negated some kind of Nehruvian consensus, it is possible to argue that they did strengthen a move away from the cloistered liberal vision of the Nehruvian kind.

Without bringing up the question of teleological readings of what democracy means or must mean, it is by now self-evident that within the frame of reference of the Nehruvian vision itself, or, in other words, the first transition, this was a failure of both political leadership and governance. Both these failures, as we have argued, arose from the cracks in the transitional regime itself — most notably the one between the profession of socialism and a political system committed to social justice and poverty eradication through a mixed economy with the state holding the commanding heights and the reality of a liberal constitutional state promoting capitalist development by building infrastructure and protecting most often 'inefficient' domestic industry through protectionist measures and a strategy of import substitution. At the heart of this, too, there was the conflation of nation and state and the valorisation of the latter, which, let us repeat, was in no way incommensurate with striking a capitalist path under the direction of a ruling bloc that combined industrial capitalist and rich peasant interests.

How these failures led to the second transition in the fields of recalibrating economic policy, governance, and the Nehruvian social engineering project which tried to radically recreate subjects and subjectivities will be dealt in greater detail in the companion volume. Its articles probe the state–citizen dialectic in its various forms as also the strategies and techniques of governance to help more clearly understand processes of subjectification.

I

The Juridical–Political Route to Norms of Governance

I

Two Constitutional Tasks: Setting Up the Indian State and the Indian Government

Ranabir Samaddar

Introduction

Though Carl Schmitt has famously remarked that the sovereign is the one who can decide exceptions, modern political societies are born on the basis of two principles, *sovereignty and democracy*, and these two principles are in general — at the same time and by turn — inseparable and in contradiction with each other. For democracy to be effective, it must create a system of law, which will create the power of the demos, stronger than any other power, and therefore stronger than any other force. Yet, in the constitution of this power, this force, *immunity* must function as the building principle, because the saliency of this power must be recognised in the beginning, in silence, in total conformity, and in an un-avowable manner. Therefore there can be endless repetition of the theory of law and endless political rhetoric, but at the moment of its demonstration, sovereignty is silent about claim and legitimacy, it is pure at the moment proper to it, its force showing its character in the decision to take and make exception to any rule that had constituted it in the first place. In India, a prisoner given the death penalty 13 years earlier, Dhananjay Chatterji, died in 2004. When there were endless debates, petitions, and legal arguments against the death penalty and for the right to life guaranteed in Article 21, and appeals therefore that the man be given mercy, the state was silent. When the given hour arrived it simply executed the man. Or, we can recall how the war in Iraq began. When millions came down to the streets appealing that Iraq be spared, the US sovereign power began the war exactly as planned and announced earlier — only in this case the attack was brought forward by 24 hours. In its moment of demonstration sovereignty is, therefore, pure. That is why people say that sovereignty cannot be represented in the sense in which in the 18th century a king could send some other *body* to represent him (his body) in another court; there could be *agents*, but the sovereign remained un-representable. In even the most democratic law making there is thus a silent consensus required to be present at the beginning, that the production of this power must be immune from any exception; if at all there is to be any exception, it is the sovereign who will decide exception. Constitution making, to be successful, therefore claims immunity — immunity from democracy and any particular or individual legality — and it is only through this process that the union of democracy and sovereignty is achieved.

In the historical and temporal thickness of democratic law making in India, from 1946–49, the grounds were those of necessity and unavoidability on the basis of which claims about immunity of the power being built were made. One who represented this juridical logic more than any other was Babasaheb Ambedkar. It was a symbolic situation. The man who opposed any nationalist hegemony during the colonial days and used legal arguments to defend group representation in democratic polities now defended the principles of republicanism, centralism, exceptionality, and juridical absoluteness to characterise the power that was there in a *constituent* form, and now being given a constitutional shape. He was chair of the Drafting Committee, he piloted the difficult proposals, he decided when to stop deliberations and ruthlessly bring out the support and strength that would carry the controversial proposals through. What is, then, intrinsic to the process that builds the legal existence of sovereignty? Can democracy ever come to terms with this experience? Or is this *the* experience with which democracy becomes operational at least at the level of juridical–political reality — the reality of legalities? It will be instructive to study at least some of the occasions when Ambedkar was engaged in building the discourse of a 'sovereign democratic power' that would mark independent India, now free from colonial rule. In this constituted form, sovereignty would represent democracy; parliament and other organs would 'represent sovereignty' to the extent that was possible; sovereignty would decide exceptions, indications of which were to be given in the constitution; and at the end of the whole process the constituted power would accrue more force than the constituent power, because it was now constitutional. No one more than Ambedkar, who had at another level been an ardent advocate of rights and dignity of the Dalits, understood the centrality of the role of the constitution in attaining the union of democracy and sovereignty and giving birth to an awesome power, called the sovereign State of India. Or probably there was a connection between the two levels — that of rights and that of sovereignty, because what was at stake was the legal constitution of a democratic sovereign power — a process that must be immune from any temporary consideration in producing legalities of a political society — these legalities included rights, rule of law, and legal separation of powers. Again, no one more than Ambedkar understood the nature of this double requirement of immunity, of the process (of constituting the sovereign) and the product (the constituted sovereign).

What I am attempting to do here is a difficult task for myself, also for a reader not familiar with the details of constitution making in India, particularly the intense socio-political strains of quarrel, rivalry, battle, and the war of words that had beneath them the social wars going on in the country at the time of transition. In some of the exchange of words I reproduce here it can be seen that the Dalit leader is scoffing at the pretensions of the upper-caste representatives in law making — law making that Ambedkar seems to say is secular and free of all social pretensions; in some cases the Dalit leader is waging his last battle against feudal remnants through trying to erect a sovereign, secular, democratic and republican force pitted against upper-caste, particularistic politics, by way of constructing a universal, *a universal power*, whose other name is sovereignty. It was the last battle, it could be said, that the lower depths were waging within the confines of modernity — therefore the universal power in defence of democracy against feudal, casteist obstacles was the ultimate dream that was now being pursued by constitutional forces. This is how democracy contributes in the making of sovereign power. The reader should follow closely the exchange of words in the Constituent Assembly. At times I have reproduced some lengthy extracts. But it will be good to listen to them attentively to make a judgement of what I argue in this article.

Yet the question remained whether the sovereign power would acquire a logic of its own, overriding the aspirations of dignity, justice, and rights — yes, rights that had called for an existence of a legally constituted sovereign power for their guarantee.

First Stake: Ensuring Juridical Authority of the State

Let us follow the exchange of words that Ambedkar had with T. T. Krishnamachari on 15 November 1948 in course of a discussion on Article 10 of the constitution.

> **A**: I do not think that I am called upon to say anything with regard to amendments Nos. 334, 336 and 337. Such observations, therefore, as I shall make in the course of my speech will be confined to the question of residence about which there has been so much debate and the use of the word "backward" in clause (3) of article 10. My friend Mr. T. T. Krishnamachari, has twitted the Drafting Committee that the Drafting Committee, probably in the interests of some members of that Committee, instead of producing a Constitution, have produced a paradise for lawyers. I am not prepared to say that this Constitution will not give rise to questions, which will involve legal interpretation or judicial interpretation. In fact, I would like to ask Mr. Krishnamachari if he can point out to me any instance of any Constitution in the world which has not been a paradise for lawyers. I would particularly ask him to refer to the vast storehouse of law reports with regard to the Constitution of the United States, Canada and other countries. I am therefore not ashamed at all if this Constitution hereafter for purposes of interpretation is required to be taken to the Federal Court. That is the fate of every Constitution and every Drafting Committee. I shall therefore not labour that point at all.

> Now, with regard to the question of residence: the matter is really very simple and I cannot understand why so intelligent a person as my friend Mr. T. T. Krishnamachari should have failed to understand the basic purpose of that amendment.

> **K**: For the same reason as my Honourable friend had for omitting to put that word originally in the article.

> **A**: I did not quite follow. I shall explain the purpose of this amendment. (It is the feeling of many persons in this House that, since we have established a common citizenship throughout India, irrespective of the local jurisdiction of the provinces and the Indian States, it is only a concomitant thing that residence should not be required for holding a particular post in a particular State because, in so far as you make residence a qualification, you are

really subtracting from the value of a common citizenship which we have established by this Constitution or which we propose to establish by this Constitution. Therefore in my judgement, the argument that residence should not be a qualification to hold appointments under the State is a perfectly valid and a perfectly sound argument.) At the same time, it must be realised that you cannot allow people who are flying from one province to another, from one State to another as mere birds of passage without any roots, without any connection with that particular province, just to come, apply for posts and, so to say, take the plums and walk away. Therefore, some limitation is necessary. It was found, when this matter was investigated, that already today in very many provinces rules have been framed by the provincial governments prescribing a certain period of residence as a qualification for a post in that particular province. Therefore the proposal in the amendment that, although as a general rule residence should not be a qualification, yet some exception might be made, is not quite out of the ordinary. We are merely following the practice, which has been already established in the various provinces. However, what we found was that while different provinces were laying down a certain period as a qualifying period for posts, the periods varied considerably. Some provinces said that a person must be actually domiciled. What that means, one does not know. Others have fixed ten years, some seven years and so on. It was therefore felt that, while it might be desirable to fix a period as a qualifying test, that qualifying test should be uniform throughout India. Consequently, if that object is to be achieved, viz., that the qualifying residential period should be uniform, that object can be achieved only by giving the power to Parliament and not giving it to the local units, whether provinces or States. That is the underlying purpose of this amendment putting down residence as a qualification ...

Now, Sir, to come to the other question which has been agitating the members of this House, *viz.,* the use of the word "backward" in clause (3) of article 10. I should like to begin by making some general observations so that members might be in a position to understand the exact import, the significance and the necessity for using the word "backward" in this particular clause. If members were to try and exchange their views on this subject, they will find that there are three points of view which it is necessary for us to reconcile if we are to produce a workable proposition which will be accepted by all. Of the three points of view, the first is that there shall be equality of opportunity for all citizens. It is the desire of many Members of this House that every individual who is qualified for a particular post should be free to apply for that post, to sit for examinations and to have his qualifications tested so as to determine whether he is fit for the post or not and that there ought to be no limitations, there ought to be no hindrance in the operation of this principle of equality of opportunity. Another view mostly shared by a section of the House is that, if this principle is to be operative — and it ought to be operative in their judgement to its fullest extent — there ought to be no reservation of any sort for any class or community at all, that all citizens, if they are qualified, should be placed on the same footing of equality so far as the public services are concerned. That is the second point of view we have. Then we have quite a massive opinion, which insists that, although theoretically it is good to have the principle that, there shall be equality of opportunity, there must at the same time be a provision made for the entry of certain communities which have so far been outside the administration. As I said, the Drafting Committee had to produce a formula which would reconcile these three points of view, firstly, that there shall be equality of opportunity, secondly that there shall be reservations in favour of certain communities which have not so far had a 'proper took-in' so to say into the administration. If Honourable members will bear these facts in mind — the three principles we had to reconcile — they will see that no better formula could be produced than the one that is embodied in sub-clause (3) of article 10 of the Constitution; they will find that the view of those who believe and hold that there shall be equality of opportunity, has been embodied in sub-clause (1) of Article 10. It is a generic principle. At the same time, as I said, we had to reconcile this formula with the demand made by certain communities that the administration which has now — for historical reasons — been controlled by one community or a few communities, that situation should disappear and that the others also must have an opportunity of getting into the public services. Supposing, for instance, we were to concede in full the demand of those communities who have not been so far employed in the public services to the fullest extent, what would really happen is, we shall be completely destroying the first proposition upon which we are all agreed, namely, that there shall be an equality of opportunity. Let me give an illustration. Supposing, for instance, reservations were made for a community or a collection of communities, the total of which came to something like 70 per cent of the total posts under the State and only 30 per cent are retained as the unreserved. Could anybody say that the reservation of 30 per cent as open to general competition would be satisfactory from the point of view of giving effect to the first principle, namely, that there shall be equality of opportunity? It cannot be in my judgement. Therefore the seats to be reserved, if the reservation is to be consistent with sub-clause (1) of Article 10, must be confined to a minority of seats. It is then only that the first principle could find its place in the Constitution and effective in operation. If Honourable Members understand this position that we have to safeguard two things, namely, the principle of equality of opportunity and at the same time satisfy the demand of communities which have not had so far representation in the State, then, I am sure they will agree that unless you use some such qualifying phrase as "backward" the exception made in favour of reservation will ultimately eat up the rule altogether. Nothing of the rule will remain. That I think, if I may say so, is the justification why the Drafting Committee undertook on its own shoulders the responsibility of introducing the word 'backward' which, I admit, did not originally find a place in the fundamental right in the way in which it was passed by this Assembly. But I think Honourable Members will realise that the Drafting Committee which has been ridiculed on more than one ground for producing sometimes a loose draft, sometimes something which is not appropriate and so on, might have opened itself to further attack that they produced a Draft Constitution in which the exception was so large, that it left no room for the rule to operate. I think this is sufficient to justify why the word "backward" has been used.

With regard to the minorities, there is a special reference to that in Article 296, where it has been laid down that some provision will be made with regard to the minorities. Of course, we did not lay down any proportion. That is quite clear from the section itself, but we have not altogether omitted the minorities from consideration. Somebody asked me: "What is a backward community"? Well, I think anyone who reads the language of the draft itself will find that we have left it to be determined by each local Government. A backward community is a community, which is backward in the opinion of the Government. My Honourable Friend Mr. T. T. Krishnamachari asked me whether this rule would be justifiable. It is rather difficult to give a dogmatic answer. Personally I think it would be a justifiable matter. If the local Government included in this category of reservations such a large number of seats; I think one could very well go to the Federal Court and the Supreme Court and say that the reservation is of such a magnitude that the rule regarding equality of opportunity has been destroyed and the court will then come to the conclusion whether the local Government or the State Government has acted in a reasonable and prudent manner. Mr. Krishnamachari asked: "Who is a reasonable man and who is a prudent man? These are matters of litigation". Of course, they are matters of litigation, but my Honourable Friend Mr. Krishnamachari will understand that the words "reasonable persons and prudent persons" have been used in very many laws and if he will refer only *to* the Transfer of Property Act, he will find that in very many cases the words "a reasonable person and a prudent person" have very well been defined and the court will not find any difficulty in defining it. I hope, therefore that the amendments I have accepted, will be accepted by the House.[1]

The jurist here was not playing with words. He was laying down the juridical authority of the State, no matter if in the process lawyers, litigants, courts, and legal commentators would have a field day in the future of nation's life. Who should have the power to decide as to who belonged to the backward community? How should the principle of equality be enforced? What legal meaning should be obtained from the principle of equality? The matter of reservation or positive discrimination raised a storm in the public legal and intellectual sphere of the country since the publication of the Mandal Commission Report and the then government's decision at the centre to implement it (1990). In that context, there is a need to see how one of the most famous principles of governing India was being decided at the time of making the constitution. It had enormous significance for the theme of rights, for the standard of rule, and for the necessity of a public power to be impartial. Not only that, here the jurist was saying to the members: Think of the legal tradition (of USA, of India) — it is on that basis that the juridical authority of the sovereign power would be built. This power would be attentive to

---

[1] In this chapter I have taken principally from Ambedkar's speeches and responses in the Constituent Assembly in its final stage of deliberations in order to show his final positions. These excerpts are from 15 November 1948–8 January 1949. All citations of his speeches and responses in exchange are from the proceedings of the Constituent Assembly. For details of the extracts see www.ambedkar.org/ambcd/63B1.CA%20Debates%2015. Accessed 17 October 2008.

inequalities and would take governmental steps to correct them; it would not allow footloose, high-flying members of the Indian affluent class to seek jobs everywhere; it would combine the contradictory pulls of domicile, nationality, and national citizenship in the economic life. Only by satisfying the imperatives of governmentality does the sovereign become the sovereign. Ambedkar here not only saw much earlier than Michel Foucault the truth of the relation between sovereign power and the governmental existence of that power, he was probably more realistic.[2] To legitimise the inherent force of this public power, called sovereignty, this sovereign power must know how to govern, must have the rules and by-rules of governing accepted by the political society — in short, it must learn how to appear and behave as a public political power not susceptible to any cold weather and knowledgeable enough to act as the guardian of public interest. Sovereign power and governmental power are not at odds with each other; they precondition each other's life in the condition of modernity.

Yet, we cannot have the luxury of forgetting that such a combination of sovereign and governmental power can be built only on legal continuities. The novelty of the task of building the legal personality of the sovereign cannot cause the giddiness of excitement. A new sovereign may appear, an old one may die, be replaced or overthrown, but the rules for governing must be there. The sovereign cannot exist in a legal void. Therefore legal continuities are vital, and no one understood the theme of legal continuity better than Ambedkar. In another exchange of words, this time on Article 13, this is what he and Thakur Dass Bhargava had to say against each other's positions:

Thakur Dass Bhargava: Anyhow I pose this question to the Chairman of the Drafting Committee whether in these circumstances, *viz.,* where there is in existence a provision in the

---

[2] Though in several of his fragmentary writings and speeches in later years Michel Foucault spoke of governmentality, the reader can principally consult his essay, 'Governmentality', presented as part of a course on 'Security, Territory, and Population' given in 1977–78 at the College de France, and later published in *Essential Works of Michel Foucault, 1954–1984*, Vol. 3, ed. James Faubion, trans. Robert Hurley, London: The Penguin Press, 1994, pp. 201–22.

Constitution itself empowering the legislature *or* the executive to pass an order or law abridging the rights mentioned in clause (1), the court can go into the merits or demerits of the order or law and declare a certain law invalid or a certain Act as not justified. In my view the court's jurisdiction is ousted by clearly mentioning in the Constitution itself that the State shall have the power to make laws relating to libel, association or assembly in the interest of public order, restrictions on the exercise of ...

A: Sir, if I might interrupt my Honourable Friend, I have understood his point and I appreciate it and I undertake to reply and satisfy him as to what it means. It is therefore unnecessary for him to dilate further on the point.

B: Similarly, at present you have the right to assemble peaceably and without arms and you have in 1947 passed a law under which even peaceable assemblage could be bombed without warning from the sky. We have today many provisions, which are against this peaceable assembling. Similarly in regard to ban on association or unions ...

A: Is it open to my Honourable friend to speak generally on the clauses?

Vice-President: That is what I am trying to draw his attention to.

A: This is an abuse of the procedure of the House. I cannot help saying that. When a member speaks on an amendment, he must confine himself to that amendment. He cannot avail himself of this opportunity of rambling over the entire field.

B: I am speaking on the amendment; but the manner in which Dr. Ambedkar speaks and expresses himself is extremely objectionable. Why should he get up and speak in a threatening mood or a domineering tone?

Vice-President: Everybody seems to have lost his temper except the Chair *(Laughter)*. I had given a warning to Mr. Bhargava and, just now, was about to repeat it when Dr. Ambedkar stood up. I am perfectly certain that he was carried away by his feeling. I do not see any reason why there should be so much feeling aroused. He has been under a strain for days together. I can well understand his position and I hope that the House will allow the matter to rest there. Now, I hope Mr. Bhargava realises the position.

A: From the speeches which have been made on article 13 and article 8 and the words "existing law", which occur in some of the provisos to article 13, it seems to me that there is a good deal of misunderstanding about what is exactly intended to be done with regard to existing law. Now the fundamental article is article 8, which, specifically, without any kind of reservation, says that any existing law, which is inconsistent with the Fundamental Rights as enacted in this part *of* the Constitution is void. That is a fundamental proposition and I have no doubt about it that any 'trained lawyer, if he was asked to interpret the words "existing law" occurring in the sub-clauses to article 13, would read "existing law" in so far as it is not inconsistent with the fundamental rights. There is no doubt that that is the way in which the phrase "existing law" in the sub-clauses would be interpreted. It is unnecessary to repeat the proposition stated in article 8 every time the phrase "existing law" occurs, because it is a rule of interpretation that for interpreting any law, all relevant sections shall be taken into account and read in such a way that one section is reconciled with another. Therefore the Drafting Committee felt that they have laid down in article 8 the full and complete proposition that any existing law, in so far as it is inconsistent with the Fundamental Rights, will stand abrogated. The Drafting Committee did not feel it necessary to incorporate some such qualification in using the phrase "existing law" in the various clauses where these words occur. As I see, many people have not been able to read the clause in that way. In reading "existing law", they seem to forget what has already been stated in article 8. In order to remove the misunderstanding that is likely to be caused in a layman's mind, I have brought forward this amendment to sub-clauses (3), (4), (5) and (6) I will read for illustration sub-clause (3) with my amendment.

"Nothing in sub-clause (b) of the said clause shall affect the operation of any existing law in so far as it imposes, or prevent the State from making any law, imposing in the interests of public order."

I am accepting Mr. Bhargava's amendment and so I will add the word "reasonable" also:

"Imposing in the interests of public order reasonable restrictions on the exercise of the right conferred by the said sub-clause."

Now, the words "in so far as it imposes" to my mind make the idea complete and free from any doubt that the existing law is saved only in so far as it imposes reasonable restrictions. I think with that amendment there ought to be no difficulty in understanding that the existing law is saved only to a limited extent, it is saved only if it is not in conflict with the Fundamental Rights ...

Now, my friend, Pandit Thakur Dass Bhargava entered into a great tirade against the Drafting Committee, accusing them of having gone out of their way to preserve existing laws. I do not know what he wants the Drafting Committee to do. Does he want us to say straightaway that all existing laws shall stand abrogated on the day on which the Constitution comes into existence?

B: Not exactly.

A: What we have said is that the existing law shall stand abrogated in so far as they are inconsistent with the provisions of this Constitution. Surely the administration of this country is dependent upon the continued existence of the laws, which are in force today. It would bring down the whole administration to pieces if the existing laws were completely and wholly abrogated.

Now, I take article 307. He said that we have made provisions that the existing laws should be continued unless amended. Now, I should have thought that a man who understands law ought to be able to realize this fact that after the Constitution comes into existence, the exclusive power of making law in this country belongs to Parliament or to the several local legislatures in their respective spheres. Obviously, if you enunciate the proposition that hereafter no law shall be in operation or shall have any force or sanction, unless it has been enacted by Parliament, what would be the position? The position would be that all the laws which have been made by the earlier legislature, by the Central Legislative Assembly or the Provincial Legislative Assembly would absolutely fall to pieces, because they would cease to have any sanction, not having been made by the parliament or by the local legislatures, which under this Constitution are the only body which are entitled to make law. It is, therefore, necessary that a provision should exist in the Constitution that any laws, which have been already made, shall not stand abrogated for the mere reason that they have not been made by Parliament. That is the reason why article 307 has been introduced into this Constitution. I, therefore, submit, Sir, that my amendment which particularises the portion of the existing law which shall continue in operation so far as the Fundamental Rights are concerned, meets the difficulty, which several Honourable Members have felt by reason of the fact that they find it difficult to read article 13 in conjunction with article 8. I, therefore, think that this amendment of mine clarifies the position and hope the House will not find it difficult to accept it.

[After this clarification several amendments were not moved.]

A: Sir I move — "That in clause (4) of article 13, for the words 'the general public' the words 'public order or morality' be substituted."

A: Mr. Vice-President, Sir, I move — "That in clause (5) of article 13, for the word 'aboriginal', the word 'scheduled' be substituted." When the Drafting Committee was dealing with the question of Fundamental Rights, the Committee appointed for the Tribal Areas had not made its Report, and consequently we had to use the word 'aboriginal' at the time when the Draft was made. Subsequently, we found that the Committee on Tribal Areas had used the phrase "Scheduled Tribes" and we have used the words "scheduled tribes" in the schedules, which accompany this Constitution. In order to keep the language uniform, it is necessary to substitute the word "Scheduled" for the word "aboriginal".

All this happened in the clause-wise discussion on the draft constitution between 15 November 1948 and 8 January 1949. The drafting was by and large over, amendments were being taken care of; and appropriately ideas (on many of the things of political life) built around those of anti-colonial days were now being taken care of summarily on the issue of the right to bear arms. Everywhere, or in every case, sovereign power was being defined and given shape to in terms of two principles as evident from the preceding exchange of words — (a) the power to make exceptions; and (b) the benefit of attaining legitimacy by way of deriving continuity from earlier laws.

On the first principle, that is the power to make exceptions, which Schmitt had claimed to be the feature of sovereign power, Ambedkar was categorical. He had this to say on one occasion:

A: ... Sir, with regard to the argument that clause (4) should be deleted, I am afraid, if I may say so without any offence, that it is a very extravagant demand, a very tall order. There can be no doubt that while there are certain fundamental rights which the State must guarantee to the individual in order that the individual may have some security and freedom to develop his own personality, it is equally clear that in certain cases where, for instance, the State's very life is in jeopardy, those rights must be subject to a certain amount of limitation. Normal peaceful times are quite different from times of emergency. In times of emergency the life of the State itself is in jeopardy and if the State is not able to protect itself in times of emergency, the individual himself will be found to have lost his very existence. Consequently, *the superior right of* *the State to protect itself in times of emergency,* so that it may survive that emergency and live to discharge its functions in order that the individual under the aegis of the State may develop, must be guaranteed as safely as the right of an individual. I know of no Constitution which gave fundamental rights but which gives them in such a manner as to deprive the State in times of emergency to protect it by curtailing the rights of the individual. You take any Constitution you like, where fundamental rights are guaranteed; you will also find that provision is made for the State to suspend these in times of emergency. So far, therefore, as the amendment to delete clause (4) is concerned, it is a matter of principle and I am afraid I cannot agree with the Mover of that amendment and I must oppose it.

Now, Sir, I will go into details. My Friend Mr. Tajarnul Husain drew a very lurid picture by referring to various articles, which are included in the Chapter dealing with Fundamental Rights. He said, here is a right to take water, there is a right to enter a shop, is freedom to go to a bathing ghat. Now, if clause (4) came into operation, he suggested that all these elementary human rights which the Fundamental part guarantees — of permitting a man to go to a well to drink water, to walk on the road, to go to a cinema or a theatre, without any let or hindrance, will also disappear. I cannot understand from where my friend Mr. Tajarnul Husain got this idea. If he had referred to article 279 which relates to the power of the President to issue a proclamation of emergency, he would have found that clause (4) which permits suspension of these rights refers only to article 13 and to no other article ...

Taking up the point of Mr. Karimuddin, what he tries to do is to limit clause (4) to cases of rebellion or invasion. I thought that if he had carefully read article 275, there was really no practical difference between the provisions contained in article 275 and the amendment, which he has proposed. The power to issue a proclamation of emergency vested in the President by article 275 is confined only to cases when there is war or domestic violence.

Syed Karimuddin: Even if war is only threatened?

A: Certainly. An emergency does not merely arise when war has taken place, the situation may very well be regarded as emergency when war is threatened ... I will now take up the amendments of my friend Mr. Kamath, No. 787 read with No. 34 in List III, and the amendment of my friend Mr. Sarwate, No. 783 as amended by No. 43. My friend Mr. Kamath suggested that it was not necessary to particularize, if I understood him correctly, the various writs as the article at present does and that the matter should be left quite open for the Supreme Court to evolve such remedies as it may think proper in the circumstances of the case. I do not think Mr. Kamath has read this article very carefully. If he had read the article carefully, he would have observed that what has been done in the draft is to give general power as well as to propose particular remedies. The language of the article is very clear ... Sir, there is one other observation which I would like to make. In the course of the debates that have taken place in this House both on the Directive Principles and on the Fundamental Rights I have listened to speeches made by many members complaining that we have not enunciated a certain right or a certain policy in our Fundamental Rights or in our Directive Principles. References have been made to the Constitution of Russia and to the Constitutions of other countries where such declarations, as members have sought to introduce by means of amendments, have found a place. Sir, I think I might say without meaning any offence to anybody who has made himself responsible for these amendments that I prefer the British method of dealing with rights. The British method is a peculiar method a very real and a very sound method. British jurisprudence insists that there can be no right unless the Constitution provides a remedy for it. It is the remedy, which makes a right real. If there is no remedy, there is no right at all, and I am therefore not prepared to burden the Constitution with a number of pious declarations which may sound as glittering generalities but for which the Constitution makes no provision by way of a remedy. It is much better to be limited in the scope of our rights and to make them real by enunciating remedies than to have a tot of piteous wishes embodied in the Constitution. I am very glad that this House has seen that the remedies that we have provided constitute a fundamental part of this Constitution. Sir, with these words I commend this article to the House ...

Kamath: I am equally anxious. Mr. Vice-President, I am here seeking only a little light from Dr. Ambedkar with regard to his amendment No. 820 moved by him. I fail to see clearly why the words in the article as it stands at present should be substituted by the words he proposes to. In case his amendment is accepted, it will mean that Parliament shall have power only for prescribing punishment for the acts referred to in Clause (b). Then what about the Parliament's power to make laws with respect to any of the matters which under this power are required to be provided for by legislation in Clause (a). Does he intend by his amendment to take away the power which is sought to be conferred by Clause

(a) of this article? I want to know exactly what the import of his amendment is and why this Clause (a) is sought to be amended in this fashion.

A: I am sorry, Mr. Kamath has not been able to understand the scheme which is embodied in article 27. This article embodies three principles. The first principle is that wherever this Constitution prescribes that a law shall be made for giving effect to any Fundamental Right or where a law is to be made for making an action punishable, which interferes with Fundamental Rights, that right shall be exercised only by Parliament, notwithstanding the fact that having regard to the List which deals with the distribution of power, such law may fall within the purview of the State Legislature. The object of this is that Fundamental Rights, both as to their nature and as to the punishments involved in the infringement thereof, shall be uniform throughout India. Therefore, if that object is to be achieved, namely, that Fundamental Rights shall be uniform and the punishments involved in the breach of Fundamental Rights also shall be uniform, then that power must be exercised only by the Parliament, so that there may be uniformity. The second thing is this. If there are already Acts, which provide punishments for breaches of Fundamental Rights, unless and until the Parliament makes another or a better provision, such laws will continue in operation. That is the whole scheme of the thing. I do not see why there should be any difficulty in understanding the provisions contained in article 27 (emphasis mine).

Thus, the power to make exception is a rationally thought out power invested in a sovereign. It was reasonable and made sense in a reading with fundamental rights. Regarding the second imperative, that is continuity with the preceding legal structure, not only was sovereign power being defined as one who or which could make exceptions on the ground of public order, safety, health, and morality — grounds, which mostly only the sovereign would define (all exceptional pieces of legislation were made on these grounds and were upheld by the court), legal continuity would reinforce the sovereign's position. In this operation of the rule of juridical abstraction, low castes or Dalits or the indigenous people would be reminded of the reality again and again on any occasion when they would claim from the State steps for positive discrimination or other rights and advantages, that they were now enabled to do so because they belonged to certain 'scheduled' groups, castes, or communities, schedules that again would be decided by the State (including local governments). This is how the public power was being built by rationalising every conceivable issue of political life; Ambedkar's position was unassailable in the Constituent Assembly because he represented, more than anyone else in that assembly, *public reason* — reason based on the imperatives of governing, law, and rational rule. That is why he could go instantly into any number of details, at times massive and astonishing, and show how they were appropriate with the task of law making and rationally governing. Democracy's own sovereign power was being produced in this way.

Thus in another reminder that times had changed and therefore every radical intention of pre-sovereign days could not now be pursued, a reminder that time had changed now that the constitution was being drafted and soon 'our' sovereign power would be ready to defend 'our' interests, and therefore people need not worry so much, not be 'schizophrenic', Ambedkar had this to say in response to a inquiry from Kamath on the right to bear arms in connection to a discussion on Article 13:

A: Now, with regard to the question of bearing arms about which my friend Mr. Kamath was so terribly excited, I think the position that we have taken is very clear. It is quite true and everyone knows that the Congress Party had been agitating that there should be right to bear arms. Nobody can deny that. That is history. At the same time I think the House should not forget the fact that the circumstances when Congress passed such resolutions no longer exist.

K: A very handy argument.

A: It is because the British Government had refused to allow Indians to bear arms, not on the ground of peace and order, but on the ground that a subject people should not have the right to bear arms against an alien government so that they could organise themselves to overthrow the Government, and consequently the basic considerations on which these resolutions were passed in my judgement have vanished. Under the present circumstances, I personally myself cannot conceive how it would be possible for the State to carry on its administration if every individual had the right to go into the market and purchase all sorts of instruments of attack without any let or hindrance from the State.

K: On a point of clarification, Sir, the proviso is there, restricting that right.

A: The proviso does what? What does the proviso say? What the proviso can do is to regulate, and the term 'regulation' has been judicially interpreted as prescribing the conditions, but the conditions can never be such as to completely abrogate the right of the citizen to bear arms. Therefore regulation by itself will not prevent a citizen who wants to exercise the right to bear arms from having them. I question very much the policy of giving all citizens indiscriminately any such fundamental right. For instance, if Mr. Kamath's proposition were accepted, that every citizen should have the fundamental right to bear arms, it would be open for thousands and thousands of citizens who are today described as criminal tribes to bear arms. It would be open to all sorts of people who are habitual criminals to claim the right to possess arms. You cannot say that under the proviso a man shall not be entitled to bear arms because he belongs to a particular class.

K: If Dr. Ambedkar understands the proviso fully and clearly, he will see that such will not be the effect of my amendment.

A: I cannot yield now. I have not got much time left. I am explaining the position that has been taken by the Drafting Committee. The point is that it is not possible to allow this indiscriminate right. On the other hand my submission is that so far as bearing of arms is concerned, what we ought to insist upon is not the right of an individual to bear arms but his duty to bear arms (An Honourable Member: *Hear, hear*.). In fact, what we ought to secure is that when an emergency arises, when there is a war, when there is insurrection, when the stability and security of the State is endangered, the State shall be entitled to call upon every citizen to bear arms in defence of the State. That is the proposition that we ought to initiate and that position we have completely safeguarded by the proviso to article 17.

K: (rose to interrupt).

Vice-President: You do not interrupt, Mr. Kamath. You cannot say that I have not given you sufficient latitude.

So that is how one of the most important questions of rule of law is settled; people have to be disarmed if the rule of law enforceable if necessary by arms has to be the basis of democracy. This is so evident to those who are in the business of law making that on this obvious matter, there cannot be much time to give on this, 'not much time left' (for this), 'sufficient latitude has been given', now be ready to serve the armed forced if the sovereign requires of you, but do not ask the right to bear arms as distinct from the arms of *the armed body* of the sovereign. Because this is the sovereignty of the democratic body, therefore the sovereign could not only ask obedience of the people, but assure the latter also that it is truly public. This was significant because it was held in the context of the discussion on Article 13:

> **A:** Coming to the question of saving personal law, I think this matter was very completely and very sufficiently discussed and debated at the time when we discussed one of the Directive Principles of this Constitution which enjoins the State to seek or to strive to bring about a uniform civil code and I do not think it is necessary to make any further reference to it, but I should like to say this that, if such a saving clause was introduced into the Constitution, it would disable the legislatures in India from enacting any social measure whatsoever. The religious conceptions in this country are so vast that they cover every aspect *of* life, from birth to death. There is nothing, which is not religion and if personal law is to be saved, I am sure about it that in social matters we will come to a standstill. I do not think it is possible to accept a position of that sort. There is nothing extraordinary in saying that we ought to strive hereafter to limit the definition of religion in such a manner that we shall not extend beyond beliefs and such rituals as may be connected with ceremonials which are essentially religious. It is not necessary that the sort of laws, for instance, laws relating to tenancy or laws relating to succession, should be governed by religion. In Europe there is Christianity, but Christianity does not mean that the Christians all over the world or in any part of Europe where they live, shall have a uniform system of law of inheritance. No such thing exists. I personally do not understand why religion should be given this vast, expansive jurisdiction so as to cover the whole of life and to prevent the legislature from encroaching upon that field. After all, what are we having this liberty for? We are having this liberty in order to reform our social system, which is so full of inequities, so full of inequalities, discriminations and other things, which conflict with our fundamental rights. It is, therefore, quite impossible for anybody to conceive that the personal law shall be excluded from the jurisdiction of the State. Having said that I should also like to point out that all that the State is claiming in his matter is a power to legislate. There is no obligation upon the State to do away with personal laws. It is only giving a power. Therefore, no one need be apprehensive of the fact that if the State has the power, the State

will proceed immediately to execute or enforce that power in a manner that may be found to be objectionable by the Muslims or by the Christians or by any other Community in India.

We must all remember — including Members of the Muslim community who have spoken on this subject, though one can appreciate their feelings very well — that sovereignty is always limited, no matter even if you assert that it is unlimited, because sovereignty in the exercise of that power must reconcile itself to the sentiments of different communities. No Government can exercise its power in such a manner as to provoke the Muslim community to rise in rebellion. I think it would be a mad Government if it did so. But that is a matter, which relates to the exercise of the power and not to the power itself.

These are significant words. There can be limits occasioned by social conditions at some point of time on the sovereign's 'exercise of power', but not on 'sovereign power itself'. 'Sovereignty is always limited' because it must not lose sight of governmental considerations, but these are limits on the exercise of power, and not on the power itself. This is, of course, a classic juridical argument. It is, as the exchanges cited above show again and again, 'mono-logical' in nature, which Kant had thought would be a rational individual's position in a society. 'Monologism' as Jurgen Habermas was to show later, meant that the individual's participation in the public sphere was limited to a simple sharing of his already constituted opinions and moral decisions in a hypothetical conversation with himself.[3] Sovereignty was thus the typical Kantian 'categorical imperative' — humanity must follow this enlightened democratic sovereign power; it was also not an inter-subjective process, but a purely subjective process, out of which sovereignty had emerged, and now must practise the process also. Deliberation had its limit — the limit posed by rational choice, decision, and imperative. Constitution making, as if Ambedkar was saying to ill-trained and ill-educated members of the Constituent Assembly, a curious mixture of ignorant representatives and upper-class dilettantes, was finally a matter of categorical imperative. Certain principles were categorical;

---

[3] Giovanna Borradori, *Philosophy in a Time of Terror – Dialogues with Jurgen Habermas and Jacques Derrida*, Chicago: University of Chicago Press, 2003, pp. 59–60.

they represented reason in its purity. Sovereignty was the foremost of such principles.

In passing, then, we must ask the following question: Is this deliberation in the Constituent Assembly a 'promise of a democracy to come'? Or, is it 'the promise of rules, institutions, and a new era of rule' after the popular assembly would be over completing its *raison d'être*? This question, of course, points to a closure because we must be aware the process is already on, and while the process today says that only some regulative ideas will be put in place in the course of deliberations, *at the end of the deliberations*, these regulative principles point to the enormous difficulty of making a transition, which a constitution aims to make. Thus the aporia, and the inevitability of a risk — of denouncing the process altogether or accepting it and then exceeding it; and what then remains of the original promise, that of democracy to come? We have to rethink many of the things in the game before an answer can even be suggested.

Second Stake: Legally Constituting a Government and a People

In any case, if this was to be the nature of the sovereign power, who were to be the people to constitute the demos and whose acceptance, ownership, and obligation make the sovereign exercise fruitful? Who were 'they' who would constitute the public? Would wealth mark them, or education, or the simple fact that they were human beings, or more elementally that they were Indians? Would the demos be homogeneous or would it consist of groups? How would it enforce accountability? In an extraordinary essay on the politics of citizenship in a society undergoing transition from colonialism to independence, Paula Banerjee has shown how aliens were marked out at the time of transition and constitution making in India, and thus how indentured Indian labour abroad and other Indians working abroad were left out, and how the emerging discourse of citizenship played itself out at a time when the colonial world was drawing to a close.[4] In giving juridical form to the 'demos' this is how the Drafting Committee

---

[4] Paula Banerjee, 'Aliens in the Colonial World', in Ranabir Samaddar (ed.), *Refugees and the State — Practices of Asylum and Care in India, 1947–2000*, Delhi: Sage Publications, 2003, Chapter 1.

chairman explained the legal vision and these were how he saw the 'demos' forming its sovereignty:

A: ... Of the other amendments, on a careful examination, I find that there is only one amendment on which I need offer any reply. That is amendment No. 1415 of my friend Mr. Karimuddin. His amendment aims at prescribing that the election to the House of the People in the various States shall be in accordance with the proportional representation by single transferable vote. Now, I do not think it is possible to accept this amendment, because, so far as I am able to judge the merits of the system of proportional representation, in the light of the circumstances existing in this country, I think, that amendment cannot be accepted. My friend Mr. Karimuddin will, I think, accept the proposition that proportional representation presupposes literacy on a large scale. In fact, it presupposes that every voter shall be literate, at least to the extent of being in a position to know the numerals, and to be in a position to mark them on a ballot paper. I think, having regard to the extent of literacy in this country, such a presupposition would be utterly extravagant. I have not the least doubt on that point. Our literacy is the smallest, I believe, in the world, and it would be quite impossible to impose upon an illiterate mass of voters a system of election, which involves marking of ballot papers. That by itself would, I think, exclude the system of proportional representation.

The second thing to which I like to draw the attention of the House is that at any rate, in my judgement, proportional representation is not suited to the form of Government which this constitution lays down. The form of Government which this constitution lays down is what is known as the parliamentary system of Government, by which we understand that a government shall continue to be in office not necessarily for the full term prescribed by law, namely, five years, but so long as the Government continues to have the confidence of the majority of the House. Obviously it means that in the House where there is the parliamentary system of government, you must necessarily have a party which is in majority and which is prepared to support the Government. Now, so far as I have been able to study the results of the systems of parliamentary or proportional representation. I think, it might be said that one of the disadvantages of proportional representation is the fragmentation of the legislature into a number of small groups. I think the House will know that although the British Parliament appointed a Royal Commission in the year 1910, for the purpose of considering whether their system of single-member constituency, with one man one vote, was better or whether the proportional representation system was better, it is, I think, a matter to be particularly noted that Parliament was not prepared to accept the recommendations of that Royal Commission. The reason which was given for not accepting it was, in my judgement, a very sound reason, that proportional representation would not permit a stable government to remain in office, because Parliament would be so divided into so many small groups that every time anything happened which displeased certain groups in Parliament, they would, on that occasion, withdraw their support from the government, with the result that the Government losing the support of certain groups and units, would fall to pieces. Now, I have not the least doubt in my mind that whatever else the future government provides for, whether it relieves the people from the wants from which they are suffering now or not, our future government must do one thing, namely, it must maintain a stable Government and maintain law and order. *(Hear, Hear!)*. I am therefore, very hesitant in accepting any system of election which would damage the stability of Government. I am therefore, on that account, not prepared to accept this arrangement.

There is a third consideration, which I think is necessary to bear in mind. In this country, for a long number of years, the people have been divided into majorities and minorities. I am not going into the question whether this division of the people into majorities and minorities was natural, or whether it was an artificial thing, or something, which was deliberately calculated and brought about by somebody who was not friendly to the progress of this country. Whatever that may be, the fact remains that there have been these majorities and minorities in our country; and also that, at the initial stage when this Constituent Assembly met for the discussion of the principles on which the future constitution of the country should be based, there was an agreement arrived at between the various minority communities and the majority community with regard to the system of representation. That agreement has been a matter of give and take. The minorities who, prior to that meeting of the Constituent Assembly, had been entrenched behind a system of separate electorates were prepared, or became prepared to give up that system and the majority which believed that there ought to be no kind of special reservation to any particular community permitted, or rather agreed that while they could not agree to separate electorates, they would agree to a system of joint electorates with reservation of seats. This agreement provides for two things. It provides for a definite quota of representation to the various minorities, and it also provides that such a quota shall be returned through joint electorates. Now, my submission is this, that while it is still open to this House to revise any part of the clauses contained in this draft constitution and while it is open to this House to revise any agreement that has been arrived at between the majority and the minority, this result ought not to be brought about either by surprise or by what I may call, a side-wind. It had better be done directly and it seems to me that the proper procedure for effecting a change in articles 292 and 293 would be to leave the matter to the wishes of the different minorities themselves. If any particular minority represented in this House said that it did not want any reservation, then it would be open to the House to remove the name of that particular minority from the provisions of article 292. If any particular minority preferred that although it did not get a cent per cent deal, namely, did not get a separate electorate, but that what it has got in the form of reservation of seats is better than having nothing, then I think it would be just and proper that the minority should be permitted to retain what the Constituent Assembly has already given to it.

Thakur Dass Bhargava: But there was no agreement about reservation of seats among the communities and a number of amendments were moved by several Members for separate electorates and so on, but they were all voted down. There was no agreement at all in regard to these matters.

A: I was only saying that it may be taken away, not by force, but by consent. That is my proposition, and therefore, I submit that this proportional representation is really taking away by the back-door what has already been granted to the minorities by this agreement, because proportional representation will not give to the minorities what they wanted, namely, a definite quota. It might give them a voice in the election of their representatives. Whether the minorities will be prepared to give up their quota system and prefer to have a mere voice in the election of their representatives, I submit, in fairness ought to be left to them. For these reasons, Sir, I am not prepared to accept the amendment of Mr. Karimuddin.

Separate electorates had been one of the most controversial points in anti-colonial politics on which the nationalist sections could not come to voluntary agreement during colonial rule. On the other hand, the Royal Commission could tell nothing of the dynamics and complexities of representation in a plural society. Year after year minority governments have ruled countries on the basis of the first-past-the-post system, and popular discontent has not been able to find any constitutional way out against a system of representation that falsifies the very ethics of representing the demos. But Ambedkar's vision was clear from the way he argued: first, (except in cases of Scheduled Castes and Tribes, and reserved non-elected seats for Anglo-Indians) there would be no separate seat for any community, similarly no break-up of the demos according to any communal profile; second, this demos would consist of a 'multitude' who may not be literate, but who must perform the first function of the demos, that of electing the sovereign. It is evident as to why the legitimisation of sovereignty required a republican demos, towards the creation of which Ambedkar, in a single-minded manner, fashioned arguments. But was the sovereign to be illiterate? No, here one could ill afford to confuse the demos with the sovereign, as was amply clear from the exchange of words involving Mahavir Tyagi, Kamath, and Ambedkar over Article 62:

T: Then there is the amendment of Prof. Shah in which he says that Ministers should know the English language for ten years, and Hindi after the next ten years. I happen to be an anarchist by faith so far as literacy is concerned, I do not believe in the present-day education. I am opposed to the notion of literacy also, even though it has its own value. If I were a boy now, I would refuse to read and write. As it was, I practically refused to read and write and hence I am a semi-literate. The majority in India are illiterate persons. Why should they be denied their share in the administration of the country? I wonder, why should literacy be considered as the supreme achievement of men? Why should it be made as the sole criterion for entrusting the governance of a country to a person, and why Art, Industry, Mechanics, Physique or Beauty be not chosen as a better criterion. Ranjit Singh was not literate. Shivaji was not literate. Akbar was not much of a literate. But all of them were administering their States very well. I submit, Sir, that we should not attach too much importance to literacy. I ask Dr. Ambedkar, does he ever write? Probably he has got writers to write for him and readers to read to him. I do not see why Ministers need read and write. Whenever they want to write anything, they can use typists. Neither reading nor writing is necessary. What are necessary are initiative, honesty, personality, integrity, intelligence and sincerity. These are the qualifications that a man should have to become a Minister. It is not literacy, which is important.

K: Does my redoubtable friend want to keep India as illiterate as she is today?

A: Have you any conscientious objection against literacy?

T: No, Sir.

A: With regard to the educational qualification, notwithstanding what my friend Mr. Mahavir Tyagi has said on the question of literary qualification, when I asked him whether in view of the fact that he expressed himself so vehemently against literary qualification whether he has any conscientious objection to literary education, he was very glad to assure me that he has none. All the same, I wonder whether there would be any Prime Minister or President who would think it desirable to appoint a person who does not know English, assuming that English remains the official language of the business of the Executive or of Parliament. I cannot conceive of such a thing. Supposing the official language was Hindi, Hindustani or Urdu — whatever it is — in that event, I again find it impossible to think that a Prime Minister would be so stupid as to appoint a Minister who did not understand the official language of the country or of the Administration and while therefore it is no doubt a very desirable thing to bear in mind that persons who would hold a portfolio in the Government should have proper educational qualification, I think it is, rather unnecessary to incorporate this principle in the Constitution itself.

How were the elections to be conducted? Of course, once the sovereign had been instituted, the sovereign could now engage as the constitutional deliberations envisaged the 'administration' to conduct and supervise elections — the public and non-partial way as against engaging any private or sectional agency to conduct the elections. Here again can be seen, in the light of our experiences of how the constitutional world was producing a virtual world of republican democracy — yes, the real world of sovereignty and the virtual world of republican democracy — by assuming that this 'administration' could ensure proper representation. Ambedkar was mindful of the administrative needs of the sovereign; hence some suggestions placed by members of the Constituent Assembly for revision of draft articles were 'unnecessary', some 'superfluous', some 'harmful', and some 'necessary'. Governmental requirements were pre-eminent in this respect and the demos had to be trained on that. Thus on technical matters legality defined the core of governmentality, as on issues involving population figures. Census figures have been extremely controversial and the root of many conflicts. The Constituent Assembly was deliberating at a time when population groups were up in arms against each other, the country had been partitioned, and demography and census were the time bombs ticking all the time. We have seen the grounds on which Ambedkar had rejected the introduction of the principle of proportional representation. His following remarks show that he was aware of the reality of the elites of different community and caste groups trying to increase their domination over the electoral arithmetic, and yet had to move on to give shape to the demos — the popular electorate constituting the nation — ironing out these unhappy realities:

A: Now, Sir, so far as the general debate on the article (Article 149 for holding of elections) is concerned, it seems to me that there are only two points that call for reply. The first point is with regard to the census figures to be adopted for the purpose of the new elections. A great deal of argument was concentrated by many speakers on the fact that the census in certain provinces is not accurate and does not represent the true state of affairs so far as the relative proportions of the different communities are concerned. I think there is a great deal of force in such arguments and, if I may say so, there is enough testimony which one can collect from the Census Commissioners' reports themselves to justify that criticism. I had intended to refer to the statements made by the Census Commissioners on this issue. But, as there is no time, I think I had better not refer to them. Further, the large majority of the members who have spoken on this subject know the facts better than I do. I only want to add one thing and that is that if any people have suffered most in the matter of these manipulations of census calculations by reason of political factors; they are the Scheduled Castes *(Hear, hear)*. In Punjab for instance, the other communities are trying to eat up the Scheduled Castes in order to augment their strength and to acquire larger representation in the legislature for themselves. These poor people who have been living mostly as landless labourers in villages scattered here and there, with no economic independence, with no support from the authorities — the police or the magistracy — have been, by certain powerful communities, either compelled to return themselves as members of that particular community or not to enumerate at the elections at all. The same thing has happened to a large extent, I know, in Bengal. For some reason, which I have not been able to understand, a large majority of the Scheduled Castes there refused to return themselves as Scheduled Castes. That fact has been noted by the Census Commissioners themselves. I therefore completely appreciate the points that have been made by various members who spoke on the subject that it would not be fair to take the figures of that census.

A Member: What about Assam?

A: It may be true of Assam also. I am not very well acquainted with it. As I said I fully appreciate the point that to take those census figures and to delimit constituencies or allocate seats between the different constituencies and between the majority and minority communities would not be fair. Something will have to be done in order to see that the next election is a proper election, related properly to the population figures of the provinces as well as of the communities. All that I can do at this stage is to give an assurance that I shall communicate these sentiments to those who will be in charge of this matter and I have not the least doubt about it that the matter will be properly attended to.

There are other significant instances to show how in the form of constitutionalist exercises and constitutional deliberations, the idea of making governmental tools the principal tools to shape the demos became an irresistible idea. It is now known how more than popular common sense and dialogic wisdom legal rationality became important in shaping these governmental tools, which in time became the core of constitutionalism and legality. It is important, therefore, to read this extraordinary exchange of deliberations in the Constituent Assembly in which Ambedkar once again played the key role. The matter related to the rights of cultural/religious groups to open their own educational institutions, and get state aid:

A: Now, with regard to the second clause I think it has not been sufficiently well understood. We have tried to reconcile the claim of a community, which has started educational institutions for the advancement of its own children either in education or in cultural matters, to permit to give religious instruction in such institutions, notwithstanding the fact that it receives certain aid from the State. The State, of course, is free to give aid, is free not to give aid; the only limitation we have placed is this, that the State shall not debar the institution from claiming aid under its grant-in-aid code merely on the ground that it is run and maintained by a community and not maintained by a public body. We have there provided also a further qualification, that while it is free to give religious instruction in the institution and the grant made by the State shall not be a bar to the giving of such instruction, it shall not give instruction to, or make it compulsory upon, the children belonging to other communities unless and until they obtain the consent of the parents of those children. That, I think, is a salutary provision. It performs two functions ...

Kamath: On a point of clarification, what about institutions and schools run by a community or a minority for its own pupils — not a school where all communities are mixed but a school run by the community for its own pupils?

A: If my Friend Mr. Kamath will read the other article he will see that once an institution, whether maintained by the community or not, gets a grant, the condition is that it shall keep the school open to all communities. That provision he has not read. Therefore, by sub-clause (2) we are really achieving two purposes. One is that we are permitting a community, which has established its institutions for the advancement of its religious or its cultural life, to give such instruction in the school. We have also provided that children of other communities who attend that school shall not be compelled to attend such religious instructions, which undoubtedly and obviously must be the instruction in the religion of that particular community, unless the parents consent to it. As I say, we have achieved this double purpose and those who want religious instruction to be given are free to establish their institutions and claim aid from the State, give religious instruction, but shall not be in a position to force that religious instruction on other communities. It is therefore not proper to say that by this article we have altogether barred religious instruction. Religious instruction has been left free to be taught and given by each community according to its aims and objects subject to certain conditions. All that is barred is this, that the State in the institutions maintained by it wholly out of public funds shall not be free to give religious instruction.

Lakshmi Kanta Maitra: May I put the Honourable Member one question? There is, for instance, an educational institution wholly managed by the Government, like the Sanskrit College, Calcutta. There the *Vedas* are taught, *Smrithis* are taught, the *Gita* is taught, the *Upanishads* are taught. Similarly in several parts of Bengal there are Sanskrit Institutions where instructions in these subjects are given. You provide in article 22 (1) that no religious instruction can be given by an institution wholly maintained out of State funds. These are absolutely maintained by State funds. My point is, would it be interpreted that the teaching of *Vedas,* or *Smrithis,* or *Shastras,* or *Upanishads* comes within the meaning of a religious instruction? In that case all these institutions will have to be closed down.

A: Well, I do not know exactly the character of the institutions to which my Friend Mr. Maitra has made reference and it is therefore quite difficult for me.

Maitra: Take for instance the teaching of Gita, Upanishads, the Vedas and livings like that in Government Sanskrit Colleges and schools.

A: My own view is this that religious instruction is to be distinguished from research or study. Those are quite different things. Religious instruction means this. For instance, so far as the Islam religion is concerned, it means that you believe in one God, that you believe that *Paigambar* the Prophet is the last Prophet and so on, in other words, what we call "dogma". A dogma is quite different from study.

Vice-President: May I interpose for one minute? As Inspector of Colleges for the Calcutta University, I used to inspect the Sanskrit College, whereas Pandit Maitra is aware, students have to study not only the University course, but also books outside it in Sanskrit literature and in fact Sanskrit sacred books, but this was never regarded as religious instruction; it was regarded as a course in culture.

Maitra: My point is this. It is not a question of research. It is a mere instruction in religion or religious branches of study. I ask whether lecturing on Gita and Upanishads would be considered as giving religious instruction? Expounding Upanishads is not a matter of research.

This is how governmentality operates. In this operation, some procedure that can standardise 'cases' must be found out with regard to the matter to be administered — in this case the issues of education and public instruction. Thus, while common sense and dialogic wisdom suggested that on the tricky issue of religious instruction, secularism, impartiality of the state, and state aid to educational efforts more deliberations were needed — more introspection towards what we call as matters of public instruction involving philosophical and theological education, a matter on which the entire 19th century educationists in India had racked their brains — law needed in their place, *in the first place*, some rational sense to put into operation to straighten the complications in civil education. This is what public voice is, and this is what Ambedkar represented in the Constituent Assembly, all the more when we see how — exactly in the way he dealt with the issue of public instruction — he dealt with the matter of personal law, an issue relevant to the Part IV of the constitution, the Directive Principles of State Policy. This is what he had to say, among other things, on one of the most contentious issues of political modernity. He counselled reason and moderation, a combination that people do not sufficiently appreciate. Reason tells us to go ahead with our agenda of reform, yet it also counsels moderation, for moderation will give us an insight into the mysteries of the working of a society; and therefore reason always brings in moderation. And has it not been exactly the political essence of constitutionalism — a unique combination of reason and moderation, the other form of sovereignty and democracy? Also, has it not been one of the principal challenges to modernity, particular modernity, to achieve reason with moderation? Ambedkar thus commented in a unique vein,

Coming to the question of saving personal law, I think this matter was very completely and very sufficiently discussed and debated at the time when we discussed one of the Directive Principles of this Constitution which enjoins the State to seek or to strive to bring about a uniform civil code and I do not think it is necessary to make any further reference to it, but I should like to say this that, if such a saving clause was introduced into the Constitution, *it would disable the legislatures in India from enacting any social measure whatsoever.* The religious conceptions in this country are so vast that they cover every aspect *of* life, from birth to death ... There is nothing extraordinary in saying that we ought to strive hereafter to limit the definition of religion in such a manner that we shall not extend beyond beliefs and such rituals as may be connected with ceremonials which are essentially religious. It is not necessary that the sort of laws, for instance, laws relating to tenancy or laws relating to succession, should be governed by religion. In Europe there is Christianity, but Christianity does not mean that the Christians all over the world or in any part of Europe where they live, shall have a uniform system of law of inheritance. No such thing exists. I personally do not understand why religion should be given this vast, expansive jurisdiction so as to cover the whole of life and to prevent the legislature from encroaching upon that field. After all, what are we having this liberty for? We have this liberty in order to reform our social system, which is so full of inequities, so full of inequalities, discriminations and other things, which conflict with our fundamental rights. It is, therefore, quite impossible for anybody to conceive that the personal law shall be excluded from the jurisdiction of the State. Having said that I should also like to point out that all that the State is claiming in his matter is a power to legislate. *There is no obligation upon the State to do away with personal laws. It is only giving a power.* Therefore, no one need be apprehensive of the fact that if the State has the power, the State will proceed immediately to execute or enforce that power in a manner that may be found to be objectionable by the Muslims or by the Christians or by any other Community in India (emphasis mine).

Thus modernity brings in power and the scope to change society slowly, gradually, at will, in measure. It does not exhort us to revolt — revolution belongs to the domain of passion. Foucault was therefore perhaps not right when he placed the political culture of revolt to the annals of modernity. There Burke was more correct when he argued that moderation was the true essence of modernity, and the French were wrong in giving into passion. This was and still is the political problem of constitutionalism — how to constitute power that will have the virtue of moderation but the characteristic of sovereign, how to constitute a sovereign that will appeal to the democratic spirit yet will rely on the everyday governmentalities characterising modern political societies — a sovereign that will not act as sovereign while keeping its exceptional power intact.

None knew more than Ambedkar — a political leader, jurist, constitutionalist, mass leader, and a moderate all at the same time — to realise that only governmental capability could enable such a unique distinction to achieve. Therefore even on an issue dearest to his heart, social justice for the Dalits and their emancipation from social bondage, he knew governmental scope and power were the most necessary attributes to bring about any change. Thus, he commented in one place,

> Now, coming to the question of the scheduled tribes and as to why I substituted the word "scheduled" for the word "aboriginal", the explanation is this. As I said, the phrase "scheduled tribe" has a fixed meaning, because it enumerates the tribes, as seen in the two schedules. Well, the word "Adibasi" is really a general term, which has no specific legal *de jure* connotation; like the untouchables, it is a general term. Anybody may include anybody in the term 'untouchable'. It has no definite legal connotation. That is why in the Government of India Act of 1935, it was felt necessary to give the word 'untouchable' some legal connotation and the only way it was found feasible to do it was to enumerate the communities which in different parts and in different areas were regarded by the local people as satisfying the test of untouchability. The same question may arise with regard to Adivasis. Who are the Adivasis? The question will be relevant, because by this Constitution, we are conferring certain privileges, certain rights on these Adivasis in order that, if the matter was taken to a court of law, there should be a precise definition as to who are these Adivasis. It was decided to invent, so to say, another category or another term to be called "'Scheduled tribes" and to enumerate the Adivasis under that head. Now I think my friend, Mr. Jaipal Singh, if he were to take the several communities which are now generally described as Adivasis and compare the communities which are listed under the head of Scheduled Tribes, he would find that there is hardly a case where a community which is generally recognised as Adivasi is not included in the Schedule ....

Governmentality, Ambedkar therefore seemed to teach, is not only relational, but also contextual. It is a technique aimed to help law and facilitate administration — administration of men and women through administering matters belonging to the affairs of men and women through a combination of standardisation and flexibility that could be achieved through a union of rational knowledge (standardisation) and flexibility (power).

Constitution Making as an Art of Governing

Is what I have pointed out while recalling some of Ambedkar's arguments in the nearly four-year-long constitution-making exercise unique? Or was his role unique? It is not my case in this article to prove them though both of these may have been true, at least true then. But my intention here has been to point out how constitution-making skill and perspicacity call for a targeted approach and that is what is unique as a modern political knowledge. As a material practice it is also remorseless in logic. If it succeeds, therefore, as a dialogic exercise, it does so only partially.

To understand the point about the Constituent Assembly and the constitution-making exercise being one of the major tools to bring about a passive revolution in a country marked by unrest, madness, revolts, and schizophrenia, we need to recall a few known facts here. The demand for a Constituent Assembly was intrinsically linked to the nation's larger goal of freedom and independence. The resolution for *purna swaraj* (full independence) in 1929 aroused great nationalist enthusiasm. Reflecting a deep desire among the people to be in control of their own destiny it also represented within itself the idea of a democratic constitution, which would provide a framework for the governance of independent India by the Indian people. Therefore *purna swaraj* had the idea of a popular assembly consisting of representatives of the people. The Indian National Congress accepted the idea of a Constituent Assembly in 1934. After that it became a significant part of the nationalist agenda for independent India, the vision of which had its first glimpse in the well-known Nehru Report on the constitution of free India. The Karachi session of the Indian National Congress held in March 1931 adopted the famous resolution moved by Gandhi, which contained the charter on fundamental rights. It was against this backdrop that the idea of a sovereign, democratic nation born through the functioning of a Constituent Assembly gradually crystallised. Yet in was precisely during this period that the nation's leaders began serious thinking on issues such as personal law reform, educational design and public instruction, planning, construction of big industries, public distribution system, and economic revival through the revival of cottage, small-scale, and middle-scale industries. War, famine, and subsequent unrest only made these governmental imperatives more urgent than ever. By the time the limited elections took place in 1946, partition had been accepted by one and all as an evil necessity, territorial considerations had become dominant in all governmental considerations, and *how to rule* had become as important a consideration as to *how to become free*. Very few constitution-making experiences match the Indian one in depth, in effecting a combination of contradictory elements, and giving the constitution a purposeful look, because very few constitutions can match the Indian one in having a targeted approach as its mode. Order, security, integrity, personal freedom, political equality, development, independent judiciary, decentralisation, local self-government — all these could have appeared in time as disjointed parts of a too unwieldy agenda. But they did not, because they all appeared as implementing tasks of a sovereign state, which would govern the people with its developmental programme through *rule of law*. That is where the constitution, the constitution-making exercise, and its principal architect and his team were successful in achieving the unique feat of which Immanuel Kant and Burke would have been equally proud. The constitutionalists set in motion a mechanism of power that would be almost self-running except requiring occasional boosts from outside. The details of combining state and the government, sovereignty and governmentality, power and welfare, and ruling and development were all laid down in the book with amazing patience — all because they knew the precise nature of the job, they knew what they had inherited as the Government of India Act of 1935 was of immense value. It was a given framework with which they could now go forward and add to.

Only in this perspective can it be understood how Ambedkar and others could discipline themselves into not getting reckless and wild with the aroma and the maddening charm of the politics and act of representation. They never thought that people could be truly represented, as if Carl Schmitt was repeating his lesson in their ears,

> That X steps up in place of an absent Y, or for several thousand such Y's, is thus not in itself a representation. A particularly simple historical example of representation obtains when a king is represented to another king through an emissary (i.e., a personal representative, not through an agent, who carries out tasks for him.) In the eighteenth century this kind of "representation in an eminent sense" was clearly distinguished from other processes of delegation.[5]

---

[5] Cited in Samuel Weber, 'The Principle of Representation — Carl Schmitt's *Roman Catholicism and Political Form*', in idem, *Targets of Opportunity — On the Militarisation of Thinking*, New York: Fordham University Press, 2005, p. 39.

Therefore the constitution, having ensured that the people's voice was behind it, and that there would be elections, universal adult franchise, local and provincial elections and governments, and that the parliament would, along British lines, be the supreme legislating authority, did not spend much time on working on the theme of representation. Thus many themes were left out such as recall and referendum; similarly were left out issues of popular will as and when expressed in direct ways; similarly were left out the complications of group representation at various levels, the many locations of citizenship, the relation of representation and participation, the issue of autonomy of people's voices and of distinct areas; and, finally, the constitution simply assumed that popular representation and the basic structure provided by the 1935 Act were compatible. Instead the constitution now devoted much more time and energy on issues of governance, financial and fiscal management, rights and obligations, powers and functions of government, and the theory and practice of separation of powers. People became the 'occupied object' in this dynamics where representatives became the actors, and as if disenchanted with the fury and madness of the people, the representatives had to form a college to (a) decide as to how to introduce the rule of moderation by elaborately laying down to the minutest details the principles and corollaries of everyday governance; and (b) invest in the sovereign the power to suspend this everyday rules of governance and life also in the interests of 'exception' — thus making up the two aspects of sovereign power.

The Final Immunity of Law

From all that has been discussed till now I can say, by way of summing up, that in this task of framing the basic law, Babasaheb Ambedkar and other lawgivers concerned with social justice, liberty, and other rights were actually concerned with two overwhelming concerns. The first concern related to *conditions of governance*, which means ensuring the right conditions of governing people, conditions of successful government, conditions of stable rule, and achieving the right mix of liberty and equality, and freedom and obligations. Therefore it is found, in the above excerpts, in fact in the entire constitutional assembly proceedings, the dominant tone of moderation, and a concern that the right conditions of rule must be guaranteed through the constitution-making exercise. The second is related to the task of finding a solution to the riddle of the perpetual imbalance between state power, which implied *centralisation*, and various forms of governmental power, which implied *decentralisation and autonomies*. Caught in these two concerns Ambedkar and his colleagues were unable to work out the full logic of representation, and created what can be called the 'final immunity' of the law.

It should be asked: How does this happen in democracy? The situation that Ambedkar faced and reinforced in turn was not unique. Precisely for the fact that democracy is not an ideal but a system of government or, more aptly, speaking a way of governing, that democratic governance means ensuring certain conditions for democratic rule — conditions that may have nothing inherently democratic in them. Therefore, on the one hand, all democratic constitutions begin and found themselves on what can be called undemocratic features (carried over from previous constitutions, laws, compacts, and policies), and on the other hand the essential fact of governing produces undemocratic results, which may be called the 'deficit of democracy' or the 'democratic deficit'. In fact, as a little historical inquiry will show, the specific 'constitutional temper', which seeks to provide solidity of rule as the overwhelming requirement of the polity, was built up through the political debates in the nationalist movement preceding the constitution-making exercise — specifically in the 1930s and 1940s, when people like Tej Bahadur Sapru and C. R. Rajagopalachari repeatedly stressed the importance of constitutional and responsible behaviour, particularly in the context of British legal proposals including the Act of 1935. The British rule was one of continuous reforms — regardless of the nationalist response, or more correctly speaking, continuously responding to nationalist politics. Therefore legal reforms became a reality of the politics of the country, as real as other features were, and jurists and lawyers became headmasters and fathers of politicians. It also posed a challenge to the nationalists to continuously defend and legitimate its behaviour in terms of the standards set by the rule. Constitutional behaviour thus gained increasing importance in politics in relation to its other imperatives, to be crowned as God's final virtue in the deliberative exercise of 1946–49.[6] Thus, people like Ambedkar, who throughout the nationalist period had tried to build an alternative idea of the nation distinct from the one developed by Gandhi and Nehru (not that the latter two had the same idea), marked by the ideals of social justice and equality also became victims of the trope. Rule of law and search for an egalitarian social order was the impossible combination that Ambedkar aimed at achieving.[7] The paradox was demonstrated clearly in the failure of Ambedkar in 1951 to pilot the Hindu Code Bill to enactment after three years of effort. Ambedkar resigned from the Law Ministry — the final comment on his efforts to put constitutional behaviour above all and yet help the nation gain social justice. This is the problem of democratic deficit I am referring to in the present context.

To be true, the problem of democratic deficit was encountered in democratic studies long back, and was most acutely described by, among others, Alexis de Tocqueville in his study of American democracy about a hundred years before Ambedkar piloted the drafting of the Indian constitution. In his study is found of the tyranny of the majority, the virtues and problems posed by equality, the consequence of the presence of religion and race relations in a democracy, centralisation, the domination of commerce, and several other phenomena the problems that democracy faced and still faces — problems that are not due to insufficiency of democracy, but arise out of its conditions, and therefore produce its deficit. The final supremacy of law and accompanying lack of dialogic condition are the results of democratic deficit. However, this is a separate theme which merits an entirely separate discussion.

Presently, it can be asked: Did democracy and dialogue suffer because of this introduction of everyday governmentality in the politics of the nation, much heralded by the constitution, and none other than Ambedkar himself, whose dreams of social justice were to suffer soon the final blow at the hands of

---

[6] On this specific challenge set by the colonial rule for Indian nationalism, see D. A. Low, *Britain and Indian Nationalism: The Imprint of Ambiguity, 1929–1942*, Cambridge: Cambridge University Press, 1997.

[7] Gail Omvedt unfortunately misses this point in her otherwise forthright study of Ambedkar in the context of Indian nationalism; see her *Ambedkar: Towards an Enlightened India*, New Delhi: Penguin Books India, 2004.

an impersonal governmental machine? Or to put the question into sharper relief: How can democracy escape the aporia that constitutionalism represents? I shall end this article with some remarks on these two questions, which will also show the purpose of this section.

First, what is this aporia? I of course speak not of aporia, but of the immunity of the process — the immunity of the constitution, of the constitution-making process, and of the constitutionalists, from the daily vagaries of the politics of the street on issues of rights, justice, claim-making politics, and enforcement of responsibility. The constitution demanded responsibility; it was responsible to none. It had the final immunity; it was the god because it had combined the power of the sovereign and the tasks of the government. It was not democracy, that is, it cannot be said that constitution is democracy, but constitution promises democracy — *a democracy to come*, if it is followed.[8] In this promise, there is both an arrival and a postponement. An arrival, because constitutional democracy has arrived, constitutional order has arrived, constitution has arrived; and a postponement because till the laid script is not followed democracy will not arrive, therefore you the constitution cannot be held responsible. To arrive, to come is therefore also to postpone — because to arrive some categorical principle has been taken recourse to, constitution is the categorical principle, and it has been decided to deal with many of the burning issues of democracy later, the interest is now in setting up the principle only. To give one instance, the constitution talks only with its citizens and the institutions to govern them. But meanwhile non-citizens grow — aliens, illegal immigrants, refugees, masses of dropouts, and a huge army of underclass, not at all addressed by the constitution. Likewise, with ever-emerging hierarchies in the landscape of citizenship, some sections are increasingly out of the constitutional gaze — women of the lower order, starving peasants, an indebted population, and the moving migrants forcibly displaced from one worksite and life site to another. The constitution promises rights, but does not address the basic rightlessness of a people or groups

---

[8] On the idea of 'democracy to come', see the discussion by Jacques Derrida in *Rogues — Two Essays on Reason*, trans. Pascale-Anne Brault and Michael Naas, California: Stanford University Press, 2005.

of people who do not have 'the right to claim rights'. Through imposing a closure of its world, there is now immunity for the constitution. A promise has been issued, and now castles of reason can be made.

But is democracy then thereby postponed, is dialogue then suspended? This is my second point. As I have shown elsewhere, social and political dialogues continue, in as much as continue new efforts to build the political society with resources lying beyond the constitutional sphere and the rule of law, absorbing constitutional democracy but going beyond. The constitution may produce the citizen, but the political subject, the collective political subject, goes beyond the founding text — this is because the political subject grows out of contentious politics, the history of claim making, and the history of building new societies. Democracy therefore has to be re-envisioned not principally as a regime of rule of law presiding over a system of rights and duties but as a process of collective politics engaged in redefining rights, claims, trust, justice, and rules of conversation.

The question that may be asked, therefore, at the end of this article is: In the age of empire and democratic deficits how can the philosophy of constitution envision its path ahead? To answer this, it needs to be recalled from the 18th century democratic revolutionaries or the mid-20th century anti-colonial nationalists did not simply propose democracy and democratic independence in their given form. They addressed the issue of scale and the emerging modes of control with the appearance of the nation form in politics, and reinvented as solution the institutional forms and practices of representation. But as I have tried to demonstrate here, at both levels of the scale — the global by which I indicate global compulsions which a constitution cannot ignore, and the local, by which I mean the micro compulsions of governing — modern forms of representation will not be able to necessarily respond to the demands of the time. Restorative constitutions, constitutions that aimed at restoring the state, are failing. The problem of combining democracy with sovereignty has to be thus rigorously studied. In India, the constitution took place amidst a civil war, or many civil wars, and sovereign power was proposed as a constituent power to produce and reproduce the people as a peaceful social union ending the cataclysmic violence. Yet as we know from the subsequent history of India, a country, which can legitimately take pride in the success of its constitutional culture, the sovereign could not put an end to violence; it ended civil war by containing violence. The sovereign reorganised violence and fear into a coherent and stable political order in which governmentality worked as the main mixer of elements. In this way, the sovereign nation-state served modernity as an answer to the problem of civil war. But now is a time when the problem of scale is acute — sovereignty neither can end civil war nor can it fine tune the limitless details of governance required to make democratic sovereignty meaningful in the lives of the millions. Two problems here define the current condition: (a) The constitution produces the citizen as the political subject — subject in a double sense: first, the citizen is the subject by being the main actor in politics, and second, by being subject to rules of governance, enmeshed in daily governmentalities, because this citizen is the constitutional product; (b) meanwhile politics has gone ahead, and the emerging political subject today is a product of legality, semi-legality, and illegalities, responding to the demands of the scale in novel ways, primarily because this subject is a product not of constitutionalism but of a new politics that is post-colonial, which includes a new vision of political society that is dialogic and hence also post-national. The production of political subjectivity is a problem for stagnant politics because stagnant politics does not know how to cope with the issue of *excess*, which occasions the emergence of the subject.

What political narrative can illustrate this fabulous condition? The condition of reason producing its limits and law is leading to its transgression, law chambers and legal assemblies leading to streets, and the rights leading to a still undefined politics of justice? Surely, the answer cannot be obtained from within the constitutional discourse, situated as we are in the discourse itself. How do we come out? The limits of juridical reason, however, indicate the space (the location of stepping out) where we have to step in — that space, which is defined by three characteristics: (a) a space marked by the coexistence of legality, semi-legality, and illegalities; (b) a space marked by dialogues of these three existences; (c) and, a space marked by new and unfamiliar institutional innovations and legal pluralism. To even discursively arrive at this space, not only must we step out of the confines of constitutional discourse, we must urge on a dialogue between the constitution and the new illegalities.

What is the reason for proposing this dialogue? Here I can propose only very briefly the reason. First, the insistent presence of new illegalities must be understood. Of course illegalities have always been there. Indian society in the colonial time was characterised by many such illegal existences. But never have they been so worrisome for a legally organised political society, because multiple social struggles accompanied by an ever-increasing reach of law are creating illegal subjects. Second, the very operation of governmentality is producing illegalities as it is ruling out dialogic solutions at the micro level. Finally, law is now so much characterised by violence (legal violence) that it is today singularly unable to contest illegality as a mode of exist-ence. For these reasons constitutionalism by itself alone cannot engage with illegality — neither at the global level nor at the local level. It is this fabulous situation, possibly unprecedented, that is now urging many voices to speak out. 'Fearless speech' is a pro-duct of dialogic situation — a situation of contested conversation, only through which the closure can be escaped. And of course, the famous jurists must be told that at times history, rather than law, plays the grand jury in making a political society.

2

The 'Nehruvian' State, Developmental Imagination, Nationalism, and the Government

Benjamin Zachariah

Introduction

I wish to explore here some of the continuities and changes in the imagining and governing of the new Indian state in the period before and after formal independence, in particular through an examination of the developmental imagination that became central to the identity and legitimation of the independent Indian state. It explores the tensions and continuities between a colonial model of the state (something that requires further exploration in the historical and political science literature) and a national model, focusing on questions of legitimation as well as on actual practices of governance.

I want to pay close attention here to the uses of nationalism (a claim to the congruence of state and nation) to legitimate the state (the monopoly of legitimate violence). Although the 'Nehruvian model' of Indian nationalism became the officially proclaimed version, it is doubtful that it was ever properly hegemonic. The question of why it was not hegemonic, and yet remained the version that was most useful with which to publicly proclaim allegiance once again raises questions about the importance of languages of legitimation in a political order: What does it enable? What does it rule out? What manoeuvres, ideological and political, does it necessitate or obviate?

State-led developmentalism has been considered preferable to a dangerous, potentially or actually exclusionary 'cultural nationalism', where 'culture' stands for sectional interests, usually of a majoritarian nature. A developmental 'nationalism' is allegedly more progressive than a 'cultural' one, because it is a version of inclusive civic belonging rather than of ethnic belonging and its concomitant exclusions. The (nation-)state is legitimised and naturalised by the state claiming to be the nation through a project of collective 'development', in which the 'people' are allegedly the ultimate beneficiaries, and whose role it is to support the state's leadership. Meanwhile, a commitment to the nation-state is underpinned by the fact that 'development' takes place within the claimed geographical boundaries of that state. This collective movement towards a common goal allegedly obviates the need for close definitions of belonging and non-belonging to the 'nation': definitions can be bypassed, therefore 'culture', 'ethnies', or various other more exclusionary ways of imagining the nation, remain less of an issue. If the issue here is that of inclusive civic belonging, everyone within the borders belongs to the state, regardless of caste, creed, or religion. Exclusions are not cultural or ethnic but economic; whether this is preferable is a debatable matter.

States and Nationalisms

Such is the hegemony that the nation-state has acquired in everyday political thinking that the adjective pertaining to 'state' is almost always rendered as 'national'. Ideal-typically, the adjectives 'civic' and 'ethnic' serve to map the pluralist versus particularist themes onto nationalisms and states (even though we might avoid the national question somewhat by speaking of 'civic belonging' instead of 'civic nationalism'). The 'national' invokes the legitimacy of popular sovereignty in the service of the state. Furthermore, we are dealing very often, at least in the international (by which is meant inter-state) domain with the assumptions of an idealised liberalism that sees the possibilities of pluralism, as contained in its own ideologies, as capable of being universalised.[1] 'Liberalism' as a category was seldom directly invoked in Indian political discussions in the 20th century; it

---

[1] It might not be misplaced to point out, following the Skinner debate — for a summary, see James Tully (ed.), *Meaning and Context: Quentin Skinner and His Critics*, Cambridge: Cambridge University Press, 1988 — that political language is both normative and descriptive, and that 'liberalism', 'pluralism', 'democracy', 'nationalism', etc. are normative claims that seek to legitimate political activity (i.e., political *claims* are made in these terms) but are often in danger of lacking any agreed upon descriptive content.

has increasingly done so in the post-Cold War environment, and Indian academic writing that in part addresses an audience in the Anglo-American world tends to use it today as if it were a self-evident category.[2]

The limitations and paradoxes of such approaches find their expression in the need to defend 'values', whether plural or otherwise. 'Liberal' pluralist sentiment is plagued by the conundrum of being forced to tolerate (others') intolerance in the name of liberalism or pluralism, and surrender progressive principles in the name of diversity and (others') 'culture'. On the other hand, particularist and communitarian values might make (their own) culturalist claims to being more progressive and more inclusive than their competitors', thereby justifying (their own) intolerance

---

[2] According to the *'Begriffsgeschichte'* approach pioneered by the editors of the *Geschichtliche Grundbegriffe*, we cannot understand the politics of a given society without understanding the relevant political concepts or categories through which that politics is rendered intelligible and practised. 'Liberalism' is not a central *Begriff* for 20th-century India, either as term or concept. On the issues involved, see for instance Reinhart Koselleck's programmatic introduction in Vol. 1 of Otto Brunner, Werner Conze and Reinhart Koselleck (eds), *Geschictliche Grundbegriffe: Historisches Lexicon zur politisch-sozialen Sprache in Deutschland* (8 vols, Stuttgart: Klett, 1972–1993), which many reviewers have pointed out is not entirely in consonance with the approaches of all contributors to the *Geschictliche Grundbegriffe*. See also Reinhart Koselleck, *'Richtlinien für das Lexicon politisch-sozialer Begriffe der Neuzeit'*, *Archiv für Begriffsgeschichte* (1967), pp. 81–99, and Reinhart Koselleck, *'Begriffsgeschichte* and Social History' in Reinhart Koselleck, *Futures Past* (Cambridge, Mass.: MIT Press, 1985, trans. Keith Tribe), pp. 73–91 [in original: Koselleck, *'Begriffsgeschichte und Sozialgeschichte'* in Koselleck, *Vergangene Zukunft* (Frankfurt a.m: Suhrkamp, 1979), pp. 107–29]. An assessment of the possibilities of *Begriffsgeschichte* from the early 1990s stressed 'the extraordinary difficulty of translating the meaning of terms and concepts from one language into another, from one cultural tradition into another, and from one intellectual climate into another': Detlef Junker, 'Preface', in Hartmut Lehmann and Melvin Richter (ed.), *The Meaning of Historical Terms and Concepts: New Studies on Begriffsgeschichte* (Washington, DC: German Historical Institute Occasional Paper No. 15, 1996), p. 6. The problem is also one of wanting to map *terms* too closely onto *concepts, which is perhaps a problem of translation of* 'Begriff', *which is both term and concept.* The same term could refer to different concepts, and the same concept could be rendered by different terms. The difficulties with the arbitrary sign have not been fully grappled within this tradition, although making something of the Saussurean distinction between the synchronic and the diachronic.

in the name of liberalism, tolerance, secularism, etc. In some cases, then, the case for defending pluralism allegedly becomes a case for defending a community of faith or 'values', whether this faith is called 'tolerance' or 'culture' or 'liberalism', or even the 'Hindu way of life', allegedly more tolerant and 'secular' than other available ideologies.[3]

Examples that come readily to mind include, for instance, the allegedly tolerant Dutch state's ability to justify stigmatising Muslims on the grounds of Islam's alleged intolerance of homosexuality or its mistreatment of women. The pattern is of course discernible in several public debates in India and elsewhere about the necessity of anti-terrorist legislation in 'democracies': 'our values' include respect for the due process of law, but anything from preventive detention to torture has been discussed in terms of the exceptional threat posed by those who threaten 'our values'. Opponents point out how these values are also under threat if they can be seen not to apply to potential 'terrorists' or outsiders, who in a circular argument are the one because they are the other. This is an international (by which, again, I mean inter-state) environment in which the current Indian political order partakes.

Such arguments have been so all-pervasive in recent times that it is useless to pretend that current discussions are not to a great extent provoked by them. At any rate, they provide a strong context for the concern with attempting to discover and/or analyse statist models of belonging to states that avoid imposing a set of obligatory 'values' on actual or potential citizens, or those otherwise subject to the state's jurisdiction. This is a question of the obligatory language in which legitimate political claims can be made, for if the inclusive, secular, democratic state is as hegemonic as is hoped, strong 'values'-based claims are likely to be discredited in advance, as too exclusionary.

Inclusion, then, and the (often merely apparent) absence of markers of 'values'-based qualification to belonging within a state,

---

[3] The dilemma I have outlined here is also central to Anne Phillips, *Multiculturalism without Culture*, Princeton: Princeton University Press, 2007: see especially pp. 1–9. Her solutions are different from mine. She also distinguishes between 'culture' on the one hand, and 'religion', 'race', 'ethnicity', etc. on the other; in this article I have subsumed all these under the category 'confessional', in an extended sense.

can themselves be (presented as) 'values'. Such a state can define its exclusions in terms of excluding those who would otherwise do the excluding: even apparently unobjectionable principles such as 'freedom of speech' (most often defended in principle even as they are constrained or mutilated by states) are 'values'. It is also perfectly possible to imagine an exclusionary and secular democratic state: a 'confessional state', in an extended sense of the term, where the right to be a full member of that state requires conformity with a set of values that are often merely implicit.

In this article, I address the question of whether the two approaches, of 'civic belonging' on the one hand, and 'values' on the other, are mutually opposed, through an analysis of the 'Nehruvian' state in India and its 'legacies'. 'Nehruvian' is treated here as something more than the views of the individual whose proper name provides the root of the adjective; and 'legacies' is treated here as a set of critical engagements with precedents, models, and practices.

I should also like to bring strongly into focus the question of legitimate political languages — languages that enable or constrain what political claims can be made, and what actions justified, in a given context. Without attention to this point, we are in danger of mistaking the conventions of political argument for the substance of politics. Further, I should also like to point out that civic belonging without delineating specific characteristics of that belonging ('values'?) can be postulated in a one-state model in which everyone simply and unproblematically belongs to the state; or in a model in which all states are so similar that they cannot find a relevant Other against which to define themselves. It is difficult to sustain when really existing states must distinguish themselves from one another ('national characteristics'?) and must find grounds for excluding or including different people (non-'nationals'?). That there are also various other layers of inclusion and exclusion within the body of persons accepted as 'nationals', levels of 'true' or 'inauthentic' national belonging, is a truism that must also be taken seriously.

Nehruvian Anti-Nationalism: The Argument

India is widely regarded as a successful, democratic, and largely secular state, which despite major difficulties has avoided being a 'confessional state', i.e., a 'distinctly modern' institution in which a particular confessional group is privileged in and controls the state. 'Confessionalisation' was characterised by the heightened training and disciplining of the clergy in rival theologies, and by the intensification of preaching, religious devotions, and pastoral pedagogy for increasingly segregated congregations, leading to the emergence of distinct and mutually hostile religious cultures.[4] In our case, it might be suggested, by extension, that 'culture', 'ethnicity', 'religion' or any number of particulars could count as 'confession' in a literal sense for the schematic characterisation 'confessional state' to work (there can, as we have accepted above, be secular 'confessional states' that make 'values' claims that are not religious as the basis of belonging to it). India has taken major steps towards achieving the goal of separating the idea of citizenship from the specifics of religion, community, ethnicity — in other words, towards that ideal-typical goal of the citizen who is citizen because the state is the state, where the specifics of neither state nor citizen are central to this equation.

It is nonetheless possible to look at the meta-narrative and the practices of Indian state building (significantly always called 'nation building' by contemporaries) in terms of their implications for minorities' sense of security and belonging. The crucial years of defining Indian national belonging by the state, in legal and constitutional terms, took place against the backdrop of the formation of Pakistan, allowing Hindu nationalists to argue that the residual Indian state would now be a Hindu state. Those on the left, backed by Jawaharlal Nehru, insisted that national belonging would not be defined by religion, ethnicity, etc. but by virtue of common belonging to India. This constituted a nationalism defined by a refusal to define in any specific sense what belonging to the nation might mean.

The question arises, then, as to whether such a nationalism functions as a nationalism: If nationalism must delineate the

---

[4] See Ian Hunter, 'The Man and the Citizen: the Pluralisation of Civil Personae in Early Modern German Natural Law', in Anna Yeatman and Magdalena Zolkos (eds), *State, Security and Subject Formation*, New York: Continuum, 2010, pp. 16–35; the quote is from p. 19. Hunter is speaking of early modern Europe, and of Lutheranism, Catholicism and Calvinism in particular, but he uses the characterisation 'confessional state' by extension for other times and places, as does this article.

distinction between one nation and another, the (then) official version of Indian nationalism singularly fails to do so. If so, what happens to such a (non)-nationalism at a time of crisis? Can implicit exclusions become more explicit?

But we are working with the 'state' as the central focus here, and should resist the temptation to conflate the state with the nation in the way that its ideologues did. Let us accept, for the moment, that the state is *sui generis* but needs a legitimating ideology, then perhaps it is logical to discover that we start from the state (the monopoly of legitimate violence,[5] an organ of coercion and class rule),[6] and find ourselves discussing the nation and nationalism (the sovereignty of the people, the claim to the congruence of nation and state).[7] The question also arises — since we are dealing not only with 'the state' as an ideal-typical model, but also with a particular state which makes claims to being different from other states (the basis of national claims) — how states distinguish themselves from one another. Is it that to justify its particularity, a state must invoke values, negatively, in the case of the ideal-typical 'civic nationalism', but as we have discussed above, can this not also become an invocation of 'our values'? And is it that to legitimately monopolise violence that the state must invoke the 'nation'? This invocation is certainly necessary at the time of the hegemony of the nation-state idea, a naturalisation delivered in a hyphen, whose moment of arrival as a central legitimating basis for statehood we might wish to date precisely to the Russian Revolution, now mistakenly referred to as the 'Wilsonian Moment';[8] but authorship and origin are less

---

[5] Max Weber, '*Politik als Beruf*', lecture, Munich University, 1918, reprinted in translation as 'Politics as a Vocation' in HH Gerth and C Wright Mills (ed. & transl), *From Max Weber: Essays in Sociology*, new edn, London: Routledge, 1991, pp. 77–128; the definition appears on p. 78: 'a state is a human community that (successfully) claims the *monopoly of the legitimate use of physical force* within a given territory'.

[6] Mikhail Bakunin, 'Statism and Anarchy' (1874), VI Lenin, *The State and Revolution* (1918), http://www.marxists.org/reference/archive/bakunin/works/1873/statism-anarchy.htm, accessed 10 September 2010 and http://www.marxists.org/archive/lenin/works/1917/staterev/, accessed 10 September 2010 respectively.

[7] Ernest Gellner, *Nations and Nationalism*, Oxford: Blackwell, 1983.

[8] See Erez Manela, *The Wilsonian Moment: Self-Determination and the International Origins of Anticolonial Nationalism*, Oxford: Oxford University

important now than its implications. The conflation of 'nation' and 'state' owes much in the Indian case to the necessity of nationalism as legitimation for an anti-colonial movement in search of a state, but this is a question we can defer in its specifics, for we do not need it for this argument. It might, however, illuminate the fact that states need a legitimating ideology, and nationalisms provide it.

The 'Nehruvian project', seen in this context, was an attempt to resist and to create something other than a confessional state, through a developmental version of a 'civil philosophy', through a separation of the personae of the (wo)man as citizen (the domain of the state) and as religious individual (the domain of salvation through a chosen route that was not the concern of the state),[9] while accepting the *sui generis* character of the state as well as, logically enough for someone from the socialist tradition, its necessary class character.[10] This was a difficult manoeuvre to pull off in a context where the rationale for a post-imperialist state was that it was a national state (in this case as opposed to an imperial state), where there were also vested interests in various sectarian 'culture'- or 'confession'-based identities that sought to be the basis of an official nationalism (which, to belabour the point, is the basis of statist inclusions and exclusions). The 'Nehruvian project', thus, attempted to create a civil philosophy using a legitimating language of nationalism while at the same time attempting to bypass nationalism as a somewhat dangerous phenomenon.

Press, 2007; compare the earlier work by Arno Mayer, *Wilson vs Lenin: Political Origins of the New Diplomacy 1917–1918*, New Haven: Yale University Press, (1959) 1963).

[9] Ian Hunter, 'The Man and the Citizen'.

[10] As Nehru acknowledged in anticipating the future state,

The middle class is too strong to be pushed out and there is a tremendous lack of human material in any other class to take its place effectively, or to run a planned society ... a premature conflict on class lines would lead to a break-up and possibly to prolonged inability to build up anything (Jawaharlal Nehru to K. T. Shah, 13 May 1939, quoted in Raghabendra Chattopadhyay, 'The Idea of Planning in India, 1930–1951', unpublished PhD dissertation, Canberra: Australian National University, Canberra, 1985, p. 106.

Developmentalism as, or instead of, Civic Nationalism

To return to the beginning of our enquiry: State-led developmentalism has been considered preferable to a potentially or actually exclusionary 'cultural nationalism'; a developmental 'nationalism' is allegedly more progressive than a 'cultural' one, because it is a version of inclusive civic belonging rather than of ethnic belonging and its concomitant exclusions. The (nation-) state is legitimised and naturalised by the state claiming to be the nation through a project of collective 'development', in which the 'people' are allegedly the ultimate beneficiaries whose role it is to support the state's leadership.[11] A commitment to the nation-state is underpinned by the fact that 'development' takes place within the claimed geographical boundaries of that state. This collective movement towards a common goal allegedly obviates the need for close definitions of belonging and non-belonging to the 'nation': definitions can be bypassed, therefore 'culture', 'ethnies', or various other more exclusionary ways of imagining the nation remain less of an issue.[12] Whose commitment to the nation-state is this, however? The citizen is invoked in this model but is not allowed much of a voice.

Does developmentalism qualify as a form of nationalism? Does it do the work of delineating those who belong to the 'nation' from those who do not? Does it replace, is it replaced by, or does it coexist with, a more 'cultural' form of nationalism? My argument here is that the 'developmental' in the Indian case was

---

[11] Partha Chatterjee, *The Nation and its Fragments: Colonial and Postcolonial Histories*, Princeton: Princeton University Press, 1993, pp. 202–205.

[12] We may cite the constructionist versus primordialist debate here: Benedict Anderson, *Imagined Communities: Reflections on the Origins and Spread of Nationalism*, London: Verso, 1983; Ernest Gellner, *Nations and Nationalism*; Eric Hobsbawm and Terence Ranger (ed.), *The Invention of Tradition*, Cambridge: Cambridge University Press, 1983, 'Introduction', versus A. D. Smith and his followers: see A. D. Smith, *Nations and Nationalism in a Global Era*, Cambidge: Polity Press, 1995, for a statement of this position, and for a restatement, A. D. Smith, 'History and National Destiny: Responses and Clarifications', *Nations and Nationalism* 10, 1–2, 2004, pp. 195–209. This strikes me as largely a non-debate: If ethnies are the basis of 'nations', who invents 'ethnies'?

the outcome of a regime that sought to bypass or underplay the national question, while inevitably having to situate itself within a language of legitimacy that depended on nationalism, which was the only available paradigm to internationally (by which is of course meant 'inter-state') legitimate the Indian state.

Closely related to this is the problem of territoriality: The 'Nehruvian' state in India, in common with many states formed after a formal decolonisation process, inherited borders and boundaries that were set in place by a colonial power. To justify the 'naturalness' of that territory in terms of a 'nation' defined in 'cultural' terms becomes extremely difficult without making major exclusions, and yet there were many who made that attempt. Equally, in 'developmental' terms the alternative is to take the post-independence state's boundaries as given and not to talk too much about them.

Certain questions emerge from this situation: Is a civic nationalism a nationalism without characteristics specific to the 'nation'? Can it distinguish between the characteristics of its own nationals and the characteristics of the nationals of other states? If it is unable to or refuses to do so, does it remain a kind of nationalism? In practice, a 'Nehruvian' nationalism is open to the charge that it has no specific characteristics (a charge often levelled at it), or that it was too 'foreign' and not 'rooted' enough in the country whose nationalism it sought to be. This is, on the one hand, what made it attractive to other states emerging from colonial rule with messy identitarian politics and heterogeneous populations. On the other hand, this is what makes it vulnerable to those who demand a 'proper' nationalism with positive ('cultural'?) characteristics that go back to 'time immemorial' or an ancient, 'classical' past. So the 'Nehruvian' ('civic') nationalism is forced to confront the non-specificity of its nationalism: it could just as easily be an Indian, an Indonesian or a Ghanaian nationalism. Since the 'Nehruvians' cannot easily admit this without abandoning the legitimating framework of the nation-state, they must draw upon some specific characteristics. This leads to a calling upon the specific, which must be at least somewhat cultural.

Developmentalism was also a way for an elite that saw itself as progressive to keep its hold on the state. The narrative of the emergence of that state is founded on a stage-ist argument, in which an early compromise with anti-colonial nationalism of a bourgeois variety leads to national independence and a progressive (nation-)state in the hands of an enlightened and socialist-leaning leadership, thereby paving the way for socialism.[13] In practice, until this socialist stage is reached (and it never is), the state is a capitalist one in which domestic industry is sheltered from foreign competition (the strategy of 'import-substituting industrialisation'); infrastructure building and early risk taking on new necessary industries is by state-owned enterprises; there is some — often rhetorical — commitment to socialism or at least social justice or social welfare, and some — often rhetorical — commitment to land reform. The details can be filled in.[14]

If we are speaking here of inclusive civic belonging, everyone within the borders belongs to the state, regardless of caste, creed, or religion. Exclusions are not civic but economic; whether this is preferable is debatable, but for the purposes of our question, a Nehruvian developmentalism appears to meet the criteria of a 'civil philosophy'. It also meets the criterion of 'educating' people in 'civility' or 'civic virtue': there was a constant pedagogic project built into the Nehruvian developmental regime.

This model has problematic implications for formal democracy. The 'masses' would be told what to do for the good of the (nation-)state, which was also (in the long run?) for their own good. If, as Nehru admitted privately, it was Hindu sectarian opinion

---

[13] This is indeed a plausible and not too inconsistent reading of Lenin's views on national bourgeoisies, suitably modified by M. N. Roy's intervention. See VI Lenin, *Draft Theses on National and the Colonial Questions*, 1920, http://marxists.org/archive/lenin/works/1920/jun/05.htm, accessed 23 August 2011, part of the 11th thesis of which reads

The Communist International must enter into a temporary alliance with bourgeois democracy in the colonial and backward countries, but should not merge with it, and should under all circumstances uphold the independence of the proletarian movement even if it is in its most embryonic form.

[14] This is an argument I make in more detail in Benjamin Zachariah, *Developing India: an Intellectual and Social History, c. 1930–1950*, New Delhi: Oxford University Press, 2005, and *Nehru*, London: Routledge, 2004.

that was in the ascendant in the period leading to and immediately after independence,[15] he would ensure that this tendency had no access to legitimate political arenas. The 'Nehruvians', and Nehru in particular, were adept at manoeuvring languages of legitimacy so that, in the context both of the Indian anti-colonial struggle led by the Indian National Congress that had always claimed to be non-sectarian, and of the post-independence period, where ethnocentric sectarianisms stood temporarily discredited in the public domain (not least after the assassination of Gandhi by a Hindu),[16] a Hindu chauvinist nationalism had limited access to the language of public legitimation. Thus, the 'cultural' in the 'national' ('culture' of course being an euphemism for any number of things) was sought to be suppressed by a form of state-led developmentalism that claimed some basis in internationalist, or at least less than nationalist, thought. But this was always very unstable.

The 'Nehruvian' Project and the Developmental Imagination

If we are to speak meaningfully of the non-confessional state that the Nehruvians attempted to build, we need to distinguish meaningfully between that position (or set of positions) and the confessional position that was counter posed to it, and yet was not completely separable from it.

'Development' was not merely a set of ideas held by 'Nehruvians' or the left, even if they dominated the language that expressed it. At the time of formal independence in 1947, the conventions of thinking and speaking about development incorporated a number of coexisting and sometimes contradictory elements. Claims to 'socialism' — or to some social concern for the poor and

---

[15] Jawaharlal Nehru to Rajendra Prasad, 7 August 1947, in S. Gopal (ed.), *Selected Works of Jawaharlal Nehru, Second Series (SWJN II)*, vol. 2, Delhi: Nehru Memorial Fund, 1984, p. 191; report of Nehru's talk with Z. A. Ahmad of the Communist Party of India, June 1945, 'not to be shown to anyone without [General Secretary] P. C. Joshi's permission', 1945/9, P. C. Joshi Archive, New Delhi: Jawaharlal Nehru University.

[16] *SWJN II*, vol. 5, pp. 35–36, 'The Light has Gone Out of our Lives', All-India Radio broadcast by Nehru, 30 January 1948; resolutions on Gandhi's death, 2 February 1948, *SWJN II*, vol. 5, pp. 37–38.

downtrodden — were obligatory, since a movement towards social justice was in public debates depicted as necessary for a poor country whose independence was supposed to provide solace to its poor. Such claims were, by the 1940s, made by capitalists and avowed socialists alike. Also invoked were 'science', technology, and technical expertise as ways of achieving 'modern' social and economic goals — even by the Gandhians, who tried to redefine the 'modern' in such a way as to justify a decentralised, village-based, and labour-intensive socio-economic order as more in keeping with 'modern' trends. To achieve these goals, a good deal of 'national discipline' was required, and the 'masses' were to have to make some sacrifices in the short-term, or in the 'transitional period'. A more explicitly conservative aspect was also present: Solutions to social, economic, or political problems were to conform to 'indigenous' values — borrowings from 'foreign' systems were to be treated with suspicion (they did not conform to 'Indian values'). This was a particularly useful tactical argument used against socialists and communists by Gandhians and by the right (often strategically merging with the Gandhians); but it was also used by socialists to argue that communists were 'foreign' elements controlled from Moscow. The appeal of the 'indigenist' strand of argument in a colonised country was rhetorically powerful, and could often put people who counted themselves in the 'progressive' camp on the defensive: here, indeed, was a 'cultural' component in the 'developmental' imagination. These views contributed to a general and conventionalised view of 'development' as 'progress', and India as a potentially 'modern' country with a rich 'tradition'.[17]

We might spot certain elements that belong on the 'values' side (the 'indigenist' strand) as well as on the side of the state 'educating' subjects in 'civility' (effectively a self-proclaimed vanguard who decides to educate the 'masses', since the state is not as impersonal as its ideologues claim it to be, and its educational role must be performed by agents, and an abstraction is not an agent). They are not mutually exclusive and must compromise with one another ('national discipline' and 'national education').

---

[17] Benjamin Zachariah, *Developing India*; 'In Search of the "Indigenous": J. C. Kumarappa and the Philosophy of the Village Movement', in Michael Mann and Harald Fischer-Tine (ed.), *Colonialism as Civilising Mission*, London: Anthem Press, 2004, pp. 248–69.

The 'Nehruvian project' had to manoeuvre within this set of conventions. In order to present a case for civic belonging devoid of confessional characteristics, it had to address the argument about the nature of the nation that was to be the basis for the new state. The problem was that all forms of national argument that claimed 'India' as a national unit relied on some form of invocation of an ancient past that was, by default at least, 'Hindu'. This could be a terminological problem rather than of confession or culture. 'Hindu' and its related expressions were never fully 'national' because their multiple meanings could not simply be reduced to the imagining of an Indian nation, or a future Indian state. However, the 'national' in the Indian case was extremely reliant on one or another version of the 'Hindu'.[18] Whether as geographical, cultural, or religious entity, the 'Hindu' past was required for the national present. 'Tradition' and 'indigeneity' tended to be euphemisms that easily gravitated towards upper-caste 'Hindu' practices; and whether it could or could not be proved that these were recently invented traditions, they were effective in creating solidarities around themselves. Debates on the national therefore, always, if often implicitly relied on some debate around the category 'Hindu'.

Nehru and the Congress left contended that 'communal' identities were not true identities; they were made possible by the poverty of the people and their consequent search for resources of rather irrational hope, and were manipulated by elites with a vested interest in sectarianism for their own narrow ends. The preferred way of overcoming this problem of false consciousness was by economic means: greater prosperity for the masses would lead to greater awareness that the real issues were economic. This, with some justification, can be seen as developmentalism in place of sectarianism or 'communalism' (as it is called in India), or indeed developmentalism in place of nationalism, for sectarianism or 'communalism' can be seen as a nationalism that sets its boundaries in the wrong place (as allegedly does what we now politely call 'sub-nationalism'). It depends, of course, on one's point of view what that wrong place is.

---

[18] See inter alia Peter van der Veer, *Religious Nationalism: Hindus and Muslims in India*, Berkeley: University of California Press, 1994 for a strong version of this argument.

It is important, therefore, to look at Nehruvian nationalism in this context: an attempt to rely on solidarities based on elective affinity, not ethnicity, religion or other forms of sectarianism. But what if elective affinities refused to take appropriate national forms? As Nehru was repeatedly to put it in public, nationalism alone was too narrow and parochial to solve any major problems. Thus, it was important to have an economic programme for the raising of living standards and incomes.[19] But it was inevitable that a people not yet free would think in terms of nationalism. When they were free they would think in more broad terms, Nehru argued, because nationalism was a 19th-century idea whose time had come and gone.[20] (He was to be less optimistic about this later in his life, as the everyday politics of independent India took aggressively nationalist forms at various points.)[21]

However, even as the left wing of a nationalist movement put forward socialism as the true solution, nationalism was implicitly — in most people's thinking — better than 'communalism' because it achieved the unity of all people against the British. Development was potentially the solvent of this problem of sectarianism. In some earlier versions of this, 'socialism' was to be the achievable basis of development and to perform this anti-sectarian role. In the post-independence Indian state, this meant a state-led development where the state led by the Nehruvian elite would stand for the nation, and use the rhetoric of collective belonging to the nation to direct developmental plans from above on behalf of the people.

The attempt to bypass the problems of sectarian definitions of belonging to the nation-state through developmentalism had to be accompanied by an attempt to disarm the 'Hindu' or 'indigenist' strand of argument. In *The Discovery of India*, his statement on the nature of Indian national belonging published in 1946, Nehru stated, as he had done before, that an obsession with nationalism was a natural response to the lack of freedom.[22]

---

[19] See Jawaharlal Nehru, *An Autobiography*, London: Jonathan Cape, 1936, pp. 266, 587–90.

[20] E.g., Message to the All-India Congress Socialist Conference at Meerut, 13 January 1936, in S. Gopal (ed.), *Selected Works of Jawaharlal Nehru (SWJN)*, vol. 7, Delhi: Nehru Memorial Fund, 1975, pp. 60–61.

[21] See, for instance, his letter to Bertrand Russell during the China crisis, in Bertrand Russell, *Unarmed Victory*, Harmondsworth: Penguin, 1963, p. 105.

[22] Jawaharlal Nehru, *The Discovery of India*, London: Signet, 1946, p. 52.

With the achievement of freedom the obsession would vanish; wider groupings of nations and states, and wider solidarities on the basis of internationalism would be possible. Nehru's concern was with trying to understand the history of India in terms of 'the burden of the past', which he believed was 'over-powering, and sometimes suffocating, more especially for those of us who belong to very ancient civilisations like those of India and China'.[23]

As a matter of central importance, Nehru confronted the 'Hindu' view of Indianness: 'It is ... incorrect and undesirable to use "Hindu" or "Hinduism" for Indian culture, even with reference to the distant past'.[24] The term 'Hindu' was used in a geographical sense to denote the Indian landmass by outsiders, derived from the river Sindhu or Indus. The 'Hindu golden age' idea had been crucially shaped by the needs of Indian nationalism. This, he believed, was understandable.

> It is not Indians only who are affected by nationalist urges and supposed national interest in the writing or consideration of history. Every nation and people seems to be affected by this desire to gild and better the past and distort it to their advantage.[25]

But it was a version that was, he argued, historically false (he could not have missed the fact that he was himself attempting something not dissimilar: to narrate an acceptable past for the 'nation', retrospectively to justify his own commitment to that 'nation'). Although he acknowledged that some basic ideas and continuities had been preserved in popular and elite cultures, it was impossible to attribute this to one group of inhabitants of India. Historically, India was 'like some ancient palimpsest on which layer upon layer of thought and reverie had been inscribed, and yet no succeeding layer had completely hidden or erased what had been written previously'.[26] Each layer had enriched Indian culture and had a place in a new national consciousness; the great rulers of India were the synthesisers who looked beyond sectional interests to bring together different layers. The alien nature of British rule rested on the British

---

[23] Ibid., p. 36.
[24] Ibid., p. 75.
[25] Ibid., p. 104.
[26] Ibid., p. 59.

refusal to accept India geographically as a home, and its exploit-ation of India economically for the benefit of outside interests.

Ancient palimpsest, this, then, was to be the acknowledged basis of a nationalism that thereafter would seek to establish the grounds for a civic rather than a confessional state: a shared, and somewhat mystic, common culture that would be acknowledged and then for all effective purposes forgotten. Thus, there were no fundamental cultural values that defined the entity 'India'; and this itself was its fundamental value. Simultaneously, Nehru also warned against a view of India that over-glorified the past — a danger, he noted, that was also present in China. He agreed that both civilisations had 'shown an extraordinary staying power and adaptability'.[27] But not all ancient things were worth preserving: caste discrimination, for instance, had to be struggled against. India was at present 'an odd mixture of medievalism, appalling poverty and misery and a somewhat superficial modernism of the middle classes'.[28] What was needed was to bring modernism to the masses, by the middle classes understanding and pro-moting the needs of the masses. He stressed his admiration for Russia and the Chinese communists in their attempts to end similar conditions.

'Culture', of course, remained the sticky question if the pur-pose was to invent an inclusive nationalism. Nehru's solutions to the problem of Indian cultural unity were rather awkward. He himself claimed to have experienced this unity emotionally rather than intellectually, in his travels through India. On the intellectual side, however, he tended to fall back on stereotypes. Nehru's own language, then and later, tended to be imbued with some of the prevalent language of race and eugenics, as well as a patronising and at times paternalistic attitude towards the 'masses': he spoke unselfconsciously of 'sturdy peasants' and 'finer physical types'.[29] His view of Indian culture as accretion and synthesis fitted in well with some cultural practices such as the worship at Sufi shrines of both 'Hindus' and Muslims.[30] In other

---

[27] Ibid., p. 144.

[28] Ibid., p. 56.

[29] Ibid., pp. 65, 68.

[30] The category 'Hindu' is a disputed one and its exact boundaries are far from clear. For a preliminary set of discussions of the issues involved see, for example, David Lorenzen, 'Who Invented Hinduism?' *Comparative Studies*

cases, this view did not work quite so well. According to Nehru, Indian peasants had a common oral tradition in versions of the great epics, the *Ramayana* and the *Mahabharata*.[31] This might have been true for some Muslim or Christian 'sturdy peasants', but was not true, for instance, of the north-eastern 'tribal' territories of India that were to be inherited by independent India because they had been within the borders of British India.

There is a strong sense here that the need for such a statement appeared in the context of the growing strength of the Pakistan movement during the World War II. It is also worth noting, perhaps in this connection, that Nehru regarded his statement as an attempt to find a consensual description of what it meant to be an Indian, rather than merely as a statement of his own positions: he had hitherto avoided making too many or too precise statements on Indian nationalism, and occasionally, for wider audiences, made his distaste for nationalism quite clear:

> All that is reactionary seeks shelter under that name — fascism, imperialism, race bigotry, and the crushing of that free spirit of enquiry which gave the semblance of greatness to Europe in the nineteenth century. ... There is virtue in it up to a certain stage — till then it is a progressive force adding to human freedom. But even then it is a narrowing creed and a nation seeking freedom, like a person who is sick can think of little besides its own struggle and its own misery.[32]

The Discovery of India attributes much of its content to its author's conversations with his fellow inmates in prison on the nature of the national, and it gives the sense of his having attempted a progressive synthesis of these statements.[33] He continuously distinguishes his personal views from those that he

---

in Society and History, 41 (4), October 1999, pp. 630–59; Arvind Sharma, 'On Hindu, Hindustan, Hinduism and *Hindutva*', *Numen*, 49, 2002, pp. 1–36; Heinrich von Stietencron, 'Hinduism: On the Proper Use of a Descriptive Term', in Günther D. Sontheimer and Hermann Kulke (ed.), *Hinduism Reconsidered* Delhi: Manohar, 1989, pp. 11–27.

[31] Jawaharlal Nehru, *Discovery of India*, p. 67.

[32] Jawaharlal Nehru, article for *Asia* magazine, n.d., c.1939, typescript, copy in Indian Political Intelligence file, India Office Records, British Library, London, L/PJ/12/94, f.9.

[33] Jawaharlal Nehru, *Discovery of India*, Preface, p. 9.

believes might have wider resonances. Moreover, he does not and cannot work his way round the problem of the slippage or identification of 'Hindu' and 'Indian'. Instead, however, he tries to dilute the significance of the category 'Hindu', disarming it of its communitarian and therefore sectarian implications. This is, of course, an impossible task.[34]

The Exclusions of the Developmental Imagination

Economics versus sectarianism: economic man would inevitably replace sectarian man, as ordinary people began to recognise their real interests. This was the formula on the basis of which many public battles were fought. But ideologues like Nehru had no answer to questions of identity and solidarity as expressed in the partition massacres and the post-independence tendency of organised mobs of Hindus or Sikhs to turn on Muslims. Through this period of violence, Nehru and his government or his socialist colleagues could do no more than make statements on the irrationality of events and muse on the atavistic tendencies of mobs.[35] The transfer of power was made according to a vastly oversimplified understanding of these events that regarded widespread and unprecedented violence as indication that Hindus and Muslims now could not live together in peace. It also contributed greatly to a view among the political leadership that the 'masses' in India were an irrational, potentially violent, and volatile rabble who could not be trusted with too much political initiative. The people were the ultimate beneficiaries of development; the state was the agent of development; the nation and the state were, if not entirely identified with each other, at least in harmony. Unless challenged, therefore, the state was the nation.

---

[34] Current and earlier versions of Hindu nationalism, for instance, have tended to argue that 'Hindu' is so inclusive a category as to be acceptable to everyone, and therefore can be the basis for an Indian national identity. This was clearly not Nehru's manoeuvre.

[35] See, for instance, Nehru's speech at Khusrupore, 4 November 1946, *SWJN II*, vol. 1, p. 55; his letter to Vallabhbhai Patel, November 5, 1946, *SWJN II*, vol. 1, pp. 62–65.

There were many within Nehru's party, the Indian National Congress, who wished to exclude Muslims in particular and non-upper-caste Hindus in general from political power and social status. Behind the scenes, they argued that after the partition of India, the matter had been decided: Pakistan was a Muslim state; the residual India would therefore be a Hindu state. Nehru disagreed strongly, refusing to reduce Muslims and other non-Hindus in India to the implicit status of foreigners. Largely on the strength of claims that the Congress had repeatedly made in public before independence, he was often able to force the issue towards a non-sectarian definition of being Indian. But there were moments where the allegedly non-sectarian Indian state betrayed an implicitly communitarian logic in its actions, as in the question of the repatriation of 'abducted women' to Pakistan and India in the years after partition. 'Repatriation' was often in disregard of the wishes of the women themselves, and with the working assumption that 'originally' Hindu women who lived with Muslims in Pakistan belonged back in India.[36]

There was a definite tension between imagining an independent India that was to be for the benefit of the masses (the 'nation', represented by the nationalists-who-were-the-Congress, who would run the state) and imagining development in and for India, in which the masses (who would allegedly ultimately be the beneficiaries) were instrumentally cast as material to be moulded. This was enabled by the construction of a language of legitimacy that simultaneously centred on and marginalised the 'masses' by subordinating them to a larger, allegedly 'national', project. This, of course, is precisely the project of 'educating' the 'masses' in 'civility'; but this educational process was also a form of exclusion at the same time as it was a form of civic inclusion.

This is evident early on in the public statements around the economy emanating from the new state. The centrality of the

---

[36] For a sense of the rhetoric surrounding this, see *SWJN II*, vol. 5, pp. 113–23. Nehru wrote to Rajendra Prasad about abducted women on both sides of the border that '[n]either side has really tried hard enough to recover them'. Letter, 22 January 1948, *SWJN II*, vol. 5, pp. 113–14. For an account, see Ritu Menon and Kamala Bhasin, 'Her Body and Her Being: Of Widows and Abducted Women in Post-Partition India', in Margaret Jolly and Kalpana Ram (ed.), *Borders of Being: Citizenship, Fertility and Sexuality in Asia and the Pacific*, Ann Arbor: University of Michigan Press, 2001, pp. 58–81.

anti-imperialist struggle had often led to a deferral of questions of labour rights, wages, and welfare, in which the left wing of the nationalist movement had been complicit and even proactive, on the grounds that the first enemy to be defeated was the imperialist one; this deferral, contrary to the claims made by the left, continued after independence. This happened simultaneously with attempts of sections of the nationalist movement, then organised on a coalitional basis, to mobilise labour behind the national movement, and thereafter behind the nationalist state. The nationalist leadership and the state it controlled thereafter claimed to represent labour and at the same time demanded discipline from the labour force for 'national' goals.

The central myth that made this possible was that the post-independence Indian state was, or would be, a benign one, or at least a lesser evil. The 'masses' were instrumentalised by the custodians of the national state, and the custodians of that state presented themselves as intermediaries between the exploiters (capitalists, landlords) and the exploited (workers, peasants). The instrumentalisation of labour, allegedly for its own future good, was institutionalised in the split in the trade union movement. The older All-India Trade Union Congress (AITUC) remained with the Communist Party of India, which had become dominant in the AITUC by the end of World War II, and refused to accept the validity of government mediation. The newer Indian National Trade Union Congress (INTUC), dominated by the Congress party, accepted the myth of the benign state: the state, being a national one, was now an impartial intermediary between business and labour, representing the interests of the 'nation' as a whole.[37]

Nehru himself made several statements on the need for collective national action, and of deferring conflict between classes for that greater cause. The rhetoric of the period after 1947 strongly stressed the need for collective and disciplined national progress, for production before distribution could be achieved, and consequently for harmonious industrial relations. With the emphasis placed on 'nation building', industrialists and workers

---

[37] For a contemporary (and perceptive) account, see Richard L. Park, 'Labor and Politics in India', *Far Eastern Survey*, 10 August 1949, pp. 181–87.

were asked to work together for the collective good.[38] Change would come, but it would be relatively gradual, consensual, and rely on the education of the masses and the initiatives of the state. Vested interests would be chipped away by the authority of the state, represented by the national government, which in effect was the Congress. But the masses were to be increasingly disarmed of their own right to decide on what their interests really were.

In its operation, therefore, the developmental imagination excluded the representatives of non-elite groups from making decisions pertaining to the 'nation'. Exclusion based on a common commitment to a developmental project claiming to be for their benefit, in a paternalistic appropriation on the part of an allegedly benign state and its government, was, in being 'developmental', also largely non-'cultural', or non-'religious'; to what extent such exclusions, based on class, and therefore not 'national' exclusions, were less exclusionary than those potentially based on 'culture' remains open to question.

The 'cultural' in the 'developmental' also needs to be highlighted. A developmental project required some sense of social reform, in the older sense known in India of reforming socio-religious institutions, as well as in the socio-economic sense, for instance, of land reforms.[39] It has been pointed out that the boundary between social reform and religious reformation in many of these debates was very difficult to draw,[40] made difficult by the fact that British-Indian political discourse positioned India as a fundamentally religious society, and to what extent this view was ever rejected thereafter is doubtful: the 'Nehruvian' project to wean the masses off 'their tribal and communal selves', as the Congress Socialist Party manifesto had put it in the 1930s, was premised on at least the partial acceptance of the

---

[38] Speech to the Associated Chambers of Commerce, Calcutta, *SWJN II,* Vol. 4, 15 December 1947, pp. 563–64.

[39] On land reform debates see Suhit Sen, 'The Transitional State: Congress and Government in U.P., c.1946–57', unpublished PhD dissertation, London: School of Oriental and African Studies, University of London, 1998.

[40] Amiya P. Sen (ed.), *Social and Religious Reform: The Hindus of British India,* New Delhi: Oxford University Press, 2003, 'Introduction'.

'backwardness' of the people.[41] Social reform of various kinds was thus central to the claimed developmental agenda of the state: 'backward' institutions should be swept away, caste distinctions abolished, and a form of citizenship that rendered questions of sectarian identity irrelevant had to be found. At the same time, all social reform also ran into questions of how far a state could interfere with 'tradition'. There was the added danger that the adjudicators of what 'tradition' ought to be ended up being conservative male leaders of sects or religious organisations. And if continuing special representation for the 'Backward Classes' or 'Scheduled Castes' ran into the question of whether this in fact militated against the avowed aim of destroying these distinctions altogether, the question of preserving or reforming 'Hindu' or 'Muslim' laws also raised the question of whether these should also be abolished.

The Nehruvian state worked largely on the basis that 'minorities' should not be made to feel insecure in the new state by having their institutions subject to attack from the state. Treading softly on matters relating to minorities, the state therefore started on the reform of 'Hindu' law, with the intention, allegedly, to tackle Muslim law at a later date, and with the avowed ultimate aim of a uniform and secular civil code. But the 'Hindu Code Bill' ran into many difficulties as the self-proclaimed defenders of the 'community' sought to defend 'tradition'. It struggled on as four separate pieces of legislation, marriage, divorce, succession, and adoption. This eventually satisfied the demand for the state to take a proactive role in social reform as part of a developmentalist agenda[42] but it also tended, paradoxically, towards establishing

---

[41] 'It is the ambition of the party to make of the masses a conscious solid phalanx by dispossessing them of their tribal and communal selves, and arousing in them the sense of class-solidarity which their class-interest demands of them.' ('Ourselves', in the inaugural issue of the *Congress Socialist*, 29 September 1934, p. 2.

[42] Flavia Agnes, *Law and Gender Inequality: The Politics of Women's Rights in India*, New Delhi: Oxford University Press, 1999; Rebecca Grapevine, 'The State and Home in Early Independent India: The Hindu Marriage Act', unpublished paper presented at the conference 'Beyond Independence', London: Royal Holloway College, University of London, 11–12 April 2007; Reba Som, 'Jawaharlal Nehru and the Hindu Code Bill: A Victory of Symbol over Substance?' *Modern Asian Studies*, 28 (1) 1994, pp. 165–94.

the 'normal' citizen as a Hindu. The details are less important for the purposes of this article than the question of how the debates operated: 'communities' had laws and rights to themselves; custodians of the rights of a 'community' were its 'leaders', usually self-appointed, and male; Muslims, by being left out of questions of social reformist legislation, were exceptional citizens. This is not to suggest that this was intentional; indeed, the purpose was to establish that the right to a peaceful existence of minorities and of difference was acknowledged by the state, and that the sense of vulnerability of minorities was recognised in a democracy based on numerical majorities. Nevertheless, the logic of the position reified the idea of 'communities', and a 'nation' of 'communities' rather than of individuals.

Educating the Periphery Within: The Limits of 'Civic Inclusion'

Nehru's statecraft, as we have seen, involved treating states as well as the nationalisms they contained or espoused as potentially disruptive, irrational and unnecessary, and attempting to find ways around them, while acknowledging the importance of the nation-state idea as a legitimating one. The erosion of this vision can be traced through two interconnected examples: the problems of the North East Frontier Agency and the Chinese borders. Just as the borders with China were ambiguous, the peripheral areas of India were only a part of the Indian Union through accidents of colonial history and its arbitrary borders. The 'tribal areas' of north-east India, under colonial administration, were separated from the rest of India by an 'inner line'; the 'outer line' then divided it from the outside world — an 'outer line' whose precise position was not clearly known.[43] This division was inherited by independent India. Potential secessionist tendencies had been identified in the Naga areas of the north-east early on by Nehru, at the time of the interim government. The retention of these areas in India was impossible to justify by virtue of 'national' models. There was no particular reason why they should have shared an Indian nationalist sentiment, as Nehru himself acknowledged:

---

[43] Neville Maxwell, *India's China War*, London: Cape, 1970, pp. 25–26, 30, 32, 34.

'Our freedom movement reached these people only in the shape of occasional rumours. Sometimes they reacted rightly and sometimes wrongly.'[44] (By this, apparently, Nehru applied to the behaviour of the 'tribals' a yardstick of legitimacy that was based on a 'right' attitude to Indian nationalism.)

After independence, Nehru believed, the Naga areas ought to be a part of India and of Assam. He offered concessions: 'It is our policy that tribal areas should have as much freedom and autonomy as possible so that they can live their own lives according to their own customs and desires'. They could expect protection from being 'swamped by people from other parts of the country' and consequently from being exploited.[45] He seemed quite unconscious of the patronising language and the colonial rhetoric of his pronouncements:

> The tribal people of India are a virile people who naturally went astray sometimes. They quarrelled and occasionally cut off each other's heads ... It is often better to cut off a hand or a head than to crush and trample on a heart. Perhaps I also felt happy with these simple folk because the nomad in me found congenial soil in their company.[46]

Here, the developmental imperative that would allegedly make nationals of reluctant potential nationals was to be central; and in some ways it was more explicit than elsewhere.[47] But a modernising agenda that depended on the prior interpretation of that agenda by outside agents, and thereafter its application to its alleged beneficiaries by force was bound to be resisted. Indian attempts at 'nation building' by force of arms, with the Indian 'defence forces' indulging in large-scale killing and rape were hardly the best ways of demonstrating to north-east India the warm and enveloping joys of belonging to the Indian state. It was

---

[44] Speech, June 1952, quoted in K. S. Singh (ed.), *Jawaharlal Nehru, Tribes and Tribal Policy*, Calcutta: Anthropological Survey of India, 1989, p. 2.

[45] Letter to Naga National Council, rpt in *National Herald*, 2/10/46, *SWJN II*, vol. 2, p. 604.

[46] Speech, June 1952, quoted in K. S. Singh (ed.), *Jawaharlal Nehru, Tribes and Tribal Policy*, pp. 2–3.

[47] See also Verrier Elwin, *A Philosophy for NEFA*, Shillong: North East Frontier Agency, 1959.

in north-east India that the Nehruvian vision took on its most brutal and violent forms.

Connections to the eventual border conflict with China are obvious: the question of inheritance of colonial borders, and the question of who belongs within them. Nehru initially argued that it was not worth fighting over wasteland that no one inhabited. Various other groups refused to cede any ground to the *mlecchas*, infidel barbarians who were defiling the sacred soil of India.[48] Nehru was gradually pushed into more and more assertive positions. Meanwhile, development planners who were looking closely at Chinese experiments with cooperative farming were forced away from these efforts as everything Chinese became anathema.[49] Then, when the border dispute flared up into direct warfare in late 1962, citizenship rights were withdrawn from Indians of Chinese origin.[50]

Since the 'problem' of Indian citizenship and belonging usually takes the form of looking at Muslims, this often goes unnoticed. But this particular pairing of examples exposes the problems of a nationalism that attempts to refuse to define itself except as a common project of citizenship intended towards collective development or progress. 'We' all belong within our borders, within which we conduct development; that assumes a stability of borders and also an enforcement of belonging within those borders. Indian developmentalism took the national territory (the territory of the state) for granted; but it is forced at times to make the question of nationalism explicit. Moments of crisis and uncertainty expose certain groups to the possibility that they will suddenly find themselves excluded. The implicit assumptions behind belonging to the nation (state) can emerge at such moments at which the implicit congruence between a territorial nationalism and developmentalism must be made explicit; and that territoriality suddenly defines as outsiders

---

[48] Maxwell, *India's China War*, passim.
[49] Francine Frankel, *India's Political Economy, 1947–1977: The Gradual Revolution*, Princeton: Princeton University Press, 1978, pp. 167–68.
[50] Srirupa Roy, *Beyond Belief: India and the Politics of Postcolonial Nationalism*, Durham: Duke University Press, 2007, p. 186, 116*n*, mentions the 'ethnicisation of the nation' in connection with the China War and cites the relevant legislation.

those who (in this case visually) do not fit: Indian citizens, constitutionally, have a fundamental right to move freely and settle in any part of India, and do not require passports or identity papers, which makes nationality difficult to prove or disprove for many people. Developmentalism is thus always also, at least potentially, a nationalism whose chauvinist assumptions are held in reserve.

Some Questions: Civic Belonging, Civic Nationalism, States

The crux of the failure of the Nehruvian project was that its non-'cultural' definition of the nation depended on the naturalness of the state's boundaries, which could not be achieved without either posing as the inheritor of the British Indian state, which for reasons of legitimacy it was impossible to do, or by claiming a cultural or historic-ethnic basis for the sanctity of the land that was India, which was ideologically impossible for someone of a Nehruvian persuasion. Since neither claim could be made explicitly, the definition was inherently unstable. The 'Nehruvian project' failed, as its claim to a non-confessional state justified by a secular/civic nationalism gave way to a confessional/cultural claim. Even if this was once again suppressed, or never became official — the cat was out of the bag.

This has been an analysis of the Nehruvian vision as a potentially inclusive form of state project of providing security and belonging to a diverse population of citizens. I have not, in this article, dealt in any depth with the failures of the project in practice, concentrating instead on the structural difficulties of instituting a model of civic belonging without specific 'values'-based characteristics.[51] Let us, then, try and formulate a set of questions.

Can civic belonging be established without 'values', in a world not of 'the state', but of 'states' that must distinguish themselves from one another? Can civic belonging be instituted without

---

[51] For a longer analysis of the difficulties of the Nehruvian state in practice, see Benjamin Zachariah, *Nehru*, pp. 169–252.

resort to nationalism? Can civic nationalism be, in effect, a 'multiculturalism without culture', to translate the Nehruvian situation into the language of our own times? Can a really existing state operate as the neutral arbiter that respects different values but imposes none itself? And if it can, can it nonetheless avoid treating that absence as itself a value? Again, if it can, can it distinguish itself from other states in a world of 'nation'-states? In other words, can the relevance of 'values', of 'cultural difference' be respected without reifying particular notions of 'culture', and can states deal with the rights of individuals, not groups ('tribals', 'Muslims', 'Hindus') at the same time as respecting the relevance of the 'culture' of these groups, but not treating it as a determinant of action?[52] These are all variations on the theme of the tension between universal and particular that we have known for a long time: The Kantian categorical imperative requires agreement with the one who wills it to be a 'universal law', and at the same time, the one who makes a judgement can only do so on the basis of his or her own criteria ('values'?). The attempt to establish universal or at least apparently unobjectionable values — freedom of speech, etc. — as the basis of belonging to a state — still leaves open the question of the state's right to impose these values on those who are not necessarily willing to accept them.

The fact that a 'nation' must have exclusions in its definitions of belonging, and even in its attempts not to define, is a reasonably obvious point made by this article. That this is not necessarily merely a definitional problem is also clear: In north-east India, for instance, it was the force of arms that sought to impose belonging. In fact, 'nation building', the phrase that has been in widespread use from the 1920s, implies that belonging must be taught, by persuasion if possible, and by force if necessary. This is a paradox: The characteristics of true national belonging were not identified clearly by the state, but people were to be punished for not truly belonging.

Was 'developmentalism' alone the basis of constructing the collectivity that was to 'belong', or were there parallel suggestions of participation-based commonality that bound citizens to the

---

[52] Anna Phillips, *Multiculturalism without Culture*, pp. 52, 131, 162.

state? Participation was in fact continually invoked in the rhetoric of the state, both developmentally, through 'community development' schemes, for instance, that appropriated a Gandhian rhetoric to statist purposes (and I have argued elsewhere that the Gandhians are both directorial and authoritarian despite the rhetoric of participation from below),[53] and in terms of state rituals (elections, the national anthem, Independence Day and Republic Day parades, etc.). But the invocation of the people and their control at the same time implied that developmental and other forms of 'participation' were in fact directed and stage-managed from above, by the state.

Civic nationalism, as a general rule, accepts the boundedness of the state without identifying this boundedness with a particular cultural identity, ethnicity, or 'confession' (in the extended sense we have used the term here). It attempts to institute the boundaries of the state with reference to that state's specificity in terms of place and history — in other words, it has characteristics that are not 'values' in any narrow sense. Can we justify and sustain a strong distinction between characteristics and 'values'?

There will be moments of conflict that lead one to question the boundedness of the state; and these can lead to the bringing out of the implicit ethnic/cultural/confessional foundations of belonging to/loyalty to the state. Does a civic nationalism have implicit cultural foundations? Or even implicit anti-cultural foundations, so that a leaning towards the specificities of 'culture' can disqualify those with those specificities from membership of the civic nation (Captain Dreyfus as a Jew, for instance)? Is this anti-culturalism a way of hiding the particulars of the majority in the allegedly universal? Or does the fragility of a civic nationalism without clear definitions slide easily into a question of 'values'? Do we allow for the irreducible idea of a civic nationalism, the non-confessional idea of the state? Are particular states, in an ideal situation, simply replicas of one another, jurisdictions rather than entities with reified histories, values, cultures, nationalisms? I find this idea appealing; but then there are no grounds for a state distinguishing between the

---

[53] Benjamin Zachariah, *Developing India*, Chapter 4.

citizens of its own or another state. I find this appealing as well. I also find it utopian.

Consequences of the 'Nehruvian' Experience

We are, however, less interested here in states and nationalisms in general, being as we are interested in the nature of the post-independent Indian state, the processes of governing, and their relationship to democracy (variously described), 'development' (variously imagined), and social justice (variously conceived). That all these are positive normative categories without a necessarily agreed upon descriptive content is what makes the questions so problematic. We can speak here, with Ayesha Jalal, of an authoritarian democracy.[54] That the developmental imagination underpinning the state's official ideology greatly contributed to this democratic authoritarianism has long been accepted; but there has been a tendency to look back to the 'Nehruvian era' as a golden age. In many ways this was so; and even economists, most of whom in the post-Cold War ideological context accepted the assumption that markets were always better than states, have come round in recent years to the opinion that industrial expansion was at its best in the Nehruvian era rather than in the post-'liberalisation' market-driven 'free' economy of the 1980s and 1990s: even capitalists never had it so good. Nevertheless, there are certain tendencies from that 'golden age' whose legacies — in terms of what they continue to legitimise — need to be highlighted.

Let us deal with the question of the state legitimating itself — the colonial state towards the end of its career sought to defer the end of empire by claiming to be the national state, albeit with links to a wider Empire that was not incompatible with nationalism. The Commonwealth idea as put forth by the Round Table group, carrying as it did the assumption of less and more developed 'nations' who would be less and then more equal members of a still-British Commonwealth: the criteria of judgement remained in the hands of this imperial and self-appointed elite.[55] The

---

[54] Ayesha Jalal, *Democracy and Authoritarianism in South Asia*, Cambridge: Cambridge University Press, 1995.
[55] Frederick Madden and D. K. Fieldhouse (eds), *Oxford and the Idea of Commonwealth*, London: Croon Helm, 1982.

idea that some people rule better, and are better equipped to do so, however, remains present in the Indian developmental imagination, and it has been said before that the administration of development — or the infliction of 'development' of various kinds upon the people — was insulated from the scrutiny of the formal democracy that India acquired and administered under universal adult franchise.[56] That some people rule better, and that others must at best be trained to do the right thing, remained central to the national elite that inherited the colonial state's repressive as well as administrative apparatuses more or less intact, and also inherited a number of the assumptions built into the administration of that predecessor state.

'Development', lest we forget, was the central justification of both the national state and the colonial state. The colonial version ran something like this: The people were better served by a disinterested elite than by nationalists with their own 'interests' that were not those of the people (the colonial state refused, in its legitimating discourse, to recognise its own 'interests'). The national state's version was much the same: It claimed neutrality and mediating capacity above and outside of the society that it sought to govern. But it did this in the name of the people: thus it claimed both to be (all of) society for the purpose of legitimation (as opposed to the colonial state, which could not make this claim), and to be above it (as the colonial state had done) for the purposes of administering development. Perhaps more ominously, the state's claim to the loyalty and sacrifices of the people and its claim to the naturalness of its territorial boundaries were made simultaneously, in a way that the colonial state never attempted, and could not have attempted. The new state 'embodied' the people, not entirely (or not only) as an organicist, *völkisch* form of 'embodiment',[57] but through knowing better about what was good for them. If this seems a relatively normal

---

[56] Partha Chatterjee, 'Development Planning and the Indian State', in Terence J. Byres (ed.), *The State and Development Planning in India*, New Delhi: Oxford University Press, 1994, pp. 51–72.

[57] For an elaboration of this argument, see Benjamin Zachariah, *Developing India*, pp. 242–52, which perhaps underplays the closeness of *völkisch* forms of nationalism associated with the Hindu right to the organicist forms of nationalism implicitly (or sometimes explicitly) present in various developmental thinkers' plans.

assumption, it needs to be remembered that it also enabled the brutality of forcible nationalisation of marginal populations.

The legitimacy of the national state was related very closely — negatively — to its predecessor state, the colonial state, or in other words it owed much to the fact that the national state was not a colonial one. The importance of preserving an image of colonialism, as what the state now was not, therefore, was paramount. The legitimation provided by this preserved image lasts a long time: it reappears in various pickled and canned forms even today, allowing the 'national' state to get away with what the colonial state could never have done.

The colonial state's bureaucracy expended much energy on its elaborate staging of 'justice', in the courts and elsewhere, even to the end, and at great risk, where the decision to try the Indian National Army at the Red Fort was based on the legitimacy provided by demonstrating the due process of law as part of the orderly progress of a proper state even in exceptional circumstances. The collapse of this ritualised staging of 'justice' had a strongly de-legitimising impact on the functioning of the state. To take a counter case as illustration of this point: The massacre at Jallianwalla Bagh created a major crisis precisely because the colonial state was seen to be acting openly (as opposed to exceptionally and under cover) in a manner that exposed it to the charge of the loss of control and sense of proportion, thereby giving the impression of a loss of control. Therefore, the staging of 'justice' (and the power and the right to stage it) was part of its attempt to retain its legitimacy as a state, in the face of claims that it was illegitimate because it was not national. The national state, at the outset most clearly, was far more unconcerned about these niceties. Its legitimacy was largely based on its being 'national', and was thus based negatively on the colonial state itself. Thus, as it took over the repressive mechanisms of the colonial state, and used them very early on in Telangana or in the Naga Hills, the niceties of staging a business-as-usual form of governance where exceptional powers were to be used exceptionally, were not deemed necessary, creating quite directly the rationale for the Armed Forces Special Powers Act, passed on 11 September 1958, with many precedents in colonial-era laws that had, however, never been used so often and for so long.

We could collapse these last thoughts into a cynical comment about states behaving like states, but this approach gets us into deep waters in which we cannot make distinctions between greater and lesser levels of state oppression, different kinds of control, and different levels of access to social justice or legal remedy in various political orders. Even if, then, in theory, the state is always already the concentration camp, given the power of the sovereign to create a state of exception,[58] different states might be at different points along this continuum. And if the Nehruvian state, now fondly remembered as a period of hope, social justice, and economic development, also produced the trends we have described, this historical background might be helpful in understanding longer-term implications of apparently unproblematic state projects, and in particular the sources of at least some of the arrogance and anti-democratic aggressions of the leadership of what is allegedly the largest democracy in the world.

---

[58] Giorgio Agamben, *Homo Sacer: Sovereign Power and Bare Life*, Stanford: Stanford University Press, (1995) 1998, via Carl Schmitt, *Political Theology*, Chicago: University of Chicago Press, (1922) (1934) 1985.

3

The Political Constitution of India: Party and Government, 1946–57

Suhit K. Sen

Introduction

While the constitution of India was being encoded between 1947 and 1950 to create the legal scaffolding for the emerging independent Indian republic, parallel processes were underway over a somewhat longer period of time — 1946 to the middle of the 1960s — through which some of the ground rules for the functioning of the new political system were being hammered out. One of the important areas in which such rules were being negotiated through an intensely fraught process of contestation was that of the relationship between party and government. This was absolutely crucial in the building of India's democratic polity especially because the political scene in India after the partition was so massively dominated by the Indian National Congress and because the polity that emerged in the 1950s was at least till the mid-1970s what was later characterised as a dominant-party system.

The evidence and the argument I shall present point in two directions. First, that the choices made in this period and the outcomes they enabled favoured a relative insulation of the sphere of the state from the direct interventions of the dominant party — this, as will become evident, made possible a democratic political system, however flawed, based on constitutional sanctions and the rule of law. On the other hand, in another direction, the valorisation of state power involved, given the history of the anti-colonial movement, a wide-ranging demobilisation of the Congress party at the centre of which lay its transformation from a broad movement for national regeneration to a party with limited political objectives and an ambitious internal disciplinary programme.

At the centre of the contest, which played a most crucial role in state building in post-colonial India, was a contest for directive authority between the Congress party organisation and what came to be known as the 'ministerialist' or 'parliamentary' wing of the party, which ran the apparatus of the state that came into the hands of the Congress with the transfer of power. The former was inclined to the view that the Congress party, or movement, had a legitimate claim to a superordinate political authority based on the anterior claim that it was the organised expression of the will of the Indian people and the nation-in-the-making. In the days of the anti-colonial struggle, the Congress party had, in fact, claimed legitimacy for its representational role on the basis of the argument that it was a microcosm of the nation and the people and was thus the uniquely legitimate locus of the national and popular will and legitimate political power as opposed to the alien, intrusive, and illegitimate colonial state and other claimants to the anti-colonial mantle. After the transfer of power, the Congress party organisation was not particularly inclined to relinquish this claim, when the foundations of a democratic, constitutional, elected republic were being laid and even after it had, in fact, been put in place. The ministerialist wing of the party, led by Jawaharlal Nehru and a fairly tight oligarchy of senior leaders, later to become widely known as the 'high command', was not prepared, however, to concede to the party organisation any superordinate, structured, or directive role in the affairs of state. The party organisation's role, as Nehru frequently stressed, had to be limited to formulating broad policy objectives and not stray into the business of policy making, let alone the implementation or execution of policy.

Background to the Contest

The contest between the party organisation and the 'ministerialist' wing of the party was carried out at two levels. First, Congress committees at various levels — mainly the All-India Congress Committee (AICC) and the Pradesh Congress Committees (PCCs), but also committees lower down at the levels of the district, the town and the *mandal* — laid claim to a role in the working of the government, especially in the arena of policy making and the execution of policy. At another level, ordinary

Congress workers in local arenas tried to exert their authority in a number of ways to influence the working of government agencies and officials. Congress party leaders — the ministerialists — while rejecting the former claims, denounced the interference at local levels. Clearly, behind this contest lay two entirely divergent ideas of what constituted sovereignty and legitimate authority and from what sources these were derived.

Before proceeding further with the story of this conflict and how it contributed to the fashioning of Indian democracy, the question of periodisation must be addressed. In his study of the Congress party, Stanley Kochanek reviewed the progress of party–government relations and found three phases in the early years. The first, 1946–51, was marked by conflict; the second, 1951–63, saw a period of convergence in which a harmonious relationship was established at the cost of the government dominating the party; and the third, 1963–67, saw the evolution of a more equitable distribution of power. While Kochanek's periodisation is unexceptionable, a longer-term perspective could suggest a different way of looking at the party-government relationship. The entire Nehruvian period, roughly extending to the middle of the 1960s, from the longer-term perspective can be seen as a period of negotiation during which one fundamental rule of the emerging polity was established — that there was very limited convergence between party and government in the sphere of the state and that the latter had a great deal of autonomy in formulating policy, implementing it, and running the affairs of state. In the process of establishing this, as the conflict between the party organisation and the ministerialists played itself out, there may have been, indeed were, shifts in either direction, but the overall drift remained clear. It is important to note that the period of contestation was protracted and it was only in the mid-1950s that it started becoming clear that the ministerial wing was triumphing.

Before I proceed further, I would like to take the story of party–government relations forward in time to put the early — and critical — years in a broad, if impressionistic, context. It was only with the advent of Indira Gandhi as the head of the party, after the Congress split, and the government, that a significant reworking of the party-government equation was effected. Once Indira Gandhi had subverted the party organisation to bring it under her personal control with the help of a very small clique and subverted the functioning of the government by concentrating power in her own hands, the issue of party-government dynamics became irrelevant because the carefully hammered out constitutional consensus and procedure itself was junked. To the extent that Indira Gandhi functioned to a large extent outside the framework of constitution practice, due procedure and convention, both party and government became vehicles sometimes yoked together, sometimes not, for driving the agenda of the state.

After Indira Gandhi's defeat in the 1977 elections and the installation of the first non-Congress government at the centre — there had, of course, been several non-Congress governments in various states — the dominant party phase in Indian politics, the Congress system, effectively came to a close and a genuinely competitive party system was from then on to become the norm. Since 1977 and prior to the 15th general elections of 2009, the Congress party has been in power for nine years as a majority government — five starting as a minority government and subsequently gaining a tenuous majority, and five as the leader of a coalition. Non-Congress governments of various descriptions have been in place for the rest of the 13 years. For most of this period, the party-government equation as far as the Congress party is concerned had followed the model set up by Indira Gandhi whether during her tenure or that of Rajiv Gandhi, both of whom in contrasting styles ran both party and government outside established procedure through a highly personalised network.

Since Rajiv Gandhi's death, however, a new equation began to emerge, especially with the emergence of Sonia Gandhi as the Congress boss in 1998. The change in the equation had much to do with further changes in the broader context of politics. The failure of the Janata Party experiment of 1977 had meant a return to unambiguous Congress party rule for almost a decade. But the failure of the next non-Congress party to cohere in 1989–91 had different consequences. Instead of a consolidation of Congress ground, for a variety of reasons beyond the purview of this article, there was a fragmentation of the political space and the inauguration of a phase, still extant, of coalition politics. The Congress took some time to recognise this change, but sometime after Sonia Gandhi took charge this realisation dawned. When that did happen, the Congress party had to adjust to the realities of coalition politics. Two spells in power in a coalition is witnessing a new party-government equation in which the government has substantial autonomy under the leadership of the prime minister, but is simultaneously substantially dependent on the party under the leadership of its president for political support. The price of this support is that the party has the final say not only in laying down fundamental policy objectives, but also in ensuring that the policy-making process does not stray from the party's political parameters. Overall, the party seems to be the senior partner though it does not 'interfere' in the conduct of government in any obvious way.

This article will be devoted primarily to exploring the contest in the Nehru years that led to the establishment of the rules of party-government relations after the transfer of power. As mentioned earlier, a serious contest between the party organisation and its ministerialist wing culminated in the establishment of the ascendancy of the latter in the sphere of the state.

Significance of Kripalani's Resignation

At the national level, the question of the relationship between the Congress as an organisation and the Congress government was thrown into high relief when the Congress party president, Acharya J. B. Kripalani, resigned in 1946, alleging that he was not being taken into confidence by members of the government, and that the Congress was becoming irrelevant. Kripalani even secured Gandhi's approval of his view that the Congress Working Committee (CWC) was not being kept adequately apprised of government policy, and that this would undermine the government because the Congress was in touch with the people and was the conduit through which public opinion could filter back to the government and help it serve the people. He also took the government to task for defending the bureaucracy which had all along been criticised by the Congress. The bureaucracy, in his opinion, might have changed its attitude to the government but had not changed its attitude to its real masters — the people. After resigning from the presidency, Kripalani devoted some of his energies to building up an organisation called the Lok Sevak Sangh to carry out Gandhi's constructive programme in the United Provinces (later Uttar Pradesh, UP). The *National*

Herald commenting editorially on the proceedings of a meeting of the Sangh pointed out that by allowing members of the Sangh to hold government office if this furthered the cause of constructive work, it was allowing itself to fall within the ambit of ambiguous government patronage; the newspaper was arguing, in effect, for retaining the independence of the Sangh as a means to strengthen the Congress organisation.[1] By itself, this editorial comment may not have amounted to a whole lot, but it did point to the increasingly uneasy relationship between the government and the party.

In his letter of resignation, Kripalani referred to the weaknesses of the Congress organisation — the disintegration of morale and the personality clashes — and expatiated on the need to undertake constructive work to strengthen the organisation. This critique was made in the context of iterating the pressing need to foster greater cooperation between Congress ministries and the Congress organisation. But, he went on to say, this cooperation was lacking between the CWC and the interim government. The reason for this lack of cooperation, he hazarded, was as follows:

> It may be due to the fact that all of us are not united upon basic policies. While these policies are clearly defined for the Congress organization, it is held that they are not so clearly defined for the Interim Government and the Governments in the provinces.

Another basic difference of opinion for Kripalani was that while he and some others felt that the Congress was the only real link between government and the people some in the government did not.[2] 'They may even feel,' he complained, 'that the organization stands in the way of their freedom of action.'[3]

Following his resignation, Kripalani refused to remain on the CWC. His explanation was:

> If I remain a member of the Working Committee, I would naturally insist, consistently with my views in the matter, upon major

---

[1] *National Herald*, 1 June 1947.

[2] This idea, that the Congress was the link between the government and the people, was an important element in the changing self-image of the Congress.

[3] Kripalani's letter of resignation from the Congress presidency, 8 April, 1947, AICC (I), File no. G 31 of 1946–47.

issues being discussed in the Committee, specially when the most important members who shape the policies in the Central Cabinet are also members of that Committee. ... My views in the matter differ fundamentally from those of our *leaders* in the Cabinet. They do not feel that the Government at the Centre is Congress Government. After August 15th they seem to make a distinction between Congress and national Government, even though no such distinction is made in the case of Provincial Governments.[4]

In a note to the working committee, Kripalani reiterated this position, deploring the fact, as he mistakenly saw it, that while the provisional governments worked under the guidance of the PCCs, the interim government did not accept the direction of the working committee. Kochanek, too, seems mistakenly to subscribe in part to such a view.[5]

Shankarrao Deo, a Gandhian and one-time general secretary of the party, and no libertarian when it came to matters of party discipline, also found the party–government relationship unsatisfactory. In his view, the party sustained the government. It was the party's privilege, therefore, to lay down policy and it was for the government to implement it — only this could sustain the party's prestige and keep intact the people's faith in it. He noted disapprovingly, however, that the government was wont to unilaterally whittle down Congress policies. 'Such an attitude towards the Congress is very detrimental to its prestige. Today there is a genuine feeling that what the Congress decide is for public consumption and will hardly have any effect on the decision of the government.'[6]

On 28 October, 1948, Pattabhi Sitaramaiyya, President, Congress, was reported to have said that the Congress was a 'second chamber' with the power to 'check, revise and review' the decisions of the government, and that the Congress's role was that of a caretaker in the task of training 'ourselves' in the art of

---

[4] Undated letter from Kripalani to either Nehru or Rajendra Prasad (the letter is a draft and does not have a salutation), AICC (1), File no. ED 7 (Pt. I) of 1947–48. The word 'leaders' (in my emphasis) replaces the word 'colleagues' which is crossed out.
[5] See Stanley A. Kochanek, *The Congress Party of India, The Dynamics of One-Party Democracy,* New Jersey, 1968, *passim.*
[6] Note by Deo on Congress reorganisation, enclosed with note dated 15 January 1950, Patel Papers Correspondence, Microfilm Reel no. 2.

responsible government. 'The great duty of the Congress,' he continued, 'is to hold the scales even between the idealistic and extravagant public on the one hand and the practical ministry on the other.' He followed this up with a circular that gave guidelines about how the party and government ought to regulate their relationship. In the context of complaints from PCCs that they were being ignored, he suggested that the provincial government invite presidents and secretaries of the PCCs to canvass their opinions on forthcoming legislation and other issues once every year. Earlier, the Congress secretary had reported to the AICC that ministries were frequently ignoring the PCCs and suggested that a mechanism be instituted for liaising between the two.[7] At around this time, a UP Congressman expressed the opinion that the Congress party was 'in the context of our political life today, in the greatest danger of being submerged by, or at any rate being overshadowed by governmental machinery. Its voice is daily growing more and more inaudible ...'.[8]

Mridula Sarabhai, the acerbic Gandhian who had been a general secretary not long before writing this note, put it equally bluntly when she criticised the Congress for having thrown all its resources into building up the parliamentary wing at the expense of working towards its broader objectives in its efforts at becoming a 'party'. She divided the Congress into two groups: one idealistic and marginal, but still trying to work towards the Congress's objectives and trying to act as a bridge between the government and the people; and the other, dominant, which used the Congress for political gains and, far from encouraging the former group, resented its activities as interference.[9]

Raghukul Tilak, a UP Congressman who was later to leave the party with the socialists, wrote, in a more circumspect vein, with suggestions for the regulation of relations between the organisation and government as a necessary condition which could lead to the refurbishment of the Congress party. After the usual bemoaning of the state of the Congress organisation, Tilak suggested two areas in which remedial action would have to be

---

[7] *National Herald*, 15 December 1948.

[8] *Leader*, 24 October 1948.

[9] Letter from Sarabhai to Rajendra Prasad, then Congress president, 10 December 1948, Patel Papers (Correspondence), Microfilm Reel no. 4.

taken. First, he said, those in government had to mend their ways. Ministers had become intolerant of public criticism, and even worse, dismissive of the party organisation which was in close touch with the masses, and tried to manipulate it. They had to become more responsive and sensitive to public criticism. He suggested that ministers attend party meetings more often to discuss their problems and matters of policy, and that the party executive, at the very least, be involved in the decision-making process. He also suggested that members of the legislative assembly (MLAs) should take a greater part in popularising the work of the ministries in a coordinated way by undertaking constituency tours and participating in the routine work of the Congress. Second, Tilak said the Congress organisation had to be strengthened. The Congress had suffered because all the top leaders of the Congress had joined the legislature. A few ministers, parliamentary secretaries, and MLAs, he suggested, should forsake parliamentary work and work on the organisational side — anticipating the Kamaraj plan. This would promote greater coordination between the organisation and the government.

Similarly, commenting on Rafi Ahmed Kidwai's withdrawal from the Uttar Pradesh Pradeshik Congress Committee (UPPCC) presidential elections, the *National Herald* pointed to the necessity of working out a relationship between the ministry and the PCC in which 'the PCC is not turned into an "aman sabha"'[10] of the government but remains free to advise, criticise, and support albeit not in an irritating and destructive manner.'[11] An undated and unsigned note which recorded the views of less august Congressmen showed the same grievances. Krishna Chandra, the Congress MLA from Mathura, expressed resentment that Congress committees and Congressmen in general were losing and MLAs and ministers gaining in importance. An ordinary Congressman, identified only as Upadhyay of Ranikhet, expressed the opinion that Congress committees were considered tools to maintain power by MLAs, and that Congress ministers mischievously brought no-confidence motions against office bearers of the PCC. He recommended that the provincial

---

[10] This was a term used for loyalist conferences organised by zamindars to express their loyalty to colonial rule, and which the colonial bureaucracy helped organise.

[11] *National Herald*, 7 July 1948.

parliamentary board come under the discipline of the PCC and not include either ministers or MLAs.[12]

An extreme statement of the hostility of the organisation to the government was recorded by Bansgopal, a UP MLA:

> The present administration is practically failing, and the popularity of the Congress is declining by leaps and bounds ...

> The officials are out to discredit the Congress and Congress workers, and the Government directly or indirectly supports them. The masses are in great trouble and their daily grievances are not met.[13]

The grievances of those representing the voice of the organisation continued well into the 1950s.[14] In a communication to the AICC, the UPPCC made suggestions for the agenda of a meeting of PCC and DCC office bearers scheduled to be held in Hyderabad. One of its suggestions was that subordinate committees had to be given the right to have official meetings with bureaucrats and ministers to solve public grievances. If such meetings were considered inappropriate, these committees would have to be given the right to criticise and agitate against the government's actions which were seen as unjust and wrong. If this right was denied the Congress organisation would lose its vitality and stagnate.[15]

In the mid-1950s, an MP and ex-Congressman wrote to the new Congress president about government control over Congress.

---

[12] Undated, unsigned note, AICC (1), File no. 6 of 1947.

[13] Bansgopal to Purushottamdas Tandon, 10 September 1947, Purushottamdas Tandon Papers (National Archives of India) (henceforth P. D. Tandon Papers), Correspondence Files, 1947.

[14] By the early 1950s Nehru's conquest of the Congress had been completed, and with the unification of control over both government and party in the person of Nehru the process of government control over the party too had been consummated. For an excellent study of this process, and the disintegration, in the 1960s, of the structures of control that were fashioned in this period, see Stanley A. Kochanek, *The Congress Party of India: The Dynamics of One-party Democracy*, New Jersey: Princeton University Press, 1968.

[15] UPPCC to AICC, General Secretary, 22 December 1952, AICC (2) File no. PG 40 of 1954.

The Congress, he wrote, had ceased to guide the policies of government. Thus, instead of Congress governments there were 'Government Congresses', because the government guided and controlled the Congress. He criticised Nehru for using the Congress as a tool for organising support for his government's policies and said: 'We have to watch how you behave, whether you behave as the head of a great non-official public body to keep the governments on the right path or as their Agent-General to manage non-official support for the existing Governments.'[16] This was, in fact, a remarkably clear reading of the issue — whether the party would guide the government along the right path or whether it would be politically demobilised.

Disquiet Reaches the High Command

At the highest organised forum of the party, too, the voice of organisational disquiet was aired. At the AICC session in Kalyani in 1954, PCC chiefs and secretaries reiterated the need for close contact between the organisation and administration, and the need for legislators to stay in close contact with their constituencies. It was said in a resolution that 'those who had gone into legislatures were constituting themselves into a separate and rigid class'.[17]

At the Guwahati session of the Congress in 1958, the Congress constitution was altered afresh. I shall not go into the details of these changes other than to mention that they tried to bring about a greater balance between the 'official' and 'non-official' presence in Congress committees at various levels — the *mandal*, the district, and the province. M. V. Rao explained in his official history of the Congress party that these changes were aimed at: the elimination of bogus membership; the strengthening of bonds between each level of the organisation as represented by the committees; giving representation to weaker sections and associating representatives of non-political associations to

---

[16] An open letter from Ramnarayan Singh to U. N. Dhebar. From U. N. Dhebar's reply, which is dated 26 March 1955, this letter can be ascribed to early 1955, AICC (2) File no. G I (3) of 1955.
[17] M. V. Ramana Rao, *A Short History of the Indian National Congress*, New Delhi: S. Chand, 1959, p. 309.

make the organisation more broad-based and effective; and the *association of legislators with organisational work.* In Rao's own words:

> The amendments thus contemplate[d] the forging of new links between the organization and the people on the one side and those in it [the organization] and in the Legislature Party. The tendency for the organisation to drift far from the masses whom it is intended to serve and feel itself as a body subordinate to the Ministry or the Legislature Congress Party, is sought to be extinguished by the amendments of the Constitution.[18]

The bemoaning of the loss of prestige for the Congress organisation and the desire that the organisation play a more positive role in the exercise of State power did not go unheard. In 1950, the *Hindustan Times* noted this increasing antipathy between the Congress organisation and the government. It editorialised on the subject, suggesting that the Congress presidency should go to an outstanding personality. It is worth quoting at length from this editorial:

> A second reason for these suggestions is that after the achievement of independence, the Governments, both Central and State, have stolen the glamour from the Congress which consequently has to take a back seat. Mr Mohanlal Saxena has given expression to these feelings in a statement in the course of which he suggests a convention that the Congress President should *ipso facto* become the Prime Minister of India.[19] This convention would help, he says, in removing the anomaly of the Congress President being "eclipsed". It is because of this feeling that he has suggested that no minister except the Prime Minister and the Deputy Prime Minister should be a member of the Working Committee or a provincial executive. He has also made the somewhat queer suggestion that except the Prime Minister and the Deputy Prime Minister at the Centre and the Chief Ministers in the States — that is, with the exception of those primarily responsible for the formulation of policy — each minister should be asked to place a

---

[18] ibid., pp. 333–36.
[19] These suggestions by Mohanlal Saksena were made in a note on the reorganisation of the Congress. A copy of the note can be found enclosed with a letter from Saksena to Patel, 22 July 1950, Patel Papers (Correspondence), Microfilm Reel no. 13.

progress report before the party annually and obtain a vote of confidence. Similar feelings animate the Provincial Congress Committees and their chiefs who seem aggrieved that though they represent the Congress in the States they cannot and do not exercise the influence they should in the Governments of the State.

For the Congress which during the British regime set itself up as a parallel government it will be certainly difficult to reconcile itself to the new circumstances created by the attainment of freedom and the promulgation of a new democratic Constitution based on adult suffrage. But the adaptation must come if confusion is to be avoided.[20]

In another editorial following soon after, it said that a second factor which had to influence the choice of the Congress president was the need for promoting greater collaboration between the Congress and the government. It underlined the possibility of great political embarrassment arising from differences between members of the government and the Congress president, as the Kripalani episode had so powerfully demonstrated. It ended by saying that in a situation where the Congress was in power both at the centre and in the states, and was likely to be returned to power, it was imperative that the Congress and government work together for the greater glory of the country, adding as an aside that such cooperation was especially desirable when there was an election to be won.[21]

A note on the reorganisation of the Congress encapsulated the ambiguity, or 'confusion', as the *Hindustan Times* put it, which could result from the Congress's political location. The note started out by saying that top priority had to be given to building up a strong central authority, and in this work, government agencies manned by the Congress would be most important. All Congressmen, therefore, needed to rally around those people on whose shoulders the burden of 'building the new State' had fallen. But, it continued, the task of building a

---

[20] *Hindustan Times*, 25 July 1950. Emphasis mine.

[21] *Hindustan Times*, 8 August 1950. Both these editorials came in the wake of a controversy over the Congress presidency. Nehru had been against Tandon's candidature, and after his election refused to join the working committee. Though he was prevailed upon to do so, further differences surfaced. In the end, Tandon had to relinquish the presidency, and Nehru assumed the office.

new State could be done only with the willing allegiance and cooperation of the people at large. It was possible only for a strong and vibrant Congress to mobilise such cooperation. Thus, it said, some major Congress leaders had to remain outside govern- ment and work in the organisation. But the Congress, while per- forming this function, could not act as a public relations office of the government; it had a duty to voice the aspirations and discontent of the people. By so doing, authoritarian tendencies could be checked.[22] This, then, was the dilemma of the Congress: working out how far it could maintain a critical attitude to and a distance from government without endangering the project of monopolising post-colonial power.

Sadiq Ali, for most of this period the permanent secretary of the AICC, also found the conflicting logic of the Congress's trans- ition a little too complex to admit of easy solutions. The following extract captures the ambivalence of the Congress position:

> The necessity for the Congress committees in districts etc. to function more effectively was obvious to all. The ministers showed their anxiety to secure this co-operation. They desire that a great deal of the relief work should be undertaken by the Congress or- ganization. What assistance, financial and other, we can get from the Government was not clear. I had an idea that their policy was one of drift. At the end of the whole series of meetings I had a talk with PCC secretaries. I asked them to get from the ministers the government's definite policy and scheme of work so that our Congress Committees know where they stand ...
>
> It is necessary that our Congress organization is not discredited for want of a definite policy [on] the part of the Government and determination to implement it.[23]

---

[22] Undated, unsigned note on Congress re-organisation, AICC(l) File no. G 47 (Pt. I) of 1946. The contents of the document make it obvious that it was authored with the blessings of the socialists. A note which is remarkably similar to this one argues the first part of the above thesis, noting the importance of the Congress re-organising itself to aid the building up of a strong central authority since in the absence of a strong non-official body those in office would find 'the fabric of the State too heavy for them'. This note is undated but authored by Rammanohar Lohia, AICC (1), File no. G 6 (KW 1) of 1947.
[23] Sadiq Ali to Shankarrao Deo, 18 October 1947, AICC(I), G 18 (Pt. II) of 1947–48.

This letter is especially instructive because of two reasons. On the one hand, it shows that the AICC recognised the need for the district organisation to function effectively, and that ministers were anxious to secure the cooperation of the organisation, while expressing deep misgivings about the commitment of the government to working with the organisation. On the other, despite the anxiety that the Congress organisation not be discredited because of the government's 'drift', this letter casts the organisation in a supplicatory light — unable to do without the assistance of the government, yet uneasily yoked to it. This dilemma of location and this uneasy connection with the government stemmed from the transitional character of the Congress. On the one hand, the pressures of the new political situation set it off in the direction of being a political party, with the limited task of providing the machinery to contest elections and mobilise votes; on the other hand, it attempted to cling to a claim of sovereignty and directive power, distinct from, and, indeed, superordinate to, the government.

The important issues and dilemmas that lie at the centre of this controversy relate to the conceptualisation of the role of the party and the content of the 'party system' in a constitutional democracy fashioned in the image of Westminster-style parliamentary government. At the heart of the controversy was the question of the location of the 'party' organisation vis-à-vis, on the one side, government, and the other, the 'people' or the electorate. The debates and contestations over the relationship of the party organisation with the government were essentially caused by a lack of political consensus, or, even worse, the absence of clearly defined parameters about constitutional practice and proprieties. The ground for such a consensus over proprieties obviously existed since the Indian polity was being encoded in an explicit, written form, seemingly by overwhelming consent, in a constituent assembly that was largely the creation and the domain of the Congress.

One of the early students of the Indian constitution, Granville Austen, advanced an argument that helps us to get to the bottom of the problem. The Constituent Assembly, he said, was a representative assembly even though it was not elected on the basis of adult franchise. It was representative, in Austen's argument, in that it represented all shades of political opinion from the

Hindu communal fringe to the socialist left; it was not, however, representative in the sense of being *democratic*. In other words, it was not merely an assembly that was elected on a very restricted franchise, but it was also unrepresentative in that it was neither responsible nor responsive to the rank and file of the party, let alone the people at large. On the contrary, it was a body that conducted its deliberations and reached its decisions with a keen self-consciousness of its own corporate identity, and was quite insulated from the Congress organisation. The political contest between the organisation and the party was thus conducted between a definite set of constitutional theories about responsible parliamentary government on one side and, on the other side, a set of political presuppositions held by large numbers of Congressmen which derived from the Congress's historic role of being an agitational/oppositional movement, and its claims of being the microcosm of the nation.[24]

Historical Contingencies of the Time

It must be noted that the problem did not arise simply because there was a contest between a defined theoretical position and a political practice which was profoundly uninformed by such theory. The problem was grounded in the historical contingencies that surrounded the theory. The Westminster system, in the classical British context, had evolved through a historically determinate process of political constitution. In this process, the role of the party in sustaining parliamentary responsibility and the limits of executive power had been defined through the evolution of convention. Durgadas Basu, a commentator and expert on constitutional matters, had made the point, for instance, that in parliamentary government the cabinet was in theory responsible to parliament and thus under its control. But in practice the cabinet/executive (which exercised the power of governance; not the parliament) actually exercised a control which had a 'dictatorial character' over the parliament because of the evolution and strengthening of the party system.[25] It is

---

[24] Granville Austen, *The Indian Constitution: Cornerstone of a Nation*, New Delhi: Oxford University Press, 1966, pp. 8–16.

[25] Durgadas Basu, *Commentary on the Constitution of India*, Kolkata: S. C. Sarkar and Sons, 1955, pp. 462–66.

important to remember that the British constitution was not a written one and was based mainly on convention; it was, and presumably still is, therefore, subject to revision by the evolution of conventions and institutions. The Indian constitution was, however, one that was explicitly codified and one in which explicit legislative amendment was the preferred mode of revision. Convention was not supposed to be either the guide to practice or the motor of political change. It is worth noting that the Indian constitution made no explicit mention of parties, nor accorded to the party system any explicit constitutional status. Thus, for instance, there was no explicit requirement that the president call upon the leader of the majority party to form the executive arm of the government; though the principle of parliamentary responsibility in practice ensured (at a time when the majority of the Congress was taken for granted) that this would indeed be the case.[26]

Though the constitution gave no explicit status to the party system, the makers of the constitution specifically and Congress leaders generally, mostly well versed in the minutiae of British constitutional practice, operated on the basis of the presumption that the conventions that were central to British constitutional practice were to be taken for granted. Thus, when in the debate over the draft constitution in the Constituent Assembly an amendment was moved making explicit mention of parliamentary responsibility, Nehru, accepting the amendment, replied that the draft had not mentioned some things because it took for granted that 'the Prime Minister would be sent for by the President because he happens to represent the largest party or group in the House, further that the Prime Minister would select his ministers and further that they would be responsible to the House'.[27]

An undated AICC note on the party system made an elaborate statement of the Congress view of what the party system was all about, and encapsulated neatly the ambiguity between

---

[26] Ibid., p. 480. Thus, for instance, the recent debates (in 1991 and 1996) in cases where no party had majorities, about whom the president should summon to form a government.

[27] Constituent Assembly Debates, Official Report, (henceforth CAD), vol. IV, no. 11, pp. 915–16.

theory and practice. The party system, the note said, was a social organism whose main task was the exercise of social control through the government. The note went on to say (not necessarily with a great amount of consistency) that the party system was an institution which was meant to supplement the government and made the following proposition: 'When the party is in power the party can be regarded as a part of the government itself, shading out from the very definite responsibility to the less definite responsibility of shaping and guiding the course of public opinion.'[28] It also clarified that the party process was one through which many different interests articulated themselves; this made it resemble the State, which was not, however, the case.

Editorial comment in newspapers tended to cloud an issue that was already less than clearly defined. Thus the *National Herald* commented that it was the responsibility of the Congress party to ensure that the party system functioned successfully since the constitution was largely its creation. This was all the more necessary because the infant polity was not strong enough to bear the weight of an egocentric party; thus, the Congress needed to 'dissociate itself from the State'.[29]

Given the confusion over theory and practice, and its own non-theoretical proclivities, the organisational wing of the Congress often failed to appreciate the niceties of constitutional practice; and sometimes this could put it on a defensive footing. This was made apparent in an incident involving Sampurnanand, a minister in Pant's ministry in UP. Sampurnanand wrote to Jugal Kishore, then General Secretary, Congress, about a letter he had received from the librarian of the AICC about the salaries of a certain class of schoolmistresses. Sampurnanand went on to enquire, in a tone that was sarcastic rather than conciliatory, whether the AICC intended to treat a matter which was of 'routine administrative detail' as having political significance, and whether in future it intended to take an interest in the salaries of other employees of the UP government and ask the provincial government to make such changes as it thought proper.[30] Jugal Kishore's conciliatory

---

[28] Undated, unsigned note on the party and the party system, AICC(2), Miscellaneous File no. 4008.

[29] *The National Herald*, 22 June 1948.

[30] Sampurnanand to Jugal Kishore, 6 June 1947, AICC (1), File no. G 6 (Pt. I) of 1947.

reply began with the explanation that the librarian's letter was written in a purely personal capacity. But it went on to say:

> Ordinarily this or any other responsible Congress organization would not like to interfere in the day to day administration of the Provincial Governments but *occasion may arise when the AICC office may be obliged to make enquiries and even to issue advice. Of course in doing so, it will be couched in an appropriate language* and when the matter assumes such importance as to justify any interference on our part. ... The AICC office, it must be presumed, is not so irresponsible as to issue directives without first making elaborate enquiries.[31]

The General Secretary, AICC, thus, even while moved to defend some ground for the organisational wing of the Congress, could at best envisage for the apex representative body of the Congress organisation a role as an advisor; an advisor, moreover, who was constrained to assure the representatives of government that advice would be tendered in befitting language.

It is to be noted, however, that it was not a matter merely of not understanding the niceties of the constitutional position, but also one of contesting them. This contestation could either be at a clearly articulated level of principle or at the level of practical politics. It may further be noted that the point at issue was not merely, as in this case, one of Sampurnanand giving Jugal Kishore a lesson in constitutional propriety; it arose, rather, because the rules governing constitutional codes, conventions, and practices were not defined and allowed often to stand in for one another. In the face of this kind of contestation and 'confusion', the prescriptions of the Congress leadership were made in the idiom of constitutional theory relating not merely to the general question of the relationship between government and organisation, but to more specific questions as well. Thus it was a matter of threshing out issues relating to, say, the relationship between the legislature 'party' and the ministry, and of the relation of these with Congress committees at various levels. Vallabhbhai Patel, for instance, was to write the following cautionary lines to Thakur Phool Singh, then an office bearer

---

[31] Jugal Kishore to Sampurnanand, 20 June 1947, AICC (1), File no. G 6 (Pt. I) of 1947.

in the UPPCC executive, possibly in reply to a query about the relationship between the PCC and the Congress party in the legislature:

> The Congress Assembly Party is an independent body and it is unwise to interfere in its day-to-day internal administration. The PCC has no direct control over the Party nor has it any over-riding authority but it can influence the Assembly Party by helpful or constructive criticism or co-operation. If the Congress Assembly Party is doing anything contrary to the policy of the Congress, the PCC can, through its President, try to set matters right or ... approach the Parliamentary Board or the Working Committee.

The Congress assembly party was not bound to consult the PCC, Patel wrote, but it would be wise for it do so to avoid friction.[32]

At a more general level, Nehru, in a secret note, while urging the CWC to deliberate upon and define the 'general relationship between the working committee and the new Government of India', did not show himself to be too eager to give any quarter to the organisational wing: *'This involves,'* he wrote,

> *the general question of the freedom of the Government to shape policies and act up to them within the larger ambit of the general policies laid down in Congress resolutions.* The Government though predominantly a Congress Government and therefore subject to general Congress policy, will not be entirely a Government of Congressmen.'[33]

There is a whiff of vagueness to this formulation. The ambiguous and ad hoc character of the 'constitutional theory' of the Congress leadership, caught as it was between codification and definition through convention and practice, was exposed in the falling out between Nehru and his second finance minister, the non-Congressman John Matthai. Matthai resigned over a dispute

---

[32] Patel to Phool Singh, 16 August 1948, Patel Papers (Correspondence), Microfilm Reel no. 48.

[33] Secret note by Nehru to the working committee, 15 July 1947, AICC (I), File no. 71 of 1946–47. Kripalani's note to the working committee (see fn 18) is in response to this note.

over the role of the Planning Commission. In the acrimonious dispute, Matthai wrote to Nehru thus:

> Your suggestion that you were bound by the decision of the Congress Working Committee is hardly relevant. If the Prime Minister is to be bound by the decision of a party caucus in so important a matter to the extent you presume, there is an end to parliamentary government as one knows it.[34]

In the light of Nehru's earlier 'theory' his reply was somewhat disingenuous. Nehru wrote:

> You refer to my being bound by the decision of a party caucus. ... If the party has gone to the country on the basis of a programme, its first duty is to follow the programme insofar as it can. Parliamentary government consists of certain policies and programmes, which the majority party has proclaimed, being given effect to.[35]

Nehru's Ambiguity amidst Conflicting Pulls and Pressures

This ambiguity in Nehru's attempts to define a constitutional position found expression in an interesting way in a somewhat different context. Nehru, while trying to define the proper relationship between the prime minister and the cabinet, also found himself reflecting on party and government. In an acrimonious correspondence with Patel, occasioned by Patel's accusation that Nehru had gone over his head in a matter pertaining to the state's ministry, Nehru had written a note on the position of the prime minister in the executive. In one passage he had written the following:

> He is the chosen leader of the party and the party naturally depends upon his personality and prestige for cohesion. His position

---

[34] Matthai to Nehru, 17 June 1950, enclosed with Nehru to Patel, 27 June 1950, Patel Papers (Correspondence), Microfilm Reel no. 9.

[35] Nehru to Matthai, 27 June 1950, Patel Papers (Correspondence), Microfilm Reel no. 9. The truth, however, was that the interim government was created through negotiations between the Congress and the colonial power, and not on the basis of a mandate secured from the people on the basis of a programme.

in the party is such that while he is himself dependent on the support of his party, the party always looks to him for guidance.[36]

The *Hindustan Times* once again put the problem in perspective while commenting on the imbroglio over the Tandon presidency and Nehru's subsequent refusal to join the working committee. The editorial began by noting that in India the relationship between party and government was complicated by the preponderant weight of the Congress and the importance attached to the Congress presidency. But incontrovertibly, the prime minister held office by virtue of being the leader of the predominant party. Nehru had headed the interim government by virtue of his undisputed leadership of the Congress. Nehru thus had to have a hand in framing party policy which as head of government he would have to implement, a position which the Nasik Congress had endorsed. Thus, the editorial continued, 'If after this Pandit Nehru had kept out of the Working Committee, he would have put himself in the anomalous position of having to execute policies in the promulgation of which he would have denied himself a voice.'[37] One of the implications of what the editorial pointed out was that Nehru's legitimacy in government arose from his connection with the Congress; therefore, the government was bound to follow the policies of the Congress. It was best, therefore, that Nehru play an important role in making that policy.

The then Congress president, Rajendra Prasad, in a secret note to working committee members echoed Nehru's formulation about the relationship between the ministries and the party organisation in the provinces in a more cautious vein. It was quite clear that the role of the provincial organisation in provincial governance was not conceived of in expansive terms. Prasad was, after all, one of the oligarchs of the Congress high command and had been chosen to replace the refractory Kripalani to bring the organisation to heel. Prasad referred to a feeling among Congressmen and Congress committees that ministries were obliged to follow their directives, and deprecated

---

[36] Undated supplement to a note by Nehru on the functions of the prime minister (the latter dated 6 January 1947, Patel Papers (Correspondence), Microfilm Reel no. 45.
[37] *Hindustan Times*, 17 October 1950.

the increasing instances of individual Congressmen trying to influence government. Only the accredited representatives of the organisation, Prasad stipulated, could approach the government; the organisation's task, anyway, was to lay down policy objectives and let the ministry carry these out.[38]

Within the organisation, the resentment against the alleged high-handedness of the 'government Congress' led to the kind of solutions proposed by Tilak. But others like Raghubir Sahai, a Congress MLA in UP, noted the feud between the provincial Congress organisation and the Congress legislature party and suggested that the PCC, while influencing the government, must leave it to formulate policies as best as it could, and use the Congress organisation to ensure the successful implementation of government policies.[39]

The organisational point of view was, however, as I have already indicated, not so much a position arrived at or articulated as a set of constitutional principles woven into a coherent body of doctrine but more a set of presumptions and beliefs that derived from the ideological claims of an anti-imperialist agitational movement, and articulated in a programmatic idiom in the terrain of quotidian political practice. The dilemmas that confronted the Congress in this field of practice had more to do with the specific political location of the Congress organisation. First, the Congress was not only the preponderant political organisation (especially after partition and the consequent elimination of the Muslim League) but was in fact the political organisation that had a virtual monopoly of the apparatus of State power. This prompted an identification of the Congress with State power itself. The leadership of the Congress was moved, from the perspective of constitutional practice, to repudiate this identification; and in practical terms it was moved also to impose political regulation that would make it possible for the supremacy of the State apparatus to be upheld. Second, the Congress, in the process of transformation from a movement of nationalist agitation to a party of governance, was caught in a tension. On the one hand, its political role arose historically from its claim to

---

[38] Confidential note to the working committee, 6 December 1948, Patel Papers (Correspondence), Microfilm Reel no. 1.

[39] *National Herald*, 16 May 1948.

being the 'mirror of the nation' and the organisational voice of the people; on the other, in the new circumstances of representative democracy and adult suffrage, it had to play the role of a political machine that was to mobilise political support and turn this support into electoral success for Congress governments on the basis of programmes that the Congress governments were at liberty to either honour or repudiate.

An AICC circular sought to resolve the dilemma in the following formulation:

> The Congress is functioning in two different capacities today — as a Government responsible for law and order and as a popular organization for the attainment of freedom and justice for the masses. It is obvious that these two arms must work in close collaboration if the Congress is to function effectively in both these capacities, Moreover in the constructive field — whereby alone can the true foundations of Swaraj for the masses be laid — they have a vast field for common action.[40]

But this fairly bland prescription had a rider attached to it: a rider that pointed in the direction of a 'ministerialist' solution to the Congress crisis. The circular thus went on to say that ministers would often have to take decisions which could not in all cases be explained publicly. In such cases, Congressmen who were dissatisfied with such decisions (as, for instance, in the case of the curtailment of civil liberties) did not have the right to publicly criticise the government, but could place their point of view to the ministers concerned through the elected bodies of the Congress organisation. This was to prevent the political opponents of the Congress from getting hold of sticks with which to beat the government. Similarly, the circular admonished, PCCs, in the event of grave differences with the ministries, were not free to give a public airing to their differences but could always approach the CWC to sort out these differences.[41]

The chief whip of the Congress party in the Constituent Assembly (Legislative), in other words the interim parliament, was also moved to make admonitory gestures in the context of a speech

---

[40] AICC circular to all PCCs, 2 February, 1947, AICC (1), File no. G 3 of 1946–47.
[41] Ibid.

made in the House by Mahavir Tyagi, a somewhat irrepressible member from UP. Tyagi had criticised the government forcefully, focusing on popular discontent with the government, the absence of a viable opposition or a channel for the voice of the people to reach the ears of those in government. The whip's position was that serious allegations of corruption, inefficiency, etc., though they often lacked foundation, lowered the prestige of 'parliament' and put the government in a spot. To protect the prestige of the assembly, members of the Congress party in the assembly were required to communicate such information as they might possess on any irregularity in the functioning of the government to the chief whip who would take up the matter with the individual ministers concerned.[42]

The ministries were not always prepared to heed the directives of even the Congress president. In 1948, Rajendra Prasad wrote to all PCCs and Congress premiers suggesting 'that some liaison should be established between the Provincial Governments and the PCCs which could help smoothe matters and remove the legitimate grievances of the public'.[43] When this circular was discussed in the UPPCC, some members, notably Jugal Kishore and Vishwambhardayal Tripathi, agreed that some liaison machinery had to be instituted with the cooperation of the PCC and MLAs, and further desired that the PCC ought to be consulted by government on all major policy issues. UP Premier Govind Ballabh Pant, however, brushed these objections aside with the comment that no liaison machinery was needed since the PCC and government worked in close harmony in any case and that the institution of any such machinery at the district level was fraught with dangers.[44]

Despite these admonitions, Congressmen of all descriptions gave frequent and often unstinting public expression to their views on the affairs of state. The master of political brinkmanship, Rafi Ahmed Kidwai, raised a storm in UP Congress affairs when he supported the secession of the socialists from the Congress.

---

[42] Satyanarain Sinha to all members of the Congress party in the Constituent Assembly (Legislative), 8 March 1949, Patel Papers (Correspondence), Microfilm Reel no. 13.

[43] Zaidi and Zaidi, *Encyclopaedia of the Indian National Congress, vol. xiii, 1946–50, India Wins Freedom,* New Delhi,1981, p. 343.

[44] UPPCC Papers, Microfilm Reel no. 2.

His speeches, as they were reported, welcomed this development on the grounds that a healthy opposition was necessary for the survival of democracy, while criticising the UP government for its myriad failings.[45] Govind Sahai, a UP Congressman and an MLA, was moved to complain that senior Congressmen were vilifying the Pant government as a puppet of capitalist forces under the garb of socialism, and were urging *kisans* to overthrow the government. He alleged that some Congressmen had gone *to the extent of setting up a parallel government in a* tahsil *in UP.*[46] Even more daringly, the Banaras City Congress Committee passed a resolution which stated that ever since the Congress government had taken over the reins of the provincial government the hardships of the people had increased rather than decreased because the government had failed to tackle most urgent problems. The resolution also called on the PCC to effect a change of ministers if the ministry could not solve the problems faced by the people.[47]

At Nasik, Rao reports, Nehru apparently opposed a resolution calling for popular government in the Patiala and East Punjab States Union, and questioned the AICC's right to intervene in day-to-day administration, arguing that the house did not know the full facts and difficulties faced by the government. The resolution was withdrawn. Rao says, however, that despite Nehru's accusation of interference there was great 'non-official' activity 'and it could be seen that the AICC, as the authentic voice of the Congress, felt it should express itself on domestic and international matters'. Nehru, in this account, approved this principle. All non-official resolutions which Nehru opposed were withdrawn. (Note the use of the term non-official.)[48]

---

[45] Undated press statement by Kidwai, enclosed with Muzaffar Hussain to Rajendra Prasad, 28 June 1948, AICC (1), File no. P 17 (Pt. I) of 1947–48. Also see Krishna Chandra to G. B. Pant, n.d. Charan Singh Papers (Second Instalment) [henceforth Charan Singh Papers (II)], Subject File no. 262 of 1948–66.

[46] Govind Sahai to the AICC, 16 October 1947. AICC (1), File no. PC 18 (Pt. III) of 1947–48. The irony of this accusation may have been lost on the AICC, but its seriousness would not have gone unheeded by Congress leaders.

[47] Resolution passed at a meeting of the Banaras City Congress Committee, 10 January 1947, AICC (I), File no. 35 of 1946–47.

[48] M. V. Ramana Rao, *A Short History of the Indian National Congress*, pp. 282–83.

A Gandhian Way Out in the Background of the Ascendancy of the Ministerialists?

By the 1950s, therefore, the resolution of this question of balance seemed to be moving in a direction favourable to the 'minister-ialist party'. Shankarrao Deo who, as we have noted, showed some jealousy in defending the prerogatives of the organisa-tion, issued a circular explaining that the PCCs were not free to dictate policy to the government just because the government emanated from the party. The government functioned with the help of a well-manned administration and if the PCCs wanted to influence government policy they would be best served by forming specialised sub-committees and research wings to study ways and means of bringing about a social revolution in the country.[49] Much earlier, writing in the wake of the Jaipur session of the Congress, a special correspondent of the *National Herald* noted that this session had been a watershed in the relation-ship between Congress and government with the balance tilting decidedly towards government.[50]

By the 1950s, the government wing of the Congress was gaining the upper hand. The supremacy of the government over the Congress meant a redefinition of the sources of political legitimacy: while the colonial State had existed the Congress had derived its own legitimacy by laying claim to being the organised expression of the 'national will' which was counterposed to the illegitimate colonial State. In the changed circumstances, the State was valorised as the supreme wielder of legitimate pol-itical authority. This involved a redefinition of the Congress's political role. The pressing necessity for such a redefinition was also fuelled by the disquiet that Rajendra Prasad, for example, gave voice to at the increasing implication of the Congress with government. Thus, in Prasad's words, 'There is a real risk for the future if the Congress Government gets identified with the Congress organization. If it can happen in the case of the Congress it can also happen in the case of any other party...' Prasad went on to argue that a line had to be drawn between the

---

[49] *Hindustan Times*, 26 March 1950.
[50] *National Herald*, 24 December 1948.

responsibility and the rights of the Congress on the one hand, and the responsibility that government owed to the legislatures (or, by extension, parliament).[51]

A specific connection between the assumption of office and the Congress's changed role of acting as a link between the people and the government was made in an AICC circular which argued for the necessity of assigning absolute priority to the constructive programme: 'If the Congress Committees are to serve the masses and to help them utilise the opportunities which are arising by the transference of political power to the people of the country, they must be activised by undertaking the constructive programme.'[52] After assuming office, this theme was taken up in earnest. A note on the constructive programme emphasised that it was only through constructive work that the Congress could justify its existence, retain mass support, and thus survive.[53]

At a conference of presidents and secretaries of all PCCs, resolutions were passed, drawing attention to the importance of constructive work in the reorganisation of the Congress. Attention was drawn, for instance, to the work of bodies such as the All-India Village Industries Association (AIVIA) and the All-India Spinning Association (AISA), and members of Congress governments were called upon to implement schemes along the lines of such associations. This exhortation was accompanied by a programmatic statement about Congress reorganisation, which envisaged the institution of a special cadre of workers trained by the PCCs and the all-India constructive organisations and attached to primary Congress committees whose function would be the maintenance of records, the organisation of panchayats which would look after sanitation and primary health of the locality and 'bring under its control the entire social, political

---

[51] Prasad to Patel, 22 September 1948, Patel Papers (Correspondence), Microfilm Reel no. 3. More distanced political observers had the same thing to say.

[52] AICC circular to all PCC secretaries, 15 April 1947, AICC (1), File no. PI (Pt. III) of 1946.

[53] Undated note on the role of the constructive programme, AICC (1), File no. CPD 2 & 6 of 1947.

and economic life through the day to day execution of the constructive programme'.[54]

Implicit in the foregoing was a counterposition of constructive work to the functioning of the Congress governments. This was made clear at the same meeting in a resolution drawing the CWC's attention to the fact that the Congress governments were not following the constructive programme of the Congress and urged it to ask them to implement this programme, aimed at promoting self-reliance among the people. The conference also urged the creation of a constructive programme committee (CPC) which would carry out the Gandhian programme with the help of the government if possible, but otherwise with the help of the people.[55] At the first meeting of the CPC, the tension between the Congress organisation and the ministries, and in that context the Congress's constructive role, found ambiguous expression. A discussion of the committee's relations with the ministries concluded that it was necessary to have agencies other than the government to carry out the constructive programme. These agencies would have the leeway to experiment and develop new schemes which the government could take up later. The CPC quite clearly envisaged for itself the role of a mediator, operating in a terrain in which the government would be out of its depth.[56]

An AICC circular echoed this conception of the constructive wing of the Congress as a mediator between the people and the government. The circular envisaged for the CPCs the task of making the people self-reliant, in a manner that would make it possible for the constructive programme to be carried out with the active assistance of the people themselves. This education in self-reliance was seen as particularly important because it would

---

[54] From resolutions passed at the conference of presidents and secretaries of PCCs at Allahabad, 22–24 February 1947, AICC (1), File no. CPD 1 (Pt. II) of 1947.

[55] From resolutions passed at the conference of presidents and secretaries of PCCs at Allahabad, 22–24 February 1947, AICC (1), File no. G 8 (KW 1) of 1947–48.

[56] Report on the first meeting of the constructive programme committee held in New Delhi, 26 April 1947, AICC (1), File no. CPD 7 of 1947. A later chapter on the Congress's development strategies and its conceptualisation of the role and character of the State will be discussed, at this point from a slightly different standpoint.

also enable the people to cooperate in working the constructive schemes of the government.[57]

The UP CPC reiterated this message in a circular to all DCCs and TCCs. It began by taking note of the impression in some Congress quarters that since the government had taken up the Congress programme there was no particular need for individual Congress workers or the Congress organisation to be involved in the constructive programme. It went on to say, however, that there could be no hermetic division between the Congress governments and the Congress organisation. Thus, while the Congress governments were officially shaping the Congress's fundamental policies, it was the duty of the Congress organisation and its workers to do their utmost to aid the governments in their endeavours. The circular also repeated the injunction that it was the duty of the Congress to ensure as far as possible that the people carried out the constructive programme themselves, where possible through panchayats. The circular ended by reiterating the vision of the Congress acting as a living link between the government and the people.[58]

I have tried to show above that even within the 'ministerial' resolution of the relationship between the Congress organisation, constructive work, and the government there was a residual tension, mainly connected to equations between the organisation and ministries. The assistant secretary of the constructive programme department in the AICC office, one Ramadhar, expressed it clearly. In letters to the two general secretaries of the time, Ramadhar wrote that it was right to cooperate with the government, as also to give them information and point out its inadequacies. But in doing so, Ramadhar wrote, propriety had

---

[57] AICC circular to all PCCs and constructive organisations, 9 July 1947, AICC (1), G 3 of 1946–47.
[58] Circular from Provincial Constructive Committee, UP to all DCCs and TCCs, 20 July 1947, AICC (I), File no. G 41 (KW I) of 1946. The secretary in the AICC office also wrote to the secretary of the DCC, Etawah, that Congress committees were expected to cooperate with local government authorities in undertaking the constructive programme. He assured the secretary that the provincial ministry wished to be in contact with the masses and undertake plans for their improvement and that DCCs should send any concrete suggestions that they might have to the government through the PCC. P Chakraverti to the secretary, DCC, Etawah 11 December 1947, AICC File no. P 17 (Pt. I) of 1947–48.

to be maintained, and it was not possible for his department to infringe this. This was the main reason for starting an office for constructive work; and it was up to the office to do some solid constructive work — be it insignificant or grand.[59] In an eloquent plea for the distancing of constructive work from the activities of government, Ramadhar wrote:

> It appears that the uncertain conditions in the country and the undefined policies of the Provincial Governments will greatly hamper our work. Under these circumstances it will be essential for us to survey the whole situation and determine our approach independently. ... I should, therefore, like to impress upon you the necessity of planning this work [so] that we might organize it absolutely independently if necessary. I repeat here that I am afraid, given the general attitude of the section of the Congress running the Government, we might have to fall back upon our resources.[60]

It is quite clear that even the neo-Gandhian conception of the Congress as an organic link between the 'people/nation' and the Congress governments was caught up and shaped in the contest for political legitimacy between the Congress ministries and the party organisation. It is also clear that this conception could not always sit comfortably with the conception of the Congress as a vast bureaucratic machine.

A note on the role of constructive workers encapsulates the political predicament in a way that bears out my basic argument. It said:

> All these whole-time and earnest constructive workers who have been silently and quietly working out the Constructive Programme

---

[59] Ramadhar to Jugal Kishore, 25 August 1947, AICC (1), File no. CPD 8 of 1947.

[60] Ramadhar to Shankarrao Deo, 22 August 1947, AICC (1), File no. CPD 8 of 1947. Somewhat later Ramadhar was, however, to qualify his pessimistic prognosis. In a letter to Deo, in the course of reviewing the progress of the constructive programme following the institution of his office, Ramadhar commended Bihar and particularly the south and said, 'Evidently Provincial Governments are co-operating. These are good signs and I have begun to hope that something might still be possible' (Ramadharto Deo, 2 December 1947, AICC (1), File no. CPD 7 of 1947).

have really helped the Congress ... to forge the sanctions for its non-violent struggle for freedom and to make it an organiza- tion of the masses. And yet they are unable today to collectively influence important Congress policies and much less the policies and programmes of the ... Congress governments.

This is mainly due to a clear and dangerous divorce that has taken place between Congress Constructive workers and their organiza- tions on the one hand and Congress political workers and the Congress organizations as such on the other.[61]

This lamentation gestures quite clearly towards the point I seek to make. While the ministerial wing of the Congress and the organisational wing was involved in a contest for power, underpinned by divergent ideas about sovereignty and political legitimacy in the sphere of the state, the leadership of the Cong- ress tried, in search of a resolution, to relocate the legitimate duties of the organisation and individual workers in the sphere of the constructive Gandhian programme. The state's sphere, encompassing as it did an ambitious programme of development and that of constructive work, was not conceived of as being a hermetically sealed box. Nevertheless, the accent in formulating the latter was within the framework of nation building; within that, again, the accent was on moral regeneration.

I would argue that constructive work was encompassed largely in a sphere of nation building in which the accent was on private initiative and the actors were citizens going about their quotidian lives. Individuals and communities were to be the targets of reformation in both moral — *ahimsa*, *satyagraha*, for instance — and material — sanitation, continence, and abstemiousness, again by way of exemplification — terms through the construc- tive programme. In Gandhi's formulations of the constructive programme, as with those of his disciples, there was an ambiguity. Thus, while the arena of constructive work was seen in some senses as that of the community as extended family — which, for instance, is why all Gandhi's ashrams both in South Africa and later India sought to replicate a familial structure and ambience — in some other senses, the objects of constructive work could

---

[61] Undated note entitled 'Constructive Workers and their role in Free India', Shankarrao Deo Papers, Subject File no. 10.

appertain to the entire nation-in-the-making in the form of the national public, whose moral and material uplift was the final desideratum.

Alongside that ambivalence, there was, too, as we have seen, an ambivalence about the way the constructive programme was positioned in relation to the arena of state and government. Nevertheless, in no construction of the constructive programme could it be subsumed entirely into the arena of the state. In its autonomous dimensions, it lay clearly in a private, communitarian, and familial sphere, leaving to the ministerial wing of the Congress, the bearer of governmental power, the prerogative of fashioning the public space of the State, its institutions and discourses. In future, as we know, particularly the work of JP, and movements led by Gandhi Ashram would create problems for the government.

II

Paradigms of Inequality, Pathways to Entitlement

4

Imaginations and Manifestos of the Political Parties on Ideals of Developmental Governance

Ashutosh Kumar

Introduction

The idea of democratic governance tied with market economy has become a critical component of the neoliberal global agenda in the post-Soviet era. The two institutions of market economy and liberal political democracy are being assumed to be not merely compatible but also complementary to each other. India's twin success stories in maintaining liberal democratic institutions[1] and also achieving significant market-oriented growth in the last one and half decade have naturally been globally acknowledged and celebrated. India as such belies the experiences of the 'new' democracies of Africa and Latin America where neoliberal

---

[1] That democracy both as an idea and as an institution has got embedded in the consciousness of the Indian people has come out in different surveys based on face-to-face interviews with the respondents. In the World Values Surveys conducted all over the world in 2001, 93 per cent of the respondents interviewed in India indicated their approval of the 'democratic system' (Sandeep Shastri, 'Citizen in Political Institutions and Processes in India: A Study of the Impact of Regional, Social and Economic Factors', unpublished paper, Stellenbosch, South Africa: World Values Survey Conference, 17–21 November 2001, http://www.worldvaluessurvey.org/wvs/articles/folder_published/conference_66, accessed 20 August 2010). Democrats also outnumbered non-democrats in the SDSA survey conducted between August 2004 and March 2005 in India. In the survey 84 per cent of the respondents in India were found to be either strong or weak democrats whereas only 15 per cent respondents were considered non-democrats (Peter Ronald deSouza, Suhas Palshikar, and Yogendra Yadav, 'Surveying South Asia', Journal of Democracy, 19 (1), Baltimore, Maryland, The Johns Hopkins University Press, January 2008, pp. 85, 90).

reforms did not lead to an improvement in terms of governance or economic performance, inviting a backlash against the globalisation.

In a world swept by 'third wave of democracy', political parties, and elections, which supposedly bring together the legitimate aspirations to the core of the people, and popular representation and accountability as the primary method of reaching this goal, are increasingly being viewed as an effective method of democratic governance. It is hardly a surprise, then, that the success of India's democracy is being assessed favourably primarily in its minimalist electoral form, encompassing a multiparty system, regularly held open elections at national, state, and the local levels, and peaceful transfer of power.[2] Unlike the 'established'/'longstanding'/'old' democracies of the West, political parties in India continue to attract a high degree of interest and involvement across the spectrum of politics, while shaping identities and economic interests.

Much as the robustness of India's democratic institutions has been rightfully celebrated in their minimalist electoral form in recent years coupled with its adherence to apparent economic success, the present article argues that they are not expected to impact upon the substantive issues of public policy making and setting the national agenda even if it means overlooking the legitimate claims of a significant section of the electorates.

This article substantiates its argument by visiting India's electoral politics since the initiation of neoliberal economic reforms and taking note of a perceptible 'disconnect' between the two. For the purpose, the article mainly refers in a comparative manner to the economic agenda as revealed in the manifestos released and campaigns undertaken by the two coalition-making, polity-wide parties,[3] namely the Congress and the Bharatiya Janata

---

[2] Sunil Khilnani has argued that 'the meaning of democracy has been menacingly narrowed to signify only 'elections', primarily due to the weakening of other democratic procedures in India (*Idea of India*, New Delhi: Penguin Books India, 1997, p. 58).

[3] Parties participating as well as winning across the country both at the federal level as well as at the state level are categorised as polity-wide parties by K. Deschouwer ('Political Parties as Multi-Level Organizations', in R. S. Katz and W. Crotty [eds], *Handbook of Party Politics*, London: Sage Publications, 2006).

Party (BJP) as well as the two mainstream left parties, namely the Communist Party of India (CPI) and Communist Party of India in the last two Lok Sabha elections[4] held in 2004 and 2009 along with the relevant data from the Centre for the Study of Developing Societies-National Election Study (CSDS-NES). The essay also refers to the survey-based, India-specific findings presented in the report of the State of Democracy in South Asia (SDSA) study undertaken by CSDS-Lokniti (SDSA 2008).[5]

Rise of the Plebeians

A recurrent theme interweaving most of the studies of electoral politics in recent India is the phenomenon designated as 'democratic upsurge'.[6] India is depicted as experimenting with 'a silent revolution' as political power is 'being transferred, on the whole peacefully, from the upper-caste elites to various subaltern groups ... The relative calm of the Indian experience is primarily due to the fact the whole process is incremental.'[7] Legitimacy of traditional social authority is being undermined. A changed mode of electoral representation is being viewed as paving the way for the assertion and subsequent empowerment

---

[4] These two 'regular, timely, well conducted', and 'normal' elections underlined 'the growing maturity of Indian democracy' (Atul Kohli, 'What are You Calling a Historical Mandate?', edit page, *The Indian Express*, 19 May 2009).

[5] The achieved sample size in SDSA study was 5,389 from as many as 26 constituent states in India.

[6] The overall turnout level in assembly elections touched around 70 per cent up from around 60 per cent in the 1990s. There has also been a substantial narrowing of the gender gap in voter turnout and an upsurge in the turnout among Dalits and *adivasi*s, though not necessarily the Muslims and the very poor (Y. Yadav and S. Palshikar, 'Revisiting "Third Electoral System": Mapping Electoral Trends in India, 2004–2009', in S. Shastri, K. C. Suri, and Y. Yadav (eds), *Electoral Politics in Indian States: Lok Sabha Elections in 2004 and Beyond*, 2009, p. 397). See Y. Yadav, 'Understanding the Second Democratic Upsurge: Trends of Bahujan Participation in Electoral Politics in the 1990s', in F. Frankel, Z. Hasan, R. Bhargava, and B. Arora (eds), *Transforming India: Social and Political Dynamics of Democracy*, New Delhi: Oxford University Press, pp. 121–45.

[7] C. Jaffrelot, *India's Silent Revolution: The Rise of Low Castes in North Indian Politics*, Delhi: Permanent Black, 2003, p. 494.

of the hitherto politically dormant poor, unprivileged, and marginalised men and women and the social groups they belong to. The turnout of these groups has been higher than the average turnout, indicating a greater level of political involvement and participation. In terms of presence, a whole new generation of political entrepreneurs representing these marginal groups have come up. All this has resulted in a high level of aggregate volatility or a high degree of swing in the vote share for all parties as well as a high level of individual volatility or the proportion of electorates who changed parties across two elections. The resultant high rate of regime alteration has kept political parties on their toes, seeking new forms of political alignments and support with increased frequency.[8]

The increased level of contestation and participation is being considered good as it apparently helps to deepen a participatory mode of democratic governance by empowering the poor and the marginal in terms of policy making. How valid is such a claim? Has it made the political class more responsive and accountable? In order to interrogate the optimism about the marginal ones getting empowered as citizens under a 'new regime of governance and governmentality', we need to consider four facts that relate the emergent nature of electoral politics to the ongoing process of neoliberal reforms and underline the implications.

National Election Studies

Fact number one, always suspect, is the empirically grounded knowledge that the new economic policies right since their initiation have been disapproved of by a significant section of the electorate, especially the poor and marginal one. In the national election studies undertaken by Lokniti, CSDS, of all the Lok Sabha elections since the 1996 elections,[9] the respondents

---

[8] O. Heath, 'Party Systems, Political Cleavages and Electoral Volatility in India: State-wise Analysis 1998–1999', *Electoral Studies*, 24 (2), 2005, pp. 177–99; Y. Yadav and S. Palishkar, 'Revisiting "Third Electoral System": Mapping Electoral Trends in India, 2004–2009', in S. Shastri, K. C. Suri, and Y. Yadav (eds), *Electoral Politics in Indian States: Lok Sabha Elections in 2004 and Beyond*, New Delhi: Oxford University Press, 2009, pp. 393–429.

[9] In the NES 1996, NES 1998, and NES 1999 the achieved sample sizes were 9,614, 8,133, and 9,418, respectively. It was 27,151 in the NES 2004. The sample

were repeatedly asked three different but related time-series questions aimed at (a) determining the level of awareness about the neoliberal economic reforms among the voters coming from different sections of the society; (b) their opinion on the entry of the foreign companies in India; and (c) their views on the privatisation of existing government companies/public sector units.[10]

The data revealed that awareness about the economic reforms was abysmally low among the electorate even after a considerable period of time since their initiation. If only 19 per cent of the respondents reported having some idea of economic reforms in 1996, it was 26 per cent in a 1998 post-poll survey.[11] Among those who were aware of the reforms, the percentage of scheduled caste (SC) and scheduled tribe (ST) respondents was much lower than of other caste groups. Among the respondents, only 13 per cent of SCs and 6 per cent of STs had awareness about the reforms in the 1996 survey. The figures were 20 and 17 per cent respectively in 1998 survey.

The data also show that there has been no consensus on new economic policies. Opinions have been divided across classes, castes, occupations, and locations. A large segment of the Indian electorate, in fact, has had a negative perception of the ongoing economic reform process.[12] The NES of 2004 found that

---

size further increased to 36,238 voters in the NES 2009 post-poll survey which covered 29 states, 2,386 locations spread across 536 parliamentary constituencies (*The Hindu*, 14 May 2009). The NES 2004 and 2009 have arguably been the two largest social scientific studies of the Indian elections, for building evidence based understanding of the electorates choices (S. Shastri, K. C. Suri, and Y. Yadav, *Electoral Politics in Indian States: Lok Sabha Elections in 2004 and Beyond*, New Delhi: Oxford University Press, 2009a. http://www.csdsdelhi.org/index_pg1.htm, accessed 20 August 2010.

[10] Ashutosh Kumar, 'Rethinking State Politics in India: Regions within Regions', *Economic and Political Weekly*, 44 (19), 2009a, pp. 14–19.

[11] The question asked was: During the last five years, the central government has made many changes in its economic policy (policy regarding money matters, tax, Indian and foreign companies, government and private sectors, industry, and agriculture). Have you heard about them?

[12] Based on the data drawn from mass and elite surveys that involved 2,851 successful interviews conducted in India in 1996 covering 96 assembly constituencies in six states with varying economic indicators and party strength, P. Chhibber and S. Eldersveld found that less than 10 per cent of

44 per cent of all respondents were of the opinion that the rich had benefited from the reforms whereas the poor had become poorer. The upper-caste respondents were split nearly equally on the question but a very large portion of the respondents from the poor and peripheral groups viewed reforms as beneficial only to the rich. Among those who shared this opinion were 45 per cent of the respondents belonging to other backward castes (OBCs), SCs and STs and nearly 55 per cent of Muslim respondents. 38 per cent of all respondents interviewed held a similar opinion in the NES, 2009.[13]

Both the 1996 and 2004 NES post-poll data also revealed the popular perception that the economic condition of the common people had worsened in the recent past. In 1996, 53 per cent of the respondents held the government responsible for increasing poverty whereas in 2004, 47 per cent had the same opinion. In 2009, 36 per cent of the respondents agreed that it was the government and not the people themselves who were responsible for their poverty.

The question whether foreign companies should be allowed free trade in India was asked repeatedly in NES of 1996, 1998, 1999, 2004, and 2009. The percentage of those who opposed such a policy was 37, 37, 33, 39, and 32 per cent respectively. There was an equally steady opposition to privatisation of government companies. The average figures were 35 and 47 per cent in 1996 and 2004. Among them, the percentage was larger in the case of

---

the respondents said that reforms were great success. 80 per cent favoured direct government control in the economy. The limited mass support for reforms was attributed by the authors to the finding that the 'local elite are still by and large not supportive of reform because the government has not made a concerted effort to bring them on board, neither has it made any institutional changes such that the incentives faced by the local elites would be sufficiently altered for them to support reform' ('Local Elites and Popular Support for Economic Reform in China and India', *Comparative Political Studies*, 33 (3), 2000, pp. 363, 370).

[13] The question asked in 2009 was: Some people say that the progress made in the last few years through development schemes and programmes of the govt has benefited only the well-to-do. Others say no, the poor and needy have also benefited from them. What would you say?

socially disadvantaged groups. The figures were 37 and 45 per cent of the SCs and 30 and 42 per cent of the STs in 1996 and 2004.

In the NES survey 2009, while 46 per cent of the respondents disagreed with the opinion that government factories and businesses should be sold/handed over to private companies, 47 per cent also opposed any measure to reduce the number of government employees. Significantly, when asked whether specific services be run mainly by the government or by private companies, an overwhelming majority of the respondents preferred the government,[14] whereas 50 per cent of the respondents expressed a great deal of trust/some trust in government officials.[15] It is obvious that electorates are not in agreement with the alternative neoliberal model of governance that envisages a 'gradual curtailment of the role of the state'.[16]

---

[14] Economic reforms have often been justified by pointing towards the appalling governance structure in the delivery of basic social services for the people. However, in NES 2009, a majority of the respondents preferred the government over private companies for the delivery of the following services: 63 per cent for running the bus service, 74 per cent for drinking water supply, 69 per cent for imparting education, 73 per cent for electricity supply, and 69 per cent for hospital facility. Stronger opposition to privatisation of public services came from less privileged groups such as poor, non-literate, and rural dwellers.

[15] Disapproval for the changes that are being effected through the practice of governance under the shadow of neoliberal reforms was also apparent in the findings of a research project on 'Rights, Representation, and the Poor' conducted by Developing Countries Research Centre, University. The study showed that majority of the respondents (80 per cent) was of the view that it was the government responsibility to meet people's basic needs. Only 1 per cent of the respondents favoured the plurality of private agencies, engaged in the business of service delivery, for the purpose. 91 per cent of the respondents held the government responsible for ensuring quality services (electricity, gas, water, sewers, roads, street lighting, public transport, garbage collection). The survey was conducted in Delhi in 2003 across different and distinct categories of residential areas ('intended' and 'unintended' ones). Data was generated on the basis of structured questionnaire administered to 1,401 residents (N. Chandhoke, '"Seeing" the State in India', *Economic and Political Weekly*, XL (11), 2005, 1035–1036).

[16] N. G. Jayal, Democracy and the State: Welfare, Secularism and Development in Contemporary India, New Delhi: Oxford University Press, 2001a.

Pursuance of Neoliberal Agenda

Now, let us juxtapose fact number one with the second one. The second fact is that the two polity-wide parties of India, namely the Congress and BJP, leading the United Progressive Alliance (UPA) and National Democratic Alliance (NDA) — the alliance of both national and state-level parties — respectively, had emphasised their unambiguous commitment to economic reforms in their election manifestos released on the eve of the 2004 and 2009 elections.

The Congress party's manifesto[17] issued on the eve of 2004 parliamentary elections titled 'Congress Agenda for 2004–2009' mentioned prominently its commitment to broaden and deepen economic reforms, to attain 8–10 per cent economic growth, to ensure efficiency and competitiveness in all production sectors. For the purpose, the party promised incentives for increased foreign direct investment. The party promised to continue with disinvestments in a selective manner.[18]

In its manifesto released before the 2009 parliamentary elections, the Congress supported the continuation of the privatisation though in a selective form, tax reforms in the form of the replacement of all the indirect taxes by goods and services tax and promised incentives for greater foreign investments with emphasis on maximum added value and export potential, private investment in resources such as coal and iron ore, new deal for small and medium enterprises (SMEs), and first-generation entrepreneurs with greater access to credit and freedom from inspectors, ensuring the highest standard of corporate governance.

Economic reforms have also figured prominently in the election manifestos of the BJP.[19] In what was grandiosely called the

---

[17] For viewing the full text of the manifestos of the Congress party visit www.aicc.org.in/new/manifesto.doc, accessed 20 August 2010.

[18] The shift in favour of the reforms can be traced in the party manifesto released on the eve of the 1996 elections in which the party vowed to carry forward the momentum of economic reforms. Economic policy was to be restructured to achieve a higher trajectory of economic growth, efficiency, and competitiveness in all production sectors and also meet the target of 8–9 per cent growth in terms of GDP per annum (*The Hindu*, 13 April 1996).

[19] For complete texts of BJP manifestos visit ibnlive.in.com/news/full...bjp-manifesto.../89404-37.html; http:/www.bjp/org//, accessed 20 August 2010.

'vision document' (released in 2004), the party committed itself to 'broaden and deepen' the process of liberalisation so that a 'modern and resurgent India' could emerge as the 'nerve centre of the global knowledge economy'. The party also committed itself to making India 'a global manufacturing hub' by enabling Indian products, services, and entrepreneurs to dominate the domestic as well as the global market. The document promised to create world-class infrastructure for the cities. The party opted for a joint 13-party NDA manifesto titled '*Agenda for Development, Good Governance and Peace*'. While referring to the need of a 'brave new India', the manifesto proposed the following measures to be taken up: raising the foreign investment limits in the insurance sector; allowing overseas investors to enter retailing; and implementing an open-sky policy and continuing the privatisation process including the mining sector to 'enhance and realize the hidden wealth in the public sector undertakings'. Drawing from the vision document, the manifesto promised to make India a global leader in the information technology sector. It also proposed urban renewal schemes that included building 10 'global cities', 10 world-class airports, 100 airstrips for day flights, roads, infrastructure, a world-class telecom sector, special economic zones, introduction of e-governance, and multi-commodity exchanges. The manifesto also promised to increase the FDI in the insurance sector and to continue the process of privatisation with vigour. In the agricultural sector, a second green revolution was promised to make India the 'food factory for the world'.

The BJP manifesto, 2009 — after a decade the party, which relied on the NDA manifesto, issued its own — reiterated the party's stand on welcoming foreign companies and also promised to frame policies for reforms in labour and tax laws. It also promised to encourage private initiative in higher education. The private sector was sought to be involved in the effort to increase spending by 9 per cent. A 'New Deal' was offered to SMEs, especially in the retail sector and to first-generation entrepreneurs, with greater access to credit and freedom from inspectors. Checking corporate fraud and bringing back the black money stashed in the foreign banks were the issues that were included as a part of economic governance by the BJP, to be picked up by left parties also.

It should emerge from the above discussion that there has been a growing ideological convergence that leaves voters very little to choose from.[20] The convergence is marked by a political consensus within the BJP and the Congress and their respective regional allies about the new economic policies. A cursory look at the manifestos find keywords and phrases common to them like reforms, privatisation, disinvestment, elimination of fiscal/revenue deficits, achieving economic growth rate up to 8–10 per cent, public–private partnership, capacity building, greater internal and external competition, a second green revolution, creation of a world-class financial sector, IT, enhanced students loans, private initiative, global hub, SEZ, good governance, and corporate governance. The similarities are amazing when it comes to the agenda relating to economic issues or governance.[21] What is more, the texts, at least in parts, read very much like global funding agencies' agenda papers.

The Puzzles

The concurrence of the above two facts would leave any discerning observer of India's electoral democracy with a set of puzzles. Let us consider two of them.

The first one relates to the question as to why political parties barring those on the left have endorsed economic reforms so

---

[20] Y. Yadav, 'Why Manifestos Matter', *The Hindu*, Edit Page, 8 April 2009, http://blogs.thehindu.com/elections2009/, accessed 20 August 2010.

[21] Take, for instance, the manifestos released by the Congress and the BJP-led NDA on the eve of 1999 Lok Sabha elections. If the NDA committed to the people to provide 'good governance' in the form of 'stable, honest, transparent and efficient government', the Congress reminded the voters of 'political stability' and 'cohesiveness' the party brought to the nation in its 45 years of governance. On the economic agenda, if the NDA promised to 'continue the reform process' involving 'legislation on fiscal responsibility' so that 'foreign investment in core areas' could be encouraged, 'capital market' could be revived, and 'comprehensive reform of public sector undertakings' could be expedited, then the Congress also promised to 'push for faster economic reforms' which was to include the adoption of the measures to 'reduce the fiscal deficit to below 4 per cent of GDP' for 'encouraging foreign institutional investors, venture capital funds and private equity funds', and carry out 'disinvestment of public sector companies'.

strongly when the sentiment among voters, especially the poor and the marginal, has been so vehemently opposed to such uncritical endorsement? This when, as the CSDS-NES, 2009, data testifies, the perceptions of people on economic issues do influence their electoral choice.[22]

The easiest explanation would be that parties have repeatedly failed to gauge popular sentiment. The fate of the BJP's 'India Shining' campaign in the 2004 elections in particular would encourage such a reading.[23] Such a simplistic answer, however, would beg a further question: Why have all major parties failed equally in their attempt to read the public mind, that too not in one but two elections that took place five years apart? Obviously, this does not seem to be the answer given the fact that the political class in India, reared on fighting an unending series of electoral battles from local to parliamentary ones, is too savvy to remain blissfully unaware of the unpopularity of neoliberal policies among the marginal ones.[24] The language of manifestos of catch-all parties like ours, even if not pleasing everybody, will seek not to displease anybody, in this case a large chunk of voters. More so, as there has been a spurt of civil society initiatives to enquire about how the manifestos are being formed within the parties themselves and how and in which form these travel then from the party to the people. The manifestos are also kept in the memory block of the electorate through campaigns like *wada na todo abhiyan* (don't break promises campaign) or through the Right to Information Act.[25]

A more complex and informed explanation would be that the political parties with their ears to the ground actually have had a fairly good idea of public sentiment but for reasons that need to be spelt out by political analysts, they nonetheless continue

[22] K. C. Suri, 'The Economy and Voting in the 15th Lok Sabha Elections', *Economic and Political Weekly*, 44 (39), 2009, p. 69.

[23] S. Kumar, 'Impact of Economic Reforms on Indian Electorate', *Economic and Political Weekly*, 39 (16), 2004, pp. 1621–1630; J. Mooij, J. (ed.), *The Politics of Economic Reforms in India*, New Delhi: Sage Publications 2005, p. 16.

[24] It gets evident in the way the state units of the polity-wide parties pick up the selective part of the manifestos to communicate to the local electorates.

[25] As a result, there has been a perceptible change in the way manifestos are being crafted, conducted, and followed up. Accountability in relation to both political manifestos and political speeches are changing.

to endorse the neoliberal policies of market reforms. If we read other parts of the manifestos not only under consideration but released earlier in the post-reform period,[26] we find the two polity-wide parties have equally been keen to reassure the electorate that the neoliberal reforms would necessarily wear a human face and the poor will not be allowed to suffer.

The 'Human Face' of Neoliberal Agenda

For instance, the Congress election manifesto in 2004 identified and emphasised six basic areas of public welfare and 'good' governance:[27] achievement of social harmony, employment for the youth, rural development, economic resurgence, women's empowerment, and equal opportunities. It expressed concern about the rise in unemployment, distress among farmers and farm labourers, and falling growth rate, and accentuated disparities as a result of skewed distribution of benefits between sectors, regions, and classes. As remedial measures, the party committed itself to expanding employment in the organised sector and to promote employment-intensive growth. Rather startling was its promise to create 100,000,000 jobs a year. To ensure employment for at least one member of a rural household, the party promised to enact a national employment guarantee act to provide at least 100 days of employment every year on asset-creating public works programmes at minimum wages. Spelling out an 'agriculture first' line, the party promised the restoration of the rural credit system based on cooperatives, easing the debt burden of the small and marginal farmers, resource allocation for public investment including construction of new irrigation

---

[26] In their 1998 manifestos, both the NDA and the Congress promised to encourage employment, eradicate poverty, and provide food security to all, ensuring subsidies for the genuinely poor and needy sections as well as the implementation of minimum wages, spending 6 per cent of the GDP on education with emphasis on elementary education, reservation for SCs, STs, and OBCs in public employment and reservation for women in legislative bodies.

[27] The 1996 and 1998 manifestos of the Congress had promised stable, responsive, open, and accountable administration. The Congress, under the leadership of Sonia Gandhi, in its 1998 election manifesto promised 'Arthik Swaraj' and 'garibon ka raj' (economic self-reliance and governance by the poor).

wells especially in the backward and poorer regions, and promotion of labour-intensive export. An agricultural stabilisation fund was proposed to increase the profitability of agriculture in consonance with a long-term export policy for agricultural products in the global market. The party promised not only to ensure that 'the terms of trade would always be maintained in favour of agriculture' but also to take steps to increase profitability in agriculture. The manifesto also talked of the need to apply the gains of information technology to the modernisation of artisan and household industries. Marking a significant reversal in terms of disinvestment policy regarding the power sector, the party now assured that the public sector units with the help of the 'creative' use of foreign exchange reserve would be bearing the larger responsibility for investment in the power generation. Catering to the urban middle classes, the party held out incentives promising allocation of 6 per cent of GDP to the education sector besides granting autonomy to institutions of higher learning to ensure academic excellence and professional competence.

In its 2009 manifesto, the Congress party promised to enact a 'right to food' law, guaranteeing access to all people, especially the vulnerable sections, to sufficient quantities of food. It also promised a new land acquisition act to protect landowners from forced acquisition of land for SEZ. Farmers were promised compensation for land at market rates, to be given up voluntarily for industrial purposes. Regarding disinvestment, it was to be selective and partial with the government retaining the majority share. It also promised that there would be no 'blind privatisation'. In terms of social policies, the Congress promised free education for SC/ST children along with free coaching facilities for entrance examinations, filling up all the reserved posts, and extending reservations for poorer sections belonging to upper castes. Taking up the gender issue, the party resolved to pass the bill reserving one-third seats in the Lok Sabha and the state assemblies for women and providing incentive for girl children to acquire school education. To protect the interests of the workers' rights the party pledged to extend additional support for labour-intensive manufacturing. Also on the agenda was the formulation of a national policy to provide health security for all.

The BJP, in its vision document of 2004, had promised to oppose the unjust practices of developed countries under the

WTO agreement in order to defend the interests of Indian farmers. It envisaged a two-pronged approach, that is, policies to achieve faster economic growth combined with effective welfare measure for the poor. It promised to completely eradicate poverty and unemployment with the help of direct governmental investment. The party promised the supply of food grains to the marginal under an 'improved and expanded Antyodaya Anna Yojana'.[28] The rural–urban divide was to be bridged and employment was to be created also by encouraging the private investment in backward and rural areas. The party promised to introduce the Antyodaya scheme to provide social security to families below the poverty line. The manifesto, revolving around the issues of development, good governance,[29] and peace, assured the pursuance of the policies that were to ensure faster growth with employment, equity, social and economic justice along with distributive justice. It promised to continue with the higher governmental allocation to the self-employment generating schemes like Sampoorn Grameen Rozgar Yojana.

In its 2009 manifesto, the BJP opposed foreign investment in retail, and asked for revision of the minimum wage and expansion of safety net to cover the unorganised sector. Strengthening national rural banks and introduction of pension schemes for the farmers were also on the agenda. The party sought to regulate private health care by setting up a national regulatory authority for the purpose. It also called for massive public investments in infrastructure to arrest loss of jobs due to the ongoing global recession. It pledged to protect the interests of the small investors by ensuring high standards of corporate governance.

---

[28] What can be called the competitive politics of rice/wheat, the BJP as well as the Congress, in order to gain electoral mileage, promised in their 2009 manifestos to make available rice/wheat at subsidised price to families living below the poverty line. Whereas the Congress promised 25 kg of rice/wheat at ₹ 3 a kg every month, the BJP went a step further, promising 35 kg of rice/wheat every month at ₹ 2.

[29] In its 1999 manifesto, released under the banner of the NDA, the BJP promised 'changing the content and culture of governance of this great nation, freeing it of the triple curses of hunger (bhookh), fear (bhay), and corruption (bhrashtachar), and transforming it into a new India that is prosperous, strong, self-confident, and at peace within itself and the world'. For the purpose, the party promised to provide 'a stable, honest, transparent, and efficient government capable of accomplishing all round development'.

The only real dissent to neoliberal policies in the electoral arena, at least on paper, however, has come from the mainstream communist parties.[30] The CPI and CPI(M), in their similar 2004 and 2009 manifestos, did agree upon the disinvestment in loss-making public sector units and also agreed upon 'rational' labour reforms[31] as well as private investments in the manufacturing and service sectors but at the same time provided a strident critique of the way 'nakedly pro-rich policies' were being pursued. The two parties called for the enactment of laws to make the right to work a fundamental right. They further asked for greater investment in public works to generate employment with specified private-sector help. The implementation of comprehensive land reforms leading to the distribution of surplus land to the landless, massive increase in public investment in agriculture and irrigation, enactment of a new land acquisition act, introduction of a universal public distribution system, refusal to admit foreign direct investment and big business in retail sector, introduction of labour laws in SEZs have been the other items in the manifestos.[32]

---

[30] The regional/state level parties, even when they form state government or participate in the coalition governments at the centre, rarely question the neoliberal economic policies of the central government, even when the states where they have electoral presence have suffered due to the economic transition. Why it has been so? There can be two possible explanations. One can be that these parties led by the 'Janus-faced' regional elites prefer constant bargaining and lobbying for financial grants/deals/lucrative portfolios for their states, in exchange for political support to the coalition government at the centre in terms of its economic agenda (A. Sinha, *The Regional Roots of Development Politics in India: A Divided Leviathan*, Bloomington: Indiana University Press, 2005; V. Sridhar, 'The Neo-liberal Consensus', *Frontline*, 23 April 2004). Another reason can be that with the dismantling of the license regime, regional states have now started competing against each other to attract the flow of foreign as well as indigenous private investment. This, Partha Chatterjee argues, has resulted in 'the involvement of state level political parties and leaders with the interests of national and international corporate capital in unprecedented way' (Partha Chatterjee, 'Democracy and Economic Transformation in India', *Economic and Political Weekly*, 43 [16], 19 April 2008, p. 57).

[31] 41 per cent of the respondents in NES 2009 disagreed with the view that the government should curb the right of the workers and employees to strike.

[32] For the complete text of the CPI (M) and CPI manifestos, respectively, visit www.cpim.org/, accessed 20 August 2010 and www.cpindia.org/, accessed 20 August 2010.

Notwithstanding the opposition, so widespread has been the penetration of the neoliberal theories and agenda into political discourse and popular beliefs that it is difficult even for the left to conceive of alternatives.[33] Moreover, Bengal's recent experience shows the duplicity in the left position as the left governments (slightly more ambiguous in the case of Kerala) have been toeing the pro-reform agenda irrespective of the doctrinaire position their unelected 'national leaders' take sitting in Delhi.[34]

Were these parties engaged in political duplicity by which they were trying to trick the electorates? What persuaded them to believe that they would be able to 'convince'[35] the electorate about the 'human face' of neoliberal economic reforms? Or were they addressing two very different kinds of audience, hoping that each kind would read only those parts which pleased it and simply ignore the other parts?

Now let us consider the third fact. This has to do with the manner in which these political parties tackled the issue of identity politics. The manifestos showed that all parties tried to address issues of the economically poor; they sought to play down divisive issues of caste and religion while holding out assurances and promises to the minorities and marginal groups.

---

[33] 'The left has always worked for the creation of a political alternative that can effect a progressive shift in the policy trajectory of the country. Such an alternative cannot, obviously, be a cut-and-paste arrangement on the eve of elections. This can only emerge through sustained popular struggles' (S. Yechuri, 'A Wish List for the Congress', edit page, Hindustan Times, 21 May 2009, p. 10).

[34] P. Bardhan, 'Nature of Opposition to Economic Reforms in India', *Economic and Political Weekly*, XL (26), 2005, p. 4995; Partha Chatterjee, 'Democracy and Economic Transformation in India', p. 57. Even when the two mainstream communist parties were part of the United Front government that came in the aftermath of the Congress minority government, credited with initiating the reforms (the CPI in the legislative coalition, the CPI (M) in the executive/ cabinet coalition), the 'Common Approach and Minimum Programme' document committed itself to economic reforms albeit with some residual items from the era of development planning. A pro-reform P. Chidambaram presided over the Finance Ministry (M. P. Singh, 'India's National Front and United Front Coalition Governments: A Phase in Federalized Governance', *Asian Survey*, 41 (2), 2001, pp. 328–50.

[35] Given the limited role of the manifestos in 'convincing' the largely illiterate/semi-literate masses about mundane policy matters, the parties, of course, do resort to 'other means'.

The Congress manifesto of 2004 began with a pledge to 'defeat the forces of obscurantism and bigotry' whereas its 2009 manifesto pledged to 'combat communalism of all kinds' in order to check the subversion of 'our millennial heritage and composite nationhood'. It promised a reasonable share of jobs in the private sector for the SCs and STs. As per the Sachar Committee's recommendation, the party's 2009 manifesto promised reservation in the government jobs for the socially and educationally backward sections among the Muslims and other religious minorities.[36] The party also pledged to establish a *wakf* development corporation for the minority Muslim community and a commission for minority educational institutions.[37] Reservations for the other backward classes in the central educational institutions, along with land redistribution and new strategies for sustainable livelihood, were also promised in the party's two manifestos. In order to regain its traditional minority support base and also to garner support among the liberal/secular electorates, the Congress has thus been making efforts to 'developmentalise' the minority question.[38]

The BJP's position has been more telling. Whereas the 'core *Hindutva* issues' like ban on conversion, cow slaughter, construction of the Ayodhya temple,[39] abolition of Article 370, and

---

[36] Significantly, as per the NES 2009 data, only 15 per cent of the respondents had heard about the Sachar Committee report whereas 85 per cent had no idea about it.

[37] The 1998 Congress manifesto had promised to launch a special drive for the recruitment of minorities to the police force, paramilitary, and armed forces. The party also had pledged to keep a special watch on communally sensitive districts and places. The BJP manifesto promised the following to the minority communities: equal opportunities for their prosperity; inducement for acquiring education which is a must for progress; all possible encouragement to artisans pursuing traditional vocations; training courses for self-employment; education for women of minority communities; restriction on employment advertisements wherein the applicant has to declare his/her religion.

[38] B. Mohapatra, 'Minorities and Politics', in N. G. Jayal and P. B. Mehta (eds), *The Oxford Companion to Politics in India*, New Delhi: Oxford University Press, 2010, pp. 219–37.

[39] In a bid to occupy a centrist space in the electoral politics and also to make it more attractive to the potential allies, the vision document reflected a shift in terms of manner of articulation on the 'core *Hindutva* issues'. Unlike its 1996 and 1998 manifestos, when the BJP had demanded the abrogation

implementation of the uniform civil code had figured prominently in the party's 1996 and 1998 election manifestos,[40] in the 2004 and 2009 manifestos they were considerably softened as the two manifestos attempted a gradual blending of the issues of identity and development. The NDA manifesto of 2004, for instance, included the Ram Temple issue but declared its commitment to finding 'an early and amicable resolution' through 'intensified dialogue' for a 'negotiated settlement' or a court verdict that 'should be acceptable to all'. The 2009 party manifesto reiterated the promise to 'explore all possibilities, including negotiations and judicial proceedings, to facilitate the construction of the Ram Temple at Ayodhya'. The party acknowledged the underprivileged status of the Muslims and pledged to provide for educational development, economic uplift, and empowerment of the minorities. Instead of demanding the abolition of the new Ministry of Minorities Affairs, established by the UPA government in 2006, the party promised to revitalise it. The manifesto also made special mention of Urdu promotion and instead of wanting to ban religious conversion, it wanted to set up a consultation on this subject.

---

of Article 370 from the constitution, the 2004 document recognised the 'transient and temporary' provisions or J&K, only stressing upon the need to eliminate terrorism and accelerate development in the state. On the Ayodhya issue in 1996, the party had promised to remove all hurdles to the road to build the temple. In 1998 it agreed to explore all consensual, legal, and constitutional means to build the temple. The 2004 document underlined the need to have dialogue and mutual trust and also to accept the judicial verdict, a position reiterated in its 2009 manifesto. On uniform civil code the party, in 1996, had pledged to put an end to polygamy to give rights to women. In 1998 it promised to ask the law commission to formulate the code. In 2004 the party presented the case for gender equality and constitutional propriety stating that 'all laws including the personal laws must be in accordance with the guarantees available to all citizens under the Indian constitution'. It added that 'a social and political consensus has to be evolved before the enactment.' For the complete text see http://www.bjp.org.in//, accessed 19 August 2010.

[40] The 1996 BJP election manifesto stated that the party agenda would be based on the four concepts of '*Suraksha, Suchita, Swadeshi* and *Samrasata. Hindutva*, or cultural nationalism, shall be the rainbow which will bridge our present to our glorious past and pave the way for an equally glorious future; it will guide the transition from *Swarajya* to *Surajya*'. The manifesto called for the 'application of these four concepts in good governance' in the '*Bharatbhoomi* that stretches from the Indus to the seas'.

The Election Campaigns

The fourth and the most significant fact is regarding the way in which the election campaigns were actually undertaken at the ground level. Whereas the manifestos had focused primarily on issues and policies related to development and governance and an assessment of the performance of governments[41] and played down issues of identity, the reportage on election campaigns/ political speeches clearly revealed that the opposite had been the case when the electorate was directly approached for votes.[42]

National economic issues were underplayed while local and regional divisions based on caste and religions were deliberately brought to the fore even when the pre-poll polls, including the one conducted by the Lokniti-CSDS in January 2009, showed that unemployment and price rise — the lack of purchasing power or insufficient income rather than what parties reduce to inflation — were the overriding concern of the electorates cutting across classes.[43] Whereas the manifestos did refer to the real issues on the ground and also offered solutions to it, the 2004 and 2009 elections campaign stories showed that the political parties did not seem inclined to mobilise people on their basis.[44] The basis for electoral mobilisation has been identity populism. The pattern has varied from state to state, but the trend has been of a marked increase in the political saliency of essentialised identities of caste, religious community, and ethnicity.

In its 2004 campaign, the BJP, in an attempt to recreate the passionate support for *Hindutva* during the *Ram Rath Yatra* led by

---

[41] The 2009 Lok Sabha election campaign witnessed political parties making widespread use of constituency-wise data on economic and social indicators to attack each other and central/state governments. The parties included statistical 'evidences' in their manifestos and press briefings. A number of large media outlets cited this 'data' as part of their efforts to 'educate' the voter. The data, however, was often found to be of doubtful value.

[42] The local cadres of the parties have been using relevant extracts of national manifestos to woo the vote bank of a particular region.

[43] The 'CNN-IBN State of Nation Survey', conducted by Lokniti-CSDS in January 2009 was carried out among more than 16,000 randomly selected respondents across 23 states (for details see Y. Yadav, 'Why Manifestos Matter').

[44] For campaign details see http://blogs.thehindu.com/elections2009/, accessed 19 August 2010.

Lal Krishna Advani in 1990, banked upon his *Bharat Uday Yatra.*
Admitting 'an intrinsic link' between the two, Advani's speeches
predictably went much beyond the concerns for mundane issues
of 'good governance, security and stability', focusing rather on
the essence of *Hindutva/Bharatiyata* and the significance of the
temple issue. Narendra Modi, the *Hindutva* mascot, was among
the leaders who not only campaigned, evoking the idiom of
cultural nationalism (Gujarati *ashmita*), but also incited the
masses by accusing the Congressmen of being 'Dawood's agents'.
The foreign origin of Sonia Gandhi was also played up. The BJP
campaign received an impetus with the help of fiery speeches
made by the leaders belonging to the Sangh Parivar organisations
like the Vishwa Hindu Parishad, whose leader Praveen Togadia
not only raised the temple issue but also spoke vehemently
against the appeasement of Muslims even by the BJP.[45] Even Atal
Behari Vajpayee, the moderate face of the party, started the party
campaign from Ayodhya, promising that 'give me five more
years and the temple will be constructed'.[46] At the same time, in
order to blunt the Muslim hostility in the Hindi heartland, the
BJP leaders also played, to use media lingo, the Muslim card.
Vajpayee welcomed the Muslims 'to come to us', assuring them
that the party did not look at them suspiciously. He flagged off
Muslim *'himayat' yatra*s, apologised for the Gujarat carnage, and
touted his peace initiative with Pakistan. A beleaguered Murli
Manohar Joshi, a prominent Ayodhya face, made frantic appeals
to the Muslim voters in his constituency by distributing pam-
phlets listing the minority-specific welfare schemes initiated by
him as Union Human Resources Development Minister.[47]

The 2009 elections saw the political arena of contestation
shifting to the state level, as even the national parties adopted
state-specific electoral campaigns that invariably catered to
identity politics.[48]

The BJP national leadership during their countrywide campaign
repeatedly referred to issues having communal underpinnings
mentioned in the party's manifesto, that is, Ram Mandir, Ram

[45] *Deccan Herald*, 18 March 2004.

[46] A. A. Engineer, 'Communal Darkness in Shining India', *Economic and Political Weekly*, 39 (9), 2004, p. 886.

[47] *Indian Express*, 'Can't Convince, So Joshi Confuses Muslim Voters', 25
April 2004.

[48] Ashutosh Kumar, 'Rethinking State Politics in India', p. 18.

Setu, cow protection, cleaning the Ganges, influx of foreigners, challenge of terrorism, the need to bring about a more stringent version of the now repealed Prevention of Terrorism Act, among others. The communally sensitive issue like the delay in hanging Afzal Guru, convicted in the Parliament attack case as well as the failure of the government to check terrorist attacks like the one in Mumbai, were used to depict the Congress as being soft on the scourge of terrorism.[49] Ironically, the arrest of Hindu fanatics in the Malegaon bombing case had earlier led the BJP to question the credibility of the personnel of the Maharashtra Anti-Terrorist Squad, including its chief who was one of the senior police officers killed by the terrorists during the Mumbai attack, apparently 'distinguishing between Hindu terrorism (good) and Muslim terrorism (bad)'.[50] BJP hardliners like Narendra Modi remained the star campaigners for the party, even lending support to NDA partners like the Akali Dal. Varun Gandhi's atrocious remarks relating to the Muslims and the BJP's brazen defence coming from the top leaders like Advani and Rajnath Singh was a desperate move to consolidate the Hindu votes in the crucial state of Uttar Pradesh.[51]

Congress national leaders sought to mobilise the voters, reiterating their commitment for affirmative policies for the Dalits, *adivasi*s, minorities, and women. Like its 2004 campaign, Congress leadership, with the help of its regional allies this time, also made a conscious effort to retain the ability of the party to connect with the Dalits and Muslims, to link minority rights and the development problem. The Jan Sampark Abhiyan, undertaken by its president Sonia Gandhi, was the highlight of the Congress campaign in 2004, with the focus of the campaign being not on highlighting the virtues of reforms but on the concerns of '*aam admi*'. The story in 2009 was no different as launching Bharat Nirman Rally, the party projected itself as a symbol of stability, social harmony, and development and not a crusader for reforms.

---

[49] The Congress hit back by raking up the release of the terrorists in Kandahar by the NDA government at a time when L. K. Advani was Home Minister.

[50] M. Desai, 'History made by Millions', edit page, *Indian Express*, 17 May 2009.

[51] Even the Election Commission of India was forced to overstep its limit by advising the BJP not to nominate Varun Gandhi for the elections, an advice which was promptly rejected by BJP.

The campaigns launched at the state level by the different parties saw the BJP raking up the statehood or autonomy issues with the help of its regional allies in Kamma-dominated Telangana in Andhra Pradesh, in the Gorkha- and Rajbanshi-dominated belt in West Bengal for Gorkhaland, and in Jat-dominated Harit Pradesh in the state of Uttar Pradesh. In Maharashtra, the BJP, with its regional ally the Shiv Sena, a *Hindutva* party, raised the issue of national security and terrorism trying to corner the ruling Congress and its coalition partner the Nationalist Congress Party, a national party, after the terrorist attack in Mumbai, raising the Pakistan bogey and also indirectly targeting the local Muslim community. Reference to the challenge of terrorism was raised by BJP leadership in almost all the states, often inciting politics of 'exclusion'. As its ally Shiv Sena demanded reservation for Marathas, the BJP demanded reservation for the Gujjars in Rajasthan.

The Congress, after withdrawing its tainted candidates from Delhi, actually played the 'Sikh card' in Punjab to woo the community, estranged since 'Operation Bluestar' in 1984 and the anti-Sikh violence following the assassination of Indira Gandhi by underlining the fact that its prime ministerial candidate was a Sikh. It figured in the election speeches of Rahul Gandhi and the local leadership. The Congress followed the Akalis by raising the issue of the imposition of *jazia* tax on the Sikhs living in Pakistan by the Taliban forces as well as the ban on use of the turban by the Sikhs in France. Looking for minority votes in Uttar Pradesh, both the Congress and the Bahujan Samaj Party (BSP) campaigned against the Samajwadi Party (SP) for taking support from Kalyan Singh, who was Chief Minister in the BJP government when the Babri Masjid was pulled down in December 1992. The SP had befriended Singh, the former BJP leader, with the aim to get a sizeable chunk of the votes of the Lodh community. The Congress, eyeing the minority vote, attacked both the Biju Janata Dal and the BJP, which had formed a coalition government in Orissa, for their failure to safeguard Christians from the attack unleashed by the *Hindutva* forces in Kandhamal district.

Regional-/state-level parties followed suit by resorting brazenly to the ethnic agenda. The Shiromani Akali Dal (Badal), an ethnic party of Punjab and a long term ally of the BJP, raised the issue of the grant of tickets to/by the Congress candidates who were accused in the anti-Sikh riots in Delhi as well as the reprieve by the CBI to one of the accused in order to mobilise the Sikh voters. The Shiromani Akali Dal (Mann) and Dal Khalsa raised the issue of demographic change in Punjab due to the presence of migrant labourers. Maharashtra Navnirman Sena, led by Raj Thakeray, also raised the issue of north Indians settling down in Maharashtra, an emotive issue that was used against the Congress and its UPA ally, the Rashtriya Janata Dal, during campaign by the ruling Janata Dal in Bihar. The Nationalist Congress Party campaigned for raising the demand for according 'other backward class' status to the dominant Maratha community, especially in the Marathwada and Western Maharashtra regions, with the aim to consolidate the fragmented Maratha vote. Mayawati, the BSP supreme leader, campaigning on the plank of becoming the first Dalit Prime Minister of India, promised job reservation to the poor among the upper castes in case of forming government at the centre. BSP also mobilised the electorate by promising reservation for lower castes in the private sectors. In Tamil Nadu, the Dravidian parties, namely the DMK, AIADMK, MDMK, and PMK all tried to mobilise the electorate by referring to the plight of Tamil people trapped in the civil war in neighbouring Sri Lanka.

We are left here with a *second* puzzle that needs to be solved. How do we make sense of the absence of new economic policies as the core issue in the electoral politics considering the fact that they were introduced more than one and half decade ago? Why do those parties, which appear as votaries of neoliberal reforms in their election manifestos, shy away from taking them up as their core electoral agenda? More specifically, why have these pro-reform parties not shown the courage and the competence to mobilise the electorate in favour of reforms by projecting them as beneficial not only to the middle and upper classes but also for the masses?

On the other hand, how do we explain the failure of the mainstream communist parties in putting up stiff resistance against 'anti-poor' economic policies that go in the name of 'reforms'? How do we explain the fact that the reform process has been further strengthened with every change of the political regime at the centre? And finally, why do the under classes vote so enthusiastically when their opinions do not count in terms of the policymaking? What does all this tell us about the 'widening and deepening' of electoral democracy in recent India?

Solving the Puzzles

It is not that political analysts engaged with the study of Indian democracy, one of the largest and in many aspects exceptional in the world, have not grappled with this set of puzzle to look for plausible explanations.[52]

One set of explanations refers to the assertion of identity politics, which has formed the immediate backdrop to the last two decades of neoliberal reforms in post-Mandal and -Mandir India. The trajectory of politics has become multiple and severely constrained as it has undergone a process of reconfiguration. The subsequent emergence of multi-party competition in the 'post-Congress' polity has encouraged the parties — both polity-wide and non-polity-wide ones — to use a language during campaign that not only sharpens but also sometimes creates social cleavages. Mass politics is employed to shape and promote the parties' own distinct social support base. Reform politics remains trapped in the language of manifestos.

Taking a longer view of electoral politics in independent India, Kohli argues that the Congress had created its electoral majority by successfully aggregating the economic interests of both classes and masses. There was a definitive class basis in terms of its electoral mobilisation. After the decline of the Congress and the one party-dominant system, the rightist parties have made a conscious effort, in recent decades, to 'cut the majority–minority pie at a different angle'. Kohli dubs it as 'an alternative strategy for seeking electoral majorities by downplaying class issues at the expense of communal ones'.[53] Their pursuit of power has been based on the idea that if the poor formed the majority by the criterion of wealth, Hindus were the majority by the criterion of religion. Considerable success achieved by this strategy has forced almost all parties, with the exception of the left, to resort to casteist and religious sentiments. In a more recent paper,

---

[52] Ashutosh Kumar, 'Disconnect between Economic Reforms and Electoral Democracy in India', *Journal of Asian and African Studies*, 44 (6), 2009b, pp. 719–39.

[53] Atul Kohli, 'Politics of Economic Liberalization in India', *World Development*, 17 (3), 1989, pp. 305–307.

Kohli has attributed the mobilisation of the common people on the basis of 'ethnic nationalism — instead of the less volatile interest-oriented appeals' — at the time of elections by 'a narrow ruling alliance at the helm' as a 'substitute for pro-poor politics'. 'Is India increasingly stuck with a two-track democracy,' Kohli asks, 'in which common people are only needed at the time of elections, and then it is best that they all go home, forget politics, and let the "rational" elite quietly run a pro-business show?'[54]

Confined to debates in the English language press and the elite circles, J. D. Sachs argues, the reforms have continued unabated without attracting much contestation or even visibility, much to the relief of the political parties and class.[55]

Varshney explains the puzzle by making a distinction between elite politics and mass politics. He suggests that elite politics comprises primarily the English-speaking upper-caste and urban citizens, English-language newspapers, television, and the Internet. Away from the heat and dust of mass politics, it takes the form of consultations between business and government, and between the Indian government and the global financial institutions. Mass politics, on the other hand, takes place primarily on the streets. Touched off by issues that unleash citizens' passions and emotions, the characteristic forms of mass politics include 'large-scale agitations, demonstrations, and civil disobedience'.[56]

Varshney's argument is that political issues like Hindu–Muslim relations, ethnic disputes, and caste animosities have come to dominate the electoral agenda aimed at ensuring large-scale mobilisation due to the manoeuvring of the parties. The economic reform measures that hardly arouse much passion continue to be implemented quietly so that they do not become mass-level political issues. Since coalitions are increasingly being

---

[54] Atul Kohli, 'Politics of Economic Growth in India, 1980–2005; Part 1: The 1980s and Part 11: The 1990s and Beyond', *Economic and Political Weekly* 41 (13 and 14), 2006, pp. 1252, 1368–1369.

[55] J. D. Sachs, A. Varshney, and N. Bajpayee (eds), *India in the Era of Economic Reforms*, New Delhi: Oxford University Press, 2000, p. 15.

[56] A. Varshney, 'Mass Politics or Elite Politics: India's Economic Reforms in Comparative Perspective', in J. D. Sachs, A. Varshney, and N. Bajpai (eds), India in the Era of Economic Reforms, New Delhi: Oxford University Press, 2000; 'India's Democratic Challenge', *Foreign Affairs*, 86 (2), 2007, p. 100.

formed against Hindu nationalists on the plank of secularism and no longer against the Congress, the anti-reform parties — both the left and the lower-caste social justice parties — have remained largely ineffective in their opposition to reforms.

Suhas Palshikar has argued that the 'expansion' of democracy in contemporary India has made it imperative for the parties to absorb the newly politicised energy of the hitherto dormant sections of the society by functioning as gatekeepers for the system to 'keep politics out' of policy process.

Pratap Bhanu Mehta has commented on the absence of 'serious, open and protracted deliberations' about policy issues during the elections campaigns which are 'both too brief and enormous in scope'. He attributes it to the 'under-institutionalised' party system suffering from 'ideological decadence'. The failure on the part of the pro-reform parties to show that there is a 'direct link between the process of economic liberalisation and distributional gains for the newly influential groups in politics like the backward castes' result into the failure to form a supportive 'new distributional coalition'.[57] As a result, the parties make efforts to consolidate their constituencies either by short-term populist handouts in their manifestos aimed at direct measures for the amelioration of poverty or desperately look for some symbolic issues that veer around politics of identity based on caste or some other ethnic affiliation.

As the 'office-seeking' parties, with the exception of the left, get closely aligned with the interests of 'business, capital and the middle classes' and therefore become committed to neoliberal economic policies even as they realise that they lead to a 'widening gap between these classes and the bulk of people', the emphasis shifts from 'distributive justice' to 'high growth' as the state goal.[58] Zoya Hasan attributes the resultant irrelevance of the ideological positioning as the factor that makes it imperative for the 'pragmatic' parties to use social cleavages for the electoral mobilisation.

---

[57] Pratap Bhanu Mehta, *The Burden of Democracy*, New Delhi: Penguin Books India, 2003, p. 171.

[58] Z. Hasan, 'Political Parties', in N. G. Jayal and P. B. Mehta (eds), *The Oxford Companion to Politics in India*, New Delhi: Oxford University Press, 2010, pp. 247–48.

Patrick Heller has argued that the political forces that have emerged in the recent decades in India are more rooted than ever in social cleavages. He attributes it to two broad developments that indicate developmental failures unleashing social conflict. The first one is the decline of the electoral dominance of Congress which was sustained on the basis of its ability to keep 'vast and vertically organised patronage networks that held together a wide range of interests and groups'. The second and deeper structural cause has been the 'social and redistributive failures of Indian state'. As a result, an 'embedded particularism' has emerged that nourishes 'rent-seeking interests at the expense of state's capacity to provide public goods and institutional reform'.[59]

Another kind of explanation is to be found in the working of the institutions in India. Rob Jenkins argues that notwithstanding the success of the formal democracy in India, the reform process has been implemented in the post-1991 period in a fairly informal manner. He attributes the strengthening of the process of economic reforms after every election to the undemocratic manner in which the democratic institutions are being worked by the political class in India. The parties, he suggests, show the courage to undertake reform measures due to the existing 'fuzziness of boundaries separating party and non-party political networks'. Reforms are implemented through underhand and often non-transparent tactics by 'arranging suitable conflict avoiding (or conflict deferring) compromises among contending interests; exploiting the faith of privileged interests in the sanctity of their privileges by assuaging the opponents of liberalisation with promises that may never be fulfilled; and harnessing the political potency of nascent groups which might emerge as the key supporters in the future if offered tacit support'.[60] The political class whose 'networks of influence span party and non-party activities and are easily detachable from any political party' introduce the changes under the guise of continuity, as it remains confident of being the beneficiary of reforms by negotiating policies and accommodating interests.

---

[59] Patrick Heller, 'Degrees of Democracy: Some Comparative Lessons from India', *World Politics*, 52, July 2000, pp. 493–494.

[60] R. Jenkins, *Democratic Politics and Economic Reforms in India*, Cambridge: Cambridge University Press, 1999, p. 152.

As to why the political class prefers to opt for 'a process of slow but steady creeping reforms' avoiding political confrontation, Pranab Bardhan has his own take. He attributes it to the two different but associated drifts of political power taking place in India towards the regions and the backward and lower castes. As the enthusiasm for the reforms among the richer regions and the upper classes/castes do not 'trickle down' to the marginal ones, naturally 'even the most avid reformist politicians find it necessary to tone down their reform rhetoric at election time, when they have to face the unwashed masses'.[61]

Commenting on the choice of 'gradualism' in implementing policy reforms, Montek Singh Ahluwalia has attributed it to the pluralistic character of Indian politics where parties have to build a 'sufficient consensus' before and after every election. Electoral endorsement, at periodic intervals, can be possible only if the reforms seem to have benefited a sufficiently large percentage of the masses, a reason enough to make parties hesitant in drumming up their support.[62]

Let us build on the above sets of arguments to make further sense of what may appear as a conspiracy of silence during the electoral campaigns undertaken by parties.[63]

We can infer from the CSDS-NES data that there is a great degree of 'awareness about' and 'agreement' with the economic policy reforms among the rich and middle classes.[64] Now, this 'agreement' part needs to be explained briefly.

---

[61] P. Bardhan, 'The Political Economy of Reform in India', in Z. Hasan (ed.), *Politics and the State in India*, New Delhi: Sage Publications, 2000, p.168.

[62] M. S. Ahluwalia, 'Understanding India's Reform Trajectory: Past Trends and Future Challenges', *India Review*, 3 (4), 2004, p. 269.

[63] Interestingly, when asked during the CSDS-NES 2009 survey about 'how interested were you in the election campaign this time', 51 per cent of the respondents interviewed (36,629 in number) said they were 'not at all' interested whereas only 10.5 per cent showed a 'great deal' of interest. 31.6 per cent of the respondents were 'somewhat' interested.

[64] For the CSDS-NES surveys over the years, five indicators have been used to identify the middle-class position, namely, education above high school level; occupation-white collar jobs; housing: living in *pucca* houses, i.e., houses built of brick and lime or cement; ownership of assets: at least three of these — car/jeep/tractor, scooter/bike, house/flat; TV; water pump; and self-identification as members of the middle class.

Ascendancy of the Entrepreneurial Class

The 'new' entrepreneurial class,[65] a dominant segment of the rich class representing organised/corporate capital/big business, saw a great opportunity for itself when in 1991 a beleaguered Congress government facing an external debt crisis had to set in motion the process of free market-oriented reforms in conformity with the prescription of global lending institutions.[66] The 'new' entrepreneurial class has welcomed and benefited from the industrial policy reforms that have created the 'operational freedom' it never had before due to the hegemonic role of the public sector. Inflow of global capital and technology has allowed it finally to look towards market/business abroad and compete successfully as 'import substitution' gave way to export optimism. With a significant attitudinal change being visible in the society regarding the profit motive and creating private wealth, which is no longer looked down upon, the entrepreneur class no longer faces a problem of ideological legitimacy. The change can partly be attributed to the fact that the burgeoning private corporate sector is no longer being overwhelmingly dominated by a relatively small number of large, family-controlled business houses drawn from traditional merchant classes as the 'new' entrepreneurs take the opportunity to break the shackles to come up and in the process are shoring up the social base of the tiny class.[67]

---

[65] Even during the days of the development planning model, 'business interests in India while not publicly represented in competitive party politics, (were) better represented than those of organised labour' (L. I. Rudolph and S. Rudolph, *In Pursuit of Lakshmi: The Political Economy of the Indian State*, Chicago: University of Chicago Press, 1987, p. 25).

[66] Significantly the manifesto of every mainstream political party for the 1991 elections, cutting across the ideological spectrum, had talked about the need for restructuring the economy (A. Bhaduri and D. Nayyar, *The Intelligent Person's Guide to Liberalization*, New Delhi: Penguin Books India, 1996, p. 49).

[67] As late as in the late 1970s, the private corporate sector continued to be 'drawn predominantly from families who belonged to the major traditional trading communities of India ... and who began moving from trade into industry during the second half of the 19th century' (Stanley A. Kochanek, 'Briefcase Politics in India', *Asian Survey*, XXVII [12], 1987, p. 1281).

The 'New' Middle Class

The entrepreneurial class has received critical support in its agenda of pushing reforms from the 'great Indian middle class',[68] which is arguably the largest in the world, numbering somewhere between 100 and 250 million[69] to 200–250 million[70] to 300–350 million,[71] with the exact number depending on the criteria used.[72] Enthused with a sense of achievement and a widening of economic opportunity as the economy shifts towards the service sector, the middle class, especially its non-agriculturist dominant urban segment consisting of 'those with advanced professional credentials or accumulated cultural capital who occupy positions of recognised authority in various fields' has turned into a great votary of the reforms.[73] This 'new' middle class eager to exploit

---

[68] P. Varma, *The Great Indian Middle Class*, New Delhi: Viking, 2000. The article purposely uses the term middle *classes* and not middle class as it argues that it is difficult to speak of the Indian middle class in singular form unlike the rich or the poor classes in India about whom no one refers to as lower upper class or upper lower class. The complexion of the middle class in India keeps changing. It is just not the upper middle class and lower middle class. The heterogeneity within the middle classes brings in a whole range of new subcategories of the middle classes in India, i.e. 'old' and 'new', underlining their markers in terms of education, values, and space. Even B. B. Misra had used the term *middle classes* while writing his classic study.

[69] E. Sridharan, 'The Growth and Sectoral Composition of India's Middle Class: Its Impact on the Politics of Economic Liberalization', *India Review*, 3 (4), 2004, pp. 405–28.

[70] V. Sanghvi, 'Two Indias', *Seminar*, 1 February 2005.

[71] Shashi Tharoor, 'Who is this Middle Class', *The Hindu*, 22 May 2005.

[72] In NES 2009, when asked about the class they belonged to, 38 per cent of the respondents interviewed said that they belonged to the middle class.

[73] L. Fernandes and P. Heller, 'Hegemonic Aspirations: New Middle Class Politics and India's Democracy in Comparative Perspective', *Critical Asian Studies*, 38 (4), 2006, p. 500. However, two segments of the middle class — the public employees and the better-off agricultural classes — are not supposed to be too enthusiastic about the neoliberal reforms if they mean cutting down the subsidies (pay scale, higher interests on public savings, better service conditions, higher education, job security, overstaffing, central and state level subsidisation in the agricultural sector, tax in the agricultural sector, power sector reforms). Such 'categories' of the middle classes would certainly have mixed response to public sector reforms, privatisation, or for macro-economic stabilisation. Backward caste/Dalit middle classes would

the new market opportunities, pushed for a political project advocating a 'distinctive combination of economic liberalism and social illiberalism'.[74] The reformist measures like the reduction in the direct taxes, deregulation, privatisation, and greater access to consumer goods cater to its interest. It is this politically articulate and vociferous class and not the common masses that follow the 'scholarly' debates about the politics of reforms in print as well as the electronic media, surf the Internet,[75] and may be following the manifestos. Playing a significant political and ideological role, it has been instrumental in according greater legitimacy to the ongoing shift in terms of policy paradigm.[76] Even as the middle-class 'new politics' is not so much visible in the arena of formal electoral politics it does get played out in the form of 'every day practices through which it reproduces its privileged position'.[77]

That the 'new' middle class definitely has a wider socio-political and economic policy impact than what its actual size suggests explains why the national parties like the Congress and the BJP clamour to win over this class by putting on record their support

---

also definitely prefer the state continuing with its affirmative policies as they are the ones who are heavily dependent on state-owned public sector and government jobs and are direct beneficiaries of the state subsidies. With the emergence of an urban middle class among the lower castes, largely due to the land reforms and also the affirmative policies of the state relating to reservations in education and employment, consolidation of horizontal identities among them and given their numerical strength, elites from these castes have broken away from the catch-all parties and formed caste-specific parties to stake their claim for power and access to resources.

[74] J. Harriss, 'Class and Politics', in N. G. Jayal and P. B. Mehta (eds), *The Oxford Companion to Politics in India*, New Delhi, Oxford University Press, 2010, p. 150.

[75] The BJP, on the eve of the 2009 elections, created 'India's largest political website' with 800 pages, 400 pictures, and 250 videos mostly highlighting the persona of Advani, the party's prime ministerial candidate (Datta-Ray 2009).

[76] Referring to Gramsci, S. Deshpande argues that the middle class undertakes the task to build hegemony. The elite fraction of the middle class specialises in the production of ideologies whereas its mass fraction 'engages in the exemplary consumption of ideologies thus investing them with social legitimacy' (*Contemporary India: A Sociological View*, New Delhi: Penguin Books India, 2003, p. 141).

[77] L. Fernandes and P. Heller, Hegemonic Aspirations', p. 497.

for market reforms.[78] The 'India Shining' campaign[79] launched by the BJP was one such strategy by confusing the concerns and feelings of the middle class with that of the entire country.[80] The Congress in its manifesto said that 'the middle class of India is the proud creation of Congress' and that the policies of the party will be in 'sync with their aspirations'.[81] Wide-ranging reforms in the education sector, especially in the institutions of higher learning, opening of more centrally funded institutions and universities as well as IITs, IIMs, and NIITs, and allowing foreign universities are the promises that figured in the 2009 manifestos as well as in the campaigns of both the BJP and the Congress. The star campaigners of the two parties also appeared on the web to address the techno-savvy middle classes.

---

[78] The 2009 Lok Sabha election, as per the CSDS survey data, saw a slight increase in the turnout among middle-class voters when compared to the figures in the 1996, 1999, and 2004 surveys (S. Kumar, 'Patterns of Political Participation: Trends and Perspective', *Economic and Political Weekly*, 44 (39), 2009, p. 50). Of late, NES data had shown a steady withdrawal of the middle classes from electoral politics.

[79] The campaign promoted India as the future global superpower of the 21st century, a country of unrestricted opportunities and achievement, with a citizenry proud of populist slogans such as 'made in India' and 'there is no better time to be an Indian' (C. Brosius, *India's Middle Class: New Forms of Urban Leisure, Consumption and Prosperity*, New Delhi: Routledge, 2010, p. 1).

[80] The BJP's rise to political power in the momentous decade of 1990s was 'accompanied by the emergence of a new social group that was defined by an overlap of social and economic privileges' (Y. Yadav, 'Electoral Politics in the Time of Change: India's Third Electoral System, 1989–99', *Economic and Political Weekly*, XXXIV [34–35], 1999, pp. 2393–2399). Both the entrepreneurial as well as professional middle classes at that time 'turned away from the Congress because they saw through the rhetoric of a socialist and bureaucratised state that was incapable of providing the consumer goods and social services for which they yearned with increasing intensity with the passage of time' (R. Kumar, 'Winds of Change across India and the Shaping of a New Polity', *Journal of South Asian Studies*, XXIX [1], April 2006).

[81] Suhas Palshikar ('Tentative Emergence of a New and Tentative Condition?', *Economic and Political Weekly*, XLIV [21], 2009, p. 10) has argued that the Congress made considered attempts in the tumultuous decade of the 1990s to 'redefine the social contract and forge a policy framework that depended only on the middle classes', which implied 'an exclusion of the poor from policy considerations'. The reliance only on the middle classes for its political survival actually led to the decline of the Congress.

The entrepreneurial class has always had a decisive influence over the political parties as, among other factors, the latter have always depended upon them for funding in the absence of any form of public financing.[82] In the absence of a radical change which can evolve alternative mechanisms for funding parties and elections, the existing system of 'exchange nexus' between the corporate elites and the parties is likely to continue. Under the circumstances, the parties enjoying a considerable degree of autonomy in the initiation and design of public policy especially related to the economy has always remained and would remain suspect.[83] During the 1950s and 1960s, the parties received the bulk of their funding from the business community.[84] It is obvious that as the election campaigns are becoming costlier [85] with every passing election, big businesses, joined now by the corporate sector, due to enormous expansion of the economy, are in a position to make serious money available to the political parties. In return, they also end up making serious demands on public policy.[86] Of late, with the 'decentring' of the polity and economy, the state-level parties, often starved of funds but playing a crucial role in policy making in a coalitional arrangement, have been beneficiaries of the corporate funding in return of their support. For instance, the Confederation of Indian Industry (CII), an all-India business association, openly lobbied with the numerous opposition parties, mainly regional, when the Congress minority government led by Narsimha Rao needed support for economic

---

[82] For an analysis of the pattern of fundraising by major political parties see Stanley A. Kochanek ('Briefcase Politics in India', pp. 1278–1301; E. Sridharan, 'Parties, the Party System and Collective Action for State Funding of Elections: A Comparative Perspective on Possible Options', in P. R. de Souza and E. Sridharan (eds), *India's Political Parties*, New Delhi: Sage Publications, 2006, pp. 322–26.

[83] Stanley A. Kochanek, 'Briefcase Politics in India', p. 1294.

[84] V. Venkatesan, 'Party Finance: Chequered Relations', *Frontline*, 16 (16), 31 July–31 August 1999, http://www.hindu.com/fline/fl1616/16160100.htm, accessed 20 August 2010.

[85] The estimated expenditure by the government to conduct the 2009 Lok Sabha elections was ₹ 16,700 crore (D. Dasgupta, 'Spent at the Vote', *Hindustan Times*, 22 April 2009).

[86] H. Khare, 'Monetisation of Political Space', edit page, *The Hindu*, 25 April 2009.

reforms it had initiated, or with the coalitional partners of the pro-reform BJP-led coalition government in 1996.[87]

Now that the entrepreneurial class, backed by global corporate capital, has also the critical mass social base in the form of the middle classes that is not only growing in terms of sheer number but also in terms of its sociological composition, it further adds to its ability to push the political class for the reforms. The pertinent question that emerges then is: Why do the parties still have to resort to what Jenkins calls reforms by stealth?

It is ironically the same electoral compulsion of a democracy that explains the inability of these catch-all parties to share their enthusiasm for the 'reform' process with the ordinary electorate who think that they would be marginalised even further as a consequence. Moreover, the political class cutting across party lines no longer enjoys the confidence of the masses that it enjoyed in the first years of independence so that it could sell the idea of reforms as well as it could in the case of planning and public sector in the Nehruvian phase. The political class had then projected a comprehensive definition of development that encompassed not merely an industrial advancement, 'but also simultaneously a programme of social transformation and political democratisation' built around the then prevailing broad consensus.[88] Planning accorded legitimacy to the political class that claimed to pursue a task that was both universal and rational — the wellbeing of the people as a whole.[89] As a result, even as the rich classes felt (quite correctly) well served by the system, the marginal did not feel completely excluded from the development process. It is obvious that the 'new' political class hardly enjoys any such leverage now to win popular support for the market-driven new economic policy even as it refers to its relative advantage in terms of the growth potential of a relatively

---

[87] A. Sinha, *The Regional Roots of Development Politics in India: A Divided Leviathan*, Bloomington: Indiana University Press, 2005, p. 4.

[88] N. G. Jayal, *Democracy and the State: Welfare, Secularism and Development in Contemporary India*. New Delhi: Oxford University Press.

[89] Partha Chatterjee, 'Development Planning and the Indian State', in Z. Hasan (ed.), *Politics and the State in India*, New Delhi: Sage Publications, 2000, p. 129. The 1957 Congress manifesto had promised a 'national minimum' for everyone: progressive participation of labour in the conduct of industry; agricultural cooperatives and cooperative village management.

open economy and the efficiency it brings, not forgetting the promise of making India a global economic power.[90] That the Indian economy has been one of the fastest growing economies in the world which along with China has attained much success in meeting the challenge of global recession hardly cuts much ice with the poor and the marginal who arguably constitute a large plurality of the electorate and ominously also tend to vote in greater number than the rich and middle classes as per the CSDS data. A much more seductive argument would be that reforms have led to a decline in the poverty level, an argument that might interest some political analysts but not the masses that see the inequalities growing around them.

Gramscian Explanation

So what does the 'political class' of India cutting across the party lines do, backed as it is now only with a much narrower support base and facing the legitimation crisis which is far greater as it attempts to bring about a 'planned' transition from a command economy to a market economy. It is here that a reconstruction of the Gramscian exposition[91] of the idea of 'transformism' as a variant of 'passive revolution' becomes instructive as the political class, acting on behalf of the entrepreneurial class, and quietly opting for a path in which the dominant class interests are nearly met 'by small doses, legally in a reformist manner ... to avoid the popular masses'.[92] Such a 'compromise' is being 'manoeuvred' with the help of middle-class intellectuals/political professionals in the political parties who in the modern context approximate Gramsci's concept of 'philosophers and traditional intellectuals'.[93]

---

[90] D. Nayyar, 'Economic Development and Political Democracy: Interaction of Economics and Politics in Independent India', in N.G. Jayal (ed.), *Democracy in India*, New Delhi: Oxford University Press, 2001, p. 362.

[91] The theoretical arguments in this part draw substantially from Ashutosh Kumar, 'Dissonance between Economic Reforms and Democracy', *Economic and Political Weekly*, 43 (1), 2008, pp. 54–60.

[92] A. Gramsci, *Selections from the Prison Notebooks*, ed. and trans. Q. Hoare and G. Smith, New Delhi: Orient Longman, 2004, p. 119.

[93] In Gramscian mode, Deshpande suggests that while the elite fraction of the middle class specialises in the production of ideologies, its mass fraction 'engages in the exemplary consumption of ideologies thus investing them with social legitimacy' (*Contemporary India*, p. 141).

The political class tends to resort to 'mass politics' to secure political support among large sections of, in Gramscian terms, the 'petty bourgeoisie and even the toiling masses' and also to incorporate the 'potential forces of socialist transition' (read Indian left).[94] This mass politics involves setting the goals and aspirations of the *'new'* developmental agenda in such a manner that even as they appear to be contradictory in the sense that the demands of the poor and marginal (read the anti-poverty programmes in the party manifestos for instance) are also accommodated along with the interests of the both local and global capital but actually, as Gramsci argues in the context of the analogous effort of the bourgeoisie to establish hegemony in a transitional society with a capital/pre-capital dualism, 'they mutually support each other in the sense that they create conditions most favourable to the expansion of the latter'.[95] It was to a large extent the same story in Nehruvian India but with the difference that the political class under the 'Congress system' was then reasonably successful in constructing its moral–cultural hegemony.[96] The 'cunningness' of capital is not working as well as of now. Why is that so?

Reading Gramsci would suggest that the decades of 'democratic structuring of political and economic life and the hope and possibility of a people's democracy'[97] referred above in the context of 'democratic upsurge' in recent India, has made the subalterns critically self-aware. The desertion of the landed rich peasantry, once a beneficiary (and, therefore votary) of capital-intensive growth (read the Green Revolution) but now experiencing the heat under the WTO regime and the onslaught of the global corporate

---

[94] Writing about the phenomenon of *'transformismo'* in the case of Risorgimento in Italy of the late 19th century where the capitalist class 'planned' the survival of capitalism by entering into compromise with the pre-capitalist classes by moving in a reformist way, Gramsci described it as a 'process whereby the so-called "historic" Left and Right parties which emerged from the Risorgimento tended to converge in terms of programme during the years that followed, until there ceased to be any substantive difference between them' (*Selections from the Prison Notebooks*, 58f).

[95] K. K. Sanyal, 'Accumulation, Poverty and State in Third World', *Economic and Political Weekly*, XXIII (5), 1988, PE-28.

[96] S. Kaviraj, 'A Critique of the Passive Revolution', *Economic and Political Weekly*, XXIII (45–47), 1989, pp. 2429–2444.

[97] D. Saldanha, 'Antonio Gramsci and the Analysis of Class Consciousness', *Economic and Political Weekly*, XXIII (5), 1988, PE-12.

sector, from the reformist agenda is a major blow. It was this numerically strong class of capitalist or semi-capitalist landed peasantry whose social power, in terms of the land ownership as well as the dominant caste status in village India, enabled the political class to gain 'representative' forms of electoral support for the economic agenda. The breakdown of the 'nationalist historical bloc' in terms of the shift in the strategic relations between the two dominant classes has resulted in a weakened entrepreneurial class that is now left only with the support of the middle classes and the global allies. So unlike the heydays of the statist developmental model when a 'general consensus' was largely achieved under the 'democratic-bureaucratic system', the entrepreneurial class now finds it increasingly difficult to continue to combine 'accumulation with legitimation while avoiding the unnecessary rigours of social conflict'.[98] If earlier for the entrepreneurial class-rich peasantry combine it meant looking for the technological path to capitalist transition in the form of heavy industrialisation and Green Revolution while avoiding the political path to land reforms and agrarian mobilisation, it now means using the manoeuvring/balancing skill of the political class increasingly with middle-class roots to try to create a hiatus between the 'political' and 'economic' so as to create a 'two-track democracy'.[99] Thus arises the critical need to go for 'reformist and molecular' changes while attempting transition to the market economy — a '*transformismo*' that does not emanate as a result of a process from within society, but is sought to be achieved from above through stealth, a 'passive revolution' of capital that is 'without mass participation (and due in large part to outside forces)'.[100]

---

[98] Partha Chatterjee, 'Development Planning and the Indian State', in idem (ed.), *State and Politics in India*, New Delhi: Oxford University Press, 1998, pp. 271–97.

[99] In Gramsci's words:

> In certain given conditions certain parties ... exercise a balancing and arbitrating function between the interests of their group and those of other groups, and succeed in securing the development of the group which they represent with the consent and assistance of the allied groups' (*Selections from the Prison Notebooks*, p. 148).

[100] A. Gramsci, *Selections from the Prison Notebooks*, p. 46.

Summing Up

We may summarise our discussion by pointing out that political parties in India are trying to address two very distinct kinds of audiences separately: the English-speaking urban middle classes consisting of a 'fully informed citizenry' on the one hand, and the poor and the marginal on the other. The 'unstoppable' rise of popular engagement in electoral politics has made it impossible for the political class to ignore the latter, howsoever influential the entrepreneurial class and its allies — the rising middle classes and global capital — may be. It is because of the apprehension about the common voters' disapproval, as reflected in the survey data, that despite having a broad agreement the two polity-wide parties are extremely reluctant in making neoliberal policies of governance central to their electoral campaigns.

The result has been a relative lack of dialogue/debate/ contestation in the public arena over a substantive issue that affects vitally a vast chunk of India's electorate, if not all of it, which remains under the classes. The challenge, therefore, is to mediate the conflicts that arise due to growing incompatibility between the 'plebeianisation' of democracy that arouses egalitarian demands and the ongoing neoliberal governance agenda that condones widening inequality. Therein lies the burden of India's electoral democracy.

5

Who will be able to Access the Provisions of Liberty?: Ability, Disability, and the Interrogation of Norms*

Kalpana Kannabiran

Introduction

'[W]e are millions and millions and we are the real owners of India. It has recently become the fashion to talk of 'Quit India'. I do hope that this is only a stage for the real rehabilitation and resettlement of the original people of India. Let the British quit. Then after that, all the later-comers quit. Then there would be left behind the original people of India.'

Jaipal Singh, Representative of the Aboriginal Tribes of Nagpur, 11 December 1946. Constituent Assembly Debates, 1989, 46–47.

The Indian constitution gives voice to counter-hegemonic imaginations of justice, rooted in resistance and argumentative traditions that blossomed in the region at different points in history. Central to an understanding of the constitution, therefore, is the fact of its historical location and specificity — the inauguration of modernity — a new social order, the signposts of which are embedded in the idea of constitutional morality and distinct both from the colonial order, and also from the social order on the subcontinent during and prior to colonialism. The constitution, far from being cradled in a harmonious, uncontested space, is confronted incessantly with the crisis of multiple identities; of demarcating and separating citizens — never clearly defined but made up of the disabled, the untouchables, the transgenders, the tribals — notified and de-notified, primitive and assimilated, forest and nomadic — the minorities, for instance.

---

* This article is part of a longer work on non-discrimination and liberty. I am grateful to Ranabir Samaddar for his incisive comments and his patience.

Evident in the cursory listing of the citizens (in these official terms in which they are listed), is the hierarchy of citizenship, and the politics of disentitlement and exclusion, which is contested relentlessly by radical activists waging dramatic struggles and in the process creating new mediums of 'constitutional communication' (to borrow Ranabir Samaddar's phrase)[1] and new constitutional conversations. Therein blooms another history of constitutionalism as well. For historically oppressed classes, constitutionalism continues to hold the promise of change.

This article is an attempt to retrace the juridical meanings of discrimination and their interlocking with the right to personal liberty using the constituting power of the constitution to posit the possibilities for a dynamic interpretation of non-discrimination in the law. The Indian constitution prohibits practices of discrimination, untouchability, and forced labour through the horizontal and vertical application of rights. And yet, there is extensive documentation in official documents put out by an insurgent bureaucracy, judiciary, and citizen collectives, sometimes acting in concert, of the ways in which derogations continue to set the standard.

It is important at the outset to note the definition of discrimination adopted by the Indian constitution. The first two clauses in Article 15, which speak about discrimination, read:

> 15.(1) The State shall not discriminate against any citizen on grounds only of religion, race, caste, sex, place of birth or any of them.
> (2) No citizen shall, on grounds only of religion, race, caste, sex, place of birth or any of them, be subject to any disability, liability, restriction or condition with regard to —
> (a) access to shops, public restaurants, hotels and places of public entertainment; or
> (b) the use of wells, tanks, bathing ghats, roads and places of public resort maintained wholly or partly out of State funds or dedicated to the use of the general public.

The first clause speaks to the vertical application of the right to non-discrimination, between the state and the citizen; the second clause speaks to the horizontal application of the right, between

---

[1] Ranabir Samaddar, 'Colonial Constitutionalism', *Bayan: Constitutional Evolution*, II, July 2004, pp. 13–28.

citizens inter se. Picking up the thread of Article 15(2) is Article 17, which bans the practice of untouchability in any form — a provision that is aimed at disciplining both the state and citizen. The key to the meaning of the phrase 'shall not discriminate' in 15(1), is contained in 15(2) — subjecting a person to any disability, liability, restriction, or condition (implicitly detrimental) on the grounds of religion, race, caste, sex, or place of birth would amount to discrimination. The idea of liberty is invoked in investing 'discrimination' with meaning — the substance of 15(2) is that no citizen's freedom may be curtailed on the specified grounds. Moving further down to 15(3), 15(4), and 15(5),[2] because discrimination is a curtailing conduct that operates indirectly as well as directly, the remedy also necessitates the creation of special provisions to combat discrimination.[3] In this framework, the use of 'protective discrimination' and 'compensatory discrimination' in jurisprudence and constitutional analysis to describe these provisions needs to be problematised as contradictions in terms that create the discursive possibility for equivocation on

---

[2] 15(3) Nothing in this article shall prevent the State from making any special provision for women and children.

(4) Nothing in this article or in clause (2) of article 29 shall prevent the State from making any special provision for the advancement of any socially and educationally backward classes of citizens or for the Scheduled Castes and the Scheduled Tribes.]

(5) Nothing in this article or in sub-clause (g) of clause (1) of article 19 shall prevent the State from making any special provision, by law, for the advancement of any socially and educationally backward classes of citizens or for the Scheduled Castes or the Scheduled Tribes in so far as such special provisions relate to their admission to educational institutions including private educational institutions, whether aided or unaided by the State, other than the minority educational institutions referred to in clause (1) of article 30).

[3] These two parts of the non-discrimination protection have also been seen by the court as subject to distinct interpretive strategies, where the strict scrutiny test would apply to derogations that infringe on liberty — 15(1) and (2), but not affirmative action laws. Naz Foundation vis. NCT to Delhi. For a more detailed analysis of strict scrutiny see Tarunabh Khaitan, 'Beyond Reasonableness: A Rigorous Standard of Review for Article 15 Infringement', *Journal of the Indian Law Institute*, 50 (2), 2008, pp. 177–208; and for an analysis of Article 15 in the context of the Naz Foundation Judgment see Tarunabh Khaitan, 'Reading Swaraj into Article 15: A New Deal for All Minorities', *NUJS Law Review*, 2 (3), July–September 2009, pp. 419–31.

the important question of reservation. More recent legislation, notably the proposed amendment to the Persons with Disabilities Act, adopts the definition of discrimination from the United Nations Convention on the Protection of Rights of Persons with Disabilities (UNCRPD), which, like the Convention on the Elimination of all forms of Discrimination against Women (CEDAW), provides a broad-based inclusive definition:

> ... any *distinction, exclusion* or *restriction* made on the basis ... which has the effect or purpose of impairing or nullifying the recognition, enjoyment or exercise by ... on a basis of equality ... of human rights and fundamental freedoms in the political, economic, social, cultural, civil or any other field.

A quick comparison will demonstrate that the combined reading of 15(1) and 15(2) of the constitution of India above produces the same result. Further, even while specifying the grounds on which discrimination is prohibited, Article 15 sets out the categories within those grounds that are disadvantaged — women (and now sexual minorities), Scheduled Castes, Scheduled Tribes, and socially and economically backward classes; elsewhere in the constitution, minorities. There is therefore little possibility in the way the non-discrimination protections are constructed in India, for a liberal flattening out of the protection to 'all have the same right not be discriminated against'. The definitional framework within the constitution to deal with discrimination is fairly unambiguous.

There are also grounds specified in the non-discrimination protection, which till very recently in India were strictly applied by courts to determine whether or not a case of discrimination is maintainable. There was a further rider that discrimination would only be held to have occurred if it is established on one of the specified grounds, that is either on grounds of race or religion or sex or caste or place of birth. While the argument that it is necessary to define discrimination in a manner that 'focuses on impact (i.e., discriminatory effect) rather than on constituent elements (i.e., the grounds of the distinction) is well taken',[4] grounds, far from being purely a legal construct, serve to

---

[4] Justice L'Heureux-Dube in Egan v. Canada, (1995) 2 S.C.R. 513 at 545, in Dianne Pothier, 'Connecting Grounds of Discrimination to Real People's

'separate people who experience discrimination from those who do not' and 'reflect a political and social reality to which the law has, belatedly, given recognition'.[5]

However, the centrality of the grounds to the legal definition of discrimination and the exclusive application of the grounds in Indian constitutional jurisprudence, where claims fail if they are found to be intersectional, can vitiate the spirit of the protection. It is necessary therefore to combine discriminatory effect with the grounds in order to extend the reach of the protection creatively, and to address the normal experience of multiple intersecting discriminations. Speaking of the Canadian situation, Dianne Pothier pertinently observes:

> [A]s a woman with a disability ... I can never experience gender discrimination other than as a person with a disability; I can never experience disability discrimination other than as a woman. I cannot disaggregate myself nor can anyone who might be discriminating against me. I do not fit into discrete boxes of grounds of discrimination. Even when only one ground of discrimination seems to be relevant, it affects me as a whole person. If I am excluded or marginalized from something because of my disability, I am also excluded or marginalized as a woman and vice versa.[6]

The effect-based approach in combination with the specification of grounds was adopted by the Expert Group on the Equal Opportunity Commission in India, which defined discrimination through its effect on 'deprived groups' as

> a group of persons defined by any of the express or implied grounds on the basis of which discrimination is prohibited under section 2(k)(i) who find themselves disadvantaged or lacking in opportunities or suffer from impaired ability to make good existing opportunities to access rights and entitlements available under law or schemes of the government.

We may in the first instance identify 'deprived groups' through the medium of the constitution, and extend it beyond, drawing on

---

Real Experiences', *Canadian Journal of Women and Law*, 13, 2001, pp. 37–33, http://heinonline.org, accessed 27 July 2010.

[5] Dianne Pothier, 'Connecting Grounds of Discrimination to Real People's Real Experiences', p. 41.

[6] Ibid., p. 60.

the logic of that identification. In identifying the possible claimants of equal opportunity, the Expert Group got over the problem of exclusion of grounds in Article 15(1) in part by including disability within the grounds of 'discrimination', although it did not figure as a stated ground in Article 15. The ground of sexual orientation, while it was discussed, had to wait for the Naz Foundation. B. D. Sharma identifies five levels of deprivation:

> (1) non recognition of rights over resources and restrictions on their use; (2) alienation of the worker from the means of production; (3) denial of due entitlement of labour; (4) bartering of personal liberty; and (5) the psychological state of accepting deprivation and destitution as justified and proper and the demise of self-respect and dignity.[7]

There is something about suffering that is chronic, as also about the isolation that suffering imposes. And yet, Martha Minnow points out, it is only in moments of crisis — when there is a sharp break with the past and the future — that the chronic gets foregrounded as something deserving of attention. This moment of crisis could be triggered, for instance, by the sudden discovery of prolonged incarceration of the sane; by death in a fire because of practices of chaining people with psychiatric disorders; by pregnancy of a young woman with intellectual disability because of persistent sexual assault in a state facility. And yet, what deserves attention far more than the crisis is the chronic condition — in this instance of incarcerating those with psychiatric disabilities; of lack of care and the routine infliction of harm in private institutions for persons with psychiatric disabilities and in state facilities for the intellectually challenged. To address the chronic condition, however, would need a complete inversion of established ways of thinking, acting, and organising resources, which keep the condition of suffering chronic. In William E. Connolly's words,

> some of the most difficult cases arise when people suffer from injuries imposed by institutionalized identities, principles and cultural understandings, when those who suffer are not entirely

---

[7] 'The Twenty-ninth Report of the Commissioner for Scheduled Castes and Scheduled Tribes' (B. D. Sharma Report), National Commission for Scheduled Castes and Scheduled Tribes, Government of India, 1990, para 13.

helpless, but are defined as threatening, contagious or dangerous to the self assurance or truth of these identities and when the suffers honor sources of ethics inconsonant or disturbing to these constituencies.

It is necessary in dealing with the chronic, however, to step clear of the charity mode ('an ethics of help for the helpless' into a 'political ethos of critical engagement between interdependent contending constituencies implicated in asymmetrical structures of power'.[8]

In its classic form, I would argue, constitutional jurisprudence depoliticises the reading of non-discrimination. To echo Wendy Brown, '[d]epoliticization involves removing a political phenomenon [the writing of the constitution] from comprehension of its historical emergence and from a recognition of the powers that produce and contour it' (Brown 2006, 15). This eschewing of power and history in the representation of its subject results in the representation itself providing a truncated 'ontological naturalness or essentialism' that then goes on to inform the entire field of constitutional jurisprudence.

It is in this broad context that this article will attempt to examine the discourse on disability in India. While disability-based discrimination is the subject of special legislation, the constitution is silent on discrimination based on disability, all cases being read within the ambit of equality before law and equal opportunity. The treatment of persons with disabilities, however, has historically been discriminatory, with practices of discrimination embodied in unparalleled ways, and providing the language and medium for the articulation of disabilities in the social sphere. Opening up a discussion on discrimination and the negation of liberty by unpacking the constitutionally inarticulate field of disability-based discrimination might present unanticipated possibilities for understanding the fundamental bases of discrimination and have unexpected outcomes in terms of an understanding of constitutional morality.

In the following sections I shall examine the jurisprudence on disability through an analysis of case law on disability in India, looking at criminal justice, equality of opportunity, and questions

---

[8] William E. Connolly, 'Suffering, Justice and the Politics of Becoming', *Culture, Medicine and Psychiatry*, 20, 1996, p. 255.

of custody and consent. While case law is recent and not very extensive, especially in comparison to the other indices of discrimination, a careful reading might foreground the theoretical/ conceptual bases for the marginality of disability rights jurisprudence to the larger discussions of non-discrimination in India. Central to this exercise is an examination of the construction of corporeal normativities, and its proliferation through the constitutional interpretation on non-discrimination. In providing this detailed assessment, I hope to make the case for a radically new approach to constitutionalism that springs from the question of ability as it is theorised in philosophy and in the practice of the disability rights movements in India.

Constitutional Position in India

> Article 326: Elections to the House of the People and to the Legislative Assemblies of States to be on the basis of adult suffrage: The elections to the House of the People and to the Legislative Assembly of every state shall be on the basis of adult suffrage that is to say, every person who is a citizen of India and who is not less that eighteen years of age ... and is not otherwise disqualified under the Constitution or any law made by the appropriate Legislature on the ground of ... *unsoundness of mind* ... shall be entitled to be registered as a voter at any such election (emphasis mine).

> Article 41: Right to work, to education and to public assistance in certain cases: The State shall *within the limits of its economic capacity and development*, make effective provision for securing the right to work, to education and to public assistance in cases of unemployment, old age, sickness and disablement, and in other cases of undeserved want (emphasis mine).

What is the constitutional position on disability in India? A seven-judge constitutional bench of the Supreme Court of India in *Indra Sawhney vs. Union of India*[9] held that the spirit of articles 14 (right to equality) and 16 (right against discrimination in public employment) allowed for equality and affirmative action for persons with disabilities.

The fundamental right to life provides the guarantee of life and liberty to all persons resident in India. Article 21 of the

---

[9] *Indra Sawhney vs. Union of India* 1992 Supp (3) SCC 217.

constitution of India protects the Right to Life and Personal Liberty, which are inclusive of the principles of inherent dignity and individual autonomy for all persons resident in India. Article 21 together with Article 14, the Right to Equality before Law, provide the conditioning environment for specific laws and policies that uphold fundamental rights for different classes of individuals. Article 38 directs the state to secure a social order that promotes welfare of the people; Article 39 enjoins the state to protect the health and strength of workers, men and women; to ensure that children are not abused; citizens are not forced by economic necessity to enter avocations unsuited to their age or strength; children are given opportunities and facilities to develop in a healthy manner and in conditions of freedom and dignity; and that childhood and youth are protected against exploitation and against moral and material abandonment. Article 47 directs the State to raise the level of nutrition and the standard of living and to improve public health.

While these are general provisions that offer protections and form the basis for state policy impacting on all people across abilities, there is a double negation of the rights of persons with disabilities in the constitutional scheme, which has far-reaching implications. The first is the absence of disability as an explicit ground of discrimination under Article 15(1); the second is the bar on voting rights for persons with any mental or intellectual disability, described by the encompassing term 'unsoundness of mind'. These negations have specific impacts individually, but in concert, it means that the denial of rights of democratic citizenship expressed through adult suffrage (not, as has hitherto been assumed, 'universal adult suffrage') cannot be brought within the meaning of discrimination against persons of 'unsound mind'. Nor does the constitution define the attributes of unsoundness of mind, considering the denial is one of a critical, indeed indispensable, political right. I suggest that by this token, 'unsoundness of mind' is a fluid category that shifts constantly, the identification of such persons being part of an exercise of power by the combined forces of the state, sometimes in concert with families and communities. This denial of political voice has immediate and serious consequences for the right to liberty of persons of 'unsound mind', as we shall see later in this article. Apart from Article 326, quoted in the beginning of this article, Item 19 of the concurrent list discussed in the Constituent Assembly on 20 August 1947 reads:

19. Lunacy and mental deficiency, including places for the reception or treatment of lunatics and mental deficients.

The language of 'deficiency', 'lack', 'impairment', 'bodily defect' stalks official discourse on disability rights, making it necessary to unpack the construction of disability before moving on to examine the articulation of constitutional rights, non-discrimination, liberty, and the problems thereof.

If 'unsoundness of mind' is a homogenising construct, the second negation, namely the refusal to bring disability within the meaning of discrimination under Article 15, results in further truncating fundamental freedoms for all persons with disabilities. This is an aspect of constitutional abridgement of rights that we will revisit at different points in this and the following sections of this article.

Social contract theory, argues Martha Nussbaum, imagines contracting agents, who design the basic structure of society as free, equal and independent citizens who are fully cooperating members of society over a complete life. Disability, then, within social contract is handed as an afterthought, which necessitates 'accommodation' and the removal of 'barriers'.[10] The erection of barriers itself is a matter not of volition, but of foundational exclusions, of inarticulate premises that structure consciousness and architectural design.

For the present, however, we may just mark the clearly discernible disjuncture between the treatment of persons with disabilities other than mental disability on the one hand, where the focus is equal opportunity as distinct from non-discrimination, and persons with mental disability on the other, where protections and special measures tend to take the form of custody and negation ranging from mild to severe methods.

Problematising Ability

There are different ways of looking at disability and positioning it in the context of law. The discourse on disability in India, it appears, focuses on a bio-medical approach which measures disability against an able-bodied norm, and medically certifies

---

[10] Martha C. Nussbaum, *Frontiers of Justice: Disability, Nationality, Species Membership*, New Delhi: Oxford University Press, 2006.

that not less that 40 per cent of any of the listed forms of disability — either singly or in combination — brings a person within the category of the 'disabled', and by that token brings her within the umbrella of state protection/custody and/or largesse.[11] Recognising that employers might have an aversion to the idea of employing persons with disabilities, legislation attempts to regulate this aversion by providing incentives to employers of the disabled under Section 41 of the Act.[12] It is in the structure of the relief itself that the inarticulate ground of discrimination is evident. Where for any of the stated grounds of discrimination under Article 15 reservation is a part of the right against non-discrimination, in the case of disability, reservation is framed in the language of tolerance, with incentives being the medium through which tolerance is fostered and discrimination left unaddressed in any substantive manner, fashioning a remedy while leaving public morality firmly in place.

As a challenge to this bio-medical approach we witness around the time the United Nations Convention on the Rights of Persons with Disabilities was ratified, the deliberations on the National Policy on Disability Rights and the 11th Five Year Plan marked a shift in policy towards the social model of disability, not quite reaching there, but straddling, as it were, the bio-medical and social domains of knowledge on disability.

However, with either of these approaches, the fundamental assumptions on the dichotomy between ability and impairment

---

[11] 'Disability' under Section 2 (i) of the Persons with Disabilities Act, 1995 is defined as blindness, low vision, leprosy cured, hearing impairment, locomotion disability, mental retardation, and mental illness — certified by a medical authority to be not less than 40 per cent. Having identified the person with disability through the biomedical validation of essentialised attributes, positions in public employment that may be offered to such persons are then identified and a reservation of 3 per cent distributed among the different categories described above under Section 33 of the Act.

[12] I echo the title of Wendy Brown's work on tolerance (*Regulating Aversion: Tolerance in the Age of Identity and Aversion*, Princeton and Oxford: Princeton University Press, 2006). However, the idea of managing or regulating aversion with specific reference to persons with disabilities goes back to Jacobus tenBroek's writing ('The Right to Live in the World: The Disabled and the Law of Torts, *California Law Review*, 54) in 1966. Speaking of public attitudes to persons with disabilities, he refers to the 'public aversion to the sight of them and the conspicuous reminder of their plight' (ibid., p. 842).

are common. The contradictions in law, jurisprudence, and policy with respect to equality (non-discrimination not yet articulated for persons with disabilities) can only be understood if we begin to unpack these assumptions and reformulate the 'problem of disability'. In doing this, I draw on the work of Minae Inahara who contests 'the binary categorical system which defines disability in opposition to an able-bodied norm and suggest[s] that the disabled body is a multiplicity of excess which undermines this able-bodied norm'.[13] Critical to this argument is the idea that the able-bodied norm is illusory with all those labelled disabled, female, child, aged, obese, homosexual and all those who suffer from chronic illness or are sick, weak, vulnerable, frail for any of a host of reasons are set against the norm that is by definition unattainable. An illustration of this conflation is contained in the single constitutional provision that speaks explicitly of disability, Article 41, which addresses the state's commitment to providing public assistance in cases of 'unemployment, old age, sickness and disablement, and in other cases of undeserved want'. Labour laws reproduce this with reference not to disability but to 'continuous ill health and disablement'.[14] And yet, labour is a many-splendoured thing, with disability sitting quite easily with manual work, provided the performance of manual work is conceptualised and organised without assuming an able-bodied norm in terms of output and the design of work-enhancing implements.[15] That the able-bodied norm is physical, and therefore also sexually coded is driven home by accounts of women who seek dissolution of arranged marriages on the ground that the husband is 'impotent', a descriptor for homosexuality.[16] That the norm is male, while being self-evident, is also interestingly

---

[13] Minae Inahara, 'This Body which is Not One: The Body, Femininity and Disability', *Body & Society*, 15 (1), 2009, p. 47, http://bod.sagepub.com/cgi/content/abstract/15/1/47, accessed 12 March 2010.

[14] N. Vasanthi, 'Disability and Labour Laws in India, *Supreme Court Journal*, 1, 2007, pp. 40–46.

[15] A different conceptualisation of manual work was in fact formulated in fair detail by a large group of persons with disabilities trying to work with the National Rural Employment Guarantee Scheme at the National Institute for the Mentally Handicapped in Hyderabad, Andhra Pradesh in January 2006.

[16] I draw here on my experience of providing legal counseling to women at Asmita Resource Centre for Women, Secunderabad since 1991.

reflected through a crooked mirror that shows women unable to bear a male child as 'deficient'. The male able-bodied norm is defined also through the politics of the womb, where femininity is constructed through the capacity to bear children, so that any claim to femininity must fall short if this capacity is absent — as for instance when Sameera, a transgender person who identifies herself as female, observed at a meeting of disability rights activists that she was the most severely disabled of all because she lacked the organs necessary for creation (*srushti*).[17] This view finds its echo in the draft legislation that contentiously places 'sexual deformities' within the definition of disabilities.

The able-bodied norm is set outside the lived experience with everybody striving to reach up to it for varying periods in differing degrees during a lifetime, or simply finding the norm un-performable, and therefore being framed as its Other. The attainment of this goal or failure thereof does not in any way reflect capacity or capability or ability — nor is there any fixity to the attainment — transient and ephemeral by definition. When a 70-year-old poet I know, a woman, says with anger sometimes, quoting Charlie Chaplin, 'there is no defence against old age', or an 80-year-old civil liberties campaigner says in a barely audible voice that he just does not feel strong anymore and that makes him feel wretched, they are setting themselves up against the physical strengths that they possessed when they were younger and 'able' and which in their view an able-bodied norm is invested with. And yet, every week, he writes a lead column in a news-paper and receives thunderous applause for the radicalism of his ideas and work, and she writes, and teaches, and cares, and performs an amazing multiplicity of tasks that no able-bodied norm can contain. It is also true that she falls frequently, feels frail in mind and body more than she used to when she was younger, that he needs support to walk, and has coordination difficulties and sporadic memory losses. In other situations, the loss of effective use of a limb creates bodily impediments to functioning — and yet there are ways of getting around the obstructions, not seeing them as obstructions, but really organising tasks differently and changing the way in which we are oriented to our immediate environment.

---

[17] State-level disability rights workshop organised by the non-governmental organisation MORE in Madanapalle, Andhra Pradesh, April 2003.

The mastery of an inability, or compensating for it through bodily moves, makes ability itself fluid and malleable. This is the case with most physical disabilities as well. As Inahara puts it so aptly, 'the complexity of disabled ability does not fit into able-bodied notions of ability'.[18] Further, the moment we attempt to demarcate the disabled body, we realise that no body is fixed and perfect, and that the diversity of abilities and disabilities challenges the logic of sameness in able-bodied understanding of ability.

The definition of 'disability' cuts across a very wide range of physical, mental, and social disabilities, many of which might coexist with sound health and ability. This throws into question the supposed homogenising of disability and its constructed opposition to the able-bodied norm evident in judicial discourse on physical disabilities.

What is striking about the case law on disability is the inability of public authorities who measure disability in percentiles against the able-bodied norm, and then fix attributes and incapacities to each measure, to comprehend that what they label as 'disability' refuses to get contained within the attributes they ascribe to the label. Instead, the disabled spill out of the confines of disability merging with ability, disabled ability matching able-bodied ability, throwing the norm into crisis. The norm, however, is quickly recovered, and the measure restored, through the observation that although X suffers from disability, he is as at ease with the tasks on hand as an able person.

In the case of persons of 'unsound mind', the case law, although very limited, reveals the ways in which, although unsoundness of mind is a transient condition, it is fixed despite medical certification to the contrary (i.e., despite the declarations from the keepers of the able-bodied norm). This fixing of a shifting and nebulous condition invites tunnelling consequences in the law that herd such persons into prison — obliterating the distinction between 'insanity' and 'sanity', between degrees and forms of 'insanity', between 'mental incapacity' and 'insanity', between the 'criminally insane' and 'non-criminally insane', and between the 'criminal' and the 'mentally ill'.

---

[18] Minae Inahara, 'This Body which is Not One', p. 56.

Law as embedded in governmentality expresses itself through policy that directs executive action. It is necessary to examine that entire field of law in order to fully appreciate the place of law in society. Outside of executive action, law as embedded in governmentality surfaces through the minutiae of 'informal law' or custom — to which is added the realm of popular representation — writing, visual media, etc. — as standard or norm-setting practices. Traditions of isomorphism cut through the entire field — but also historically assertions and resistance cut through this entire field as well.

Criminal Injustice, Sound Minds, and the Idea of Liberty

> Personal liberty is one of the most precious rights of a human being and it cannot be allowed to be smothered by bureaucratic or judicial inadequacy or inefficiency.
>
> *Veena Sethi vs. State of Bihar*, 1983 AIR (SC) 339

The Criminal Procedure Code sets out the signposts for fair trial, which is a constitutional guarantee. More importantly, it prescribes down to the last detail the procedure to be followed by courts of trial if a person is to be denied the right to life and personal liberty under Article 21 of the constitution. In doing this, it also sets out the broad parameters for the safeguarding of personal liberty. There are, however, ambiguities in the provisions that deal with 'unsoundness of mind' that could be interpreted in a range of very different ways. There is a plethora of case law on the question of insanity, especially when it concerns a person accused of a serious offence.[19] My concern here is both more specific and more general. Specifically, I am concerned about the relationship between discrimination and the loss of liberty — How does 'unsoundness of mind' make persons so classified more vulnerable to incarceration? How does it disable defence against custody both during periods when unsoundness of mind prevails, and after sanity returns? How does unsoundness of mind become a justification for the judicial rationalisation of

---

[19] Amita Dhanda, *Legal Order and Mental Disorder*, New Delhi and Thousand Oaks: Sage Publications, 2000, pp. 79–180.

degrading forms of punishment — namely prolonged incarceration? My more general concern focuses on the linkages/intersections in the discrimination–liberty problematic.

In general, with respect to criminal law, sections 328–39 of Chapter XXV of the Criminal Procedure Code prescribes the procedure in relation to 'accused persons of unsound mind'. In summary, these provisions require that a magistrate, if necessary, will, through a medical examination, determine whether an accused is of unsound mind, record the fact, and postpone proceedings; a court or magistrate during a trial may also try the fact of unsoundness of mind and postpone the trial; when the trial is postponed, the accused may be released on bail, on 'sufficient surety', or may be detained in safe custody, with detention in a lunatic asylum being in accordance with the provisions of the Indian Lunacy Act, 1912; the trial *may* be resumed '*at any time after the person has ceased to be of unsound mind*' (Section 331 Criminal Procedure Code, my emphasis); where a person is acquitted on grounds that she/he was of unsound mind at the time of commission of the offence, the judgement shall state clearly whether she/he committed the offence or not; if the offence was found to have been committed by the accused, she/he will be detained in safe custody after acquittal, *or be delivered to any relative or friend of such person* (sections 335 and 339, Criminal Procedure Code). There is no prescribed time limit for postponement. Between postponement and resumption of trial, the accused may be released on surety of safe conduct, or may be detained in safe custody of a jail or a mental hospital. The discretion available to courts and executive authorities in these provisions is wide and amenable to amplification even through a strict reading. It is this piece of procedure that we will examine in this section to understand the meanings of custody and incarceration for persons found to be of 'unsound mind'.

The case of *Veena Sethi vs State of Bihar*[20] is extremely significant because it sets out the terrain of legitimate illegality, and the meanings of incarceration and loss of liberty for persons declared to be of 'unsound mind'. The case is about 16 prisoners, held in prison because they were at the time of their admission 'of unsound mind', but continued to be in custody for periods

---

[20] *Veena Sethi vs State of Bihar* 1983 AIR (SC) 339.

ranging from 25–35 years despite having been cleared for release by psychiatrists.

> It was a letter dated 15 January 1982, addressed by the Free Legal Aid Committee, Hazaribagh, to one of us (Bhagwati, J.) ... which drew the attention of the Court to the atrociously illegal detention of [sixteen] prisoners in the Hazaribagh Central Jail for almost two or three decades without any justification what-soever ... [They were] of unsound mind at the date when they were received in the jail and barring two out of them, are still rotting in jail.

Of these 16, six — Sadal Chamar, Khedu Bhattacharya, Mohamadin, Kali Singh, Ambika Lal, and Jagannath Mahto — were examined by a psychiatrist a year before the case came up for hearing in the Supreme Court, and found to be of 'unsound mind'.

> We cannot in the circumstances order their release, because having regard to the mental condition of these prisoners, *it would not be in the interest of the society* as also in their own interest to set them free. It does not appear from the record as to whether there is anyone prepared to take care of them and hence it would not be desirable to release them, because if released in the present condition, they would not be able to secure proper medical treatment and would not even be able to look after themselves. *It is indeed unfortunate that most of these prisoners have been in jail for over 25 years* and it is a *matter of shame for the society* that these prisoners have had to be detained in jail because there are not adequate institutions for treatment of the mentally sick. We are told that there is only one institution in the State of Bihar *for treatment of lunatics and persons of unsound mind* and that is the Mansik Arogyashala, Kanke and it is already over-crowded and there is no room for admitting these prisoners. We have had occasions to see lunatic asylums in one or two States and we find that *the conditions in these lunatic asylums are wholly revolting and one begins to wonder whether they are places for making insane persons sane or sane persons insane* (my emphasis).

The line of argument adopted by the Court is very interesting because it gives voice to the inarticulate premises that have historically provided justification for the incarceration of the mentally ill, mental illness in jurisprudential frameworks being conflated with criminality — especially in terms of consequences.

A condition of morbidity and an act of volition with respect to the commission of a crime invite the same treatment, even when the condition of morbidity is in fact a mitigating circumstance in fixing criminal liability. The resulting situation is paradoxical. A person of 'unsound mind' accused of committing a crime cannot be held criminally liable, and cannot be sentenced to imprisonment or death. And yet, a person who is of 'unsound mind' whether or not he is accused of commission of an offence, and whether he is acquitted on grounds that he did not commit the offence or on grounds that he did, is held in custody for an entire lifetime, in the manner in which he would be if he were sane and had been convicted for a capital offence. On review, the Supreme Court justifies the obliteration of this important distinction, affirming that 'unfortunate' and 'shameful' as it may be, a jail is better than a 'lunatic asylum', and if they cannot be treated, they must be locked away. This despite the court's recognition of the fact that 'the practice of sending lunatics or persons of unsound mind to the jail for safe custody is not at all a healthy or desirable practice, because jail is hardly a place for treating those who are mentally sick'.

The mentally ill, by this argument advanced in 1983, have no inherent right to personal liberty. What of the mandatory sentence these six persons would serve, had they been convicted of an offence? Section 428 of the Criminal Procedure Code provided for setting off the term served during trial against the sentence awarded, and Section 433A provides for remission or commutation even for cases where life imprisonment or death penalty has been awarded, to a period of 14 years in prison. Since these prisoners had already spent 25 years in prison, the Court directed the state government to drop the cases pending against them 'as it would be purely academic to pursue these cases'. Having dropped the cases, and having taken note of the 25-year prison term that had already been served, did the court order them to be set at liberty? No, it ordered them to be retained in custody till it was established medically that they were no longer mentally ill. The engagement of the court in this case with reference to these six persons therefore was to use the court's terms, 'purely academic' — but that would imply that academic exercises are disengaged by definition, a sweeping and untenable generalisation. This is in fact an early instance of the practice of jurisprudential dissociation — a strategy devised by constitutional courts in India to skirt around providing critical protections to vulnerable communities, against discrimination and loss of liberty, even while acknowledging in unequivocal terms in the same case, that it was the duty of the court to protect fundamental rights of every citizen:

> The rule of law does not exist merely for those who have the means to fight for their rights and very often for perpetuation of the status quo which protects and preserves their dominance and permits them to exploit large sections of the community but it exists also for the poor and the down-trodden, the ignorant and the illiterate who constitute the large bulk of humanity in this country.[21]

Gomia Ho, Bhondua Kurmi, Hiralal Gope, Raghunandan Gope, Francis Purti, Gulam Jileni, Kamal Singh, and Hira Lal were eight other prisoners in this case that the court was concerned about.

> The cases of these prisoners disclose a shocking state of affairs involving total disregard of basic human rights. They constitute an affront to the dignity of man and it is surprising, indeed shocking to the conscience of mankind, that such a situation should prevail in any civilized society. *What meaning has the rule of law if the poor are allowed to languish in jails without the slightest justification as if they are the castaways of the society?*[22] (my emphasis)

It is useful to look carefully at each of these people the court is trying to do justice to.

Gomia Ho was convicted on 26 March 1945 for the offence under Section 304 of the Indian Penal Code — culpable homicide not amounting to murder and sentenced to rigorous imprisonment for a period of three years and to pay a fine of ₹ 100 and in default to undergo rigorous imprisonment for a further period of six months. In 1948, while he was in Hazaribagh Central Jail and close to completion of his prison term, he was directed to be retained in 'safe custody' in the jail and given medical treatment as he 'appeared to be of unsound mind'. While he was serving

---

[21] *Veena Sethi v State of Bihar*, All India Reporter (Supreme Court) 339, AIR (SC) 339, 1983.
[22] Ibid.

term in 1946, he attempted suicide, but could not be prosecuted although an offence was registered under Section 309 since he was incapable of making the defence in the view of the civil surgeon who medically examined him periodically.

The medical examination on 25 December 1966 noted that Gomia Ho had regained his sanity, and correspondence went back and forth on the need to release him till 1972 — six years. In 1972, the Law Department directed the prison authorities to trace 'relatives of Gomia Ho who would be prepared to take delivery of him and to take care and custody and proper security'. The last reminder in Gomia's case was sent in April 1974. In 1982, he was medically examined again and found to be sane. He had already spent 37 years in prison when he had been convicted for an offence to three years rigorous imprisonment.

> Till 1966 *at least he was insane and perhaps therefore not in a position to realise that he was in jail and we might sadistically say that insanity was perhaps a blessing for him* but, since 1966 he was completely sane and fully conscious that he was detained in jail and he must have been wondering in helpless despair as to why he was kept in jail, deprived of his freedom and liberty, for well nigh 16 years ... [After release] He will be a stranger in his own land. He will perhaps hear for the first time after 35 years that his country became free from foreign bondage, though his own bondage in jail continued indefinitely and interminably ...[23]

Bhondua Kurmi was accused of an offence under Section 302, IPC — murder. He was acquitted in 1956 because the sessions judge found him to be of unsound mind. After acquitting him, the judge directed that he be sent to the Hazaribagh Central Jail for medical treatment. The acquittal itself here is an act of jurisprudential dissociation because the same judgement pronounces both acquittal and incarceration. Be that as it may, five years later, in 1961 he was found to be sane on medical examination. In 1969, for the first time, the superintendent of the prison requested the inspector-general of prisons to secure Bhondua's release. For nine years thereafter, there was a controversy between different departments of government about whether this prisoner was Bondua Kurmi or Bandhu Mahter. And Bondhua Kurmi

---

[23] Ibid.

continued to be in custody — acquitted and sane — till the Supreme Court ordered his release in 1983 on the same terms as it ordered the release of Gomia Ho — journey expenses and one week's maintenance to be paid by the state. The Supreme Court despaired yet again over how this was at all possible:

> Have we lost all regard for human values? Have we become so dehumanised that we are now oblivious to all human misery and suffering? Does a human being who is the highest creation of God and whom the Upanishads call Amrutsay Putraha 'children of immortality' mean nothing but chattel to us, simply because he is poor and ignorant and there is no one to fight for him. Must he be subjected to incarceration and privation without any reason or justification? One day the cry and despair of large numbers of people like Bhondua Kurmi will shake the very foundations of the society and imperil and entire democratic structure of our polity and if that happens, we shall only have ourselves to blame.[24]

Hiralal Gope was remanded to judicial custody to stand trial for an offence under Section 302 IPC in 1963. In 1964, the magistrate stayed the criminal proceedings after finding him incapable of making his defence and directed that he be placed under treatment at Darbhanga Jail. He was then transferred to Hazaribagh Central Jail, where no reports on his alleged insanity were available.[25] When he was examined in 1982, he was found to be sane, after having spent 19 years in prison without trial. The criminal proceeding was quashed and his sentence set off under Section 428 CrPC in 1983 by the Supreme Court.

Raghunandan Gope was charged with murder under section 302 IPC, when he killed a person 'in a fit of insanity' in 1950. Finding that he was incapable of making his defence, the court ordered that he be held in custody till such time that he become capable of making his defence after which the trial would resume. 32 years later, he was found to be sane on medical examination; through three decades not a single medical report had

---

[24] Ibid.

[25] The Supreme Court Commission on the Hospital for Mental Diseases, Shahdara found a general laxity in filing and reviewing medical reports on progress of treatment of the mentally ill under observation both by the magistracy and the institution. See Amita Dhanda, *Legal Order and Mental Disorder*, p. 41.

been filed on the status of his 'insanity', and his trial had not commenced. According to procedure he could not be prosecuted for an offence committed in a fit of insanity. He was therefore held in judicial custody without being prosecuted for a term that far exceeded the term he might have served had he been sane and been convicted for the offence of murder. The Supreme Court's exercise of jurisprudential dissociation in the case of Raghunandan was expressed in the reduction of a blatant derogation of a fundamental right to a 'difficulty', that can only be reflected on in impersonal terms, the responsibility for which cannot be fixed:

> *The difficulty is* that when a prisoner is lodged in Jail on the ground that he is of unsound mind, and therefore, required to be kept in safe custody, *the custody becomes so 'safe' that the prisoner has no opportunity of ever getting out of it* even though he has become sane and the raison d'etre of his custody has disappeared (my emphasis).

Francis Purti was remanded to jail custody in 1966 for commission of an offence under Section 302, murder. After the case was committed to the Court of Sessions, he was acquitted on grounds that he was of 'unsound mind' at the time of commission of offence and was detained in jail for purposes of medical treatment. Despite the requirement of the half-yearly report on his mental condition, no such report was filed. Yet, in 1972, a communication to the effect that Purti was sane and could be released was sent by the superintendent of Hazaribagh Jail to the inspector-general of prisons. In 1983, Purti was still in prison, acquitted of criminal charges and sane.

Ghulam Jileni was sent to prison in 1968, with a reception order for medical treatment for insanity. He was not accused of any criminal offence. There was no record of any treatment. When he was examined in 1972, he was found to be sane. He continued to be held in custody till his release in 1983.

Kamal Singh was charged with an offence under Section 302, murder, convicted by the sessions court, but acquitted by the high court and directed to be held in Hazaribagh Jail for treatment for mental illness in 1956. He was then sent to the Mansik Arogyashala in Kanke and returned to the jail after treatment with a certificate that he was sane. The case gives no details of when he was shifted to the mental health facility, how long he stayed there, or when he returned sane to jail. The first communication in this regard was from the superintendent of the jail in 1979. Kamal Singh, now declared sane, still needed to point to a relative who was willing to take care of him, which he did. There were written records where the relative was identified. Communication kept tossing from the Law Department to the sessions judge, Gaya to the High Court, Patna, to the Hazaribagh Jail for four more years till he was finally released in 1983.

Hiralal was held in custody for an offence under Section 302, murder, committed in 1948. The trial had to be suspended because the judge found that he was incapable of making his defence. Half-yearly reports were submitted by the Superintendent till 1953. After 30 years, when he was examined in 1982, he was found to be sane, with no indication of how long he had remained in custody while he was sane.

The immediate relief these prisoners, who had spent an entire lifetime in custody with no justification whatsoever, received from the Supreme Court were 'freedom', journey expenses, and one week's maintenance. The lifetimes of these 14 men — six retained in custody on orders from the Supreme Court in 1983, and eight released on orders from the Supreme Court with no burden placed on the state for the most gross derogation of the right to life and personal liberty that stretched from the foundational moment of the constitution to three decades later — tell the story of impunity with respect to the mentally ill practised by society, bolstered by the state, and legitimised by the judiciary. It is no accident that they were all poor, in all probability illiterate, in many cases men from *adivasi*, Dalit–Bahujan, and minority communities — all factors that locked discrimination with the denial of life and liberty in the most literal and direct sense.

It has been argued that the confinement of under-trials after they had regained sanity has been held to be an infringement of the right to life under Article 21 in the Veena Sethi case.[26] However, this is only a small part (a minor one at that, because it is not reflected in the consequences determined by the Supreme Court) of the judicial position. The equivocation in the delineation of the right to life in that case through the elision between

---

[26] Amita Dhanda, *Legal Order and Mental Disorder*, pp. 92–93.

misfortune, shame, and derogation on the one hand, and directions of continued custody or release with journey expenses and one week's maintenance on the other points to the troubling absence of the principle of harm and the reparations that must follow. This, I argue, is an important part of the inarticulate premise of exclusion as normal where persons with mental illness/disability are concerned. Although *mens rea* cannot be established where persons with intellectual disabilities or mental illness are concerned, and therefore there is no possibility to fix criminal liability, sentencing assumes criminal liability a priori — through the argument on the propensity to cause harm or injury where the person confined is acquitted without a finding of 'liability'; or through the argument on the proven capacity to cause harm where a person confined is *acquitted with a finding* of criminal liability. The confinement is inescapable.

The frameworks of judicial deliberation at the peak of the public interest litigation era, we find, pitched the critical issue of denial of liberty in terms of misfortune, so that the remedy lay in mere release. The harm suffered through 19–35 years in prison without trial or after acquittal or with no criminal charges whatsoever. The review of the cases by the Supreme Court does not result in any level of reparations for those who have suffered harm. Yet another problem that this case draws attention to is a derogation of Article 14, the right to equality — which implies that equality is established through the recognition of both similarity and difference. Several important differences are blurred — the distinction between mental retardation (a developmental condition) and mental illness (which could be a transient condition); the distinction between under-trials whose trial has been postponed and persons who have stood trial and been acquitted on grounds of 'unsoundness of mind'; persons who are deemed incapable of making a defence and persons against whom there are no criminal charges; and finally persons of 'unsound mind' and persons who are sane according to medical examination reports. Across all these categories, persons with varying degrees of 'unsoundness of mind', and persons with a past history of such condition were denied the right to personal liberty for reason of that condition alone by the combined might of the state — of which the judiciary was an important part.

In the case of *Sheela Barse vs. Union of India*[27] the Court made a significant shift when it criticised the widespread practice of housing women and children with mental and physical disabilities in jail for 'safe custody' as unconstitutional and placed responsibility on the state governments to move them to an environment where they could receive proper care, medical treatment, and vocational training when possible.

There have been more than a couple of instances of torture in custody that have resulted in disabilities among under-trials and convicted prisoners — blinding under-trial prisoners in custody,[28] and women subjected to sexual torture in custody becoming 'mentally ill' are known cases. Meena, brought to India from Nepal by a Brahmin, was abandoned. She was sentenced to seven days in jail for vagrancy. She arrived (in Hissar Jail) in a fearful state, delirious, unable to walk, her rectum and vaginal area torn and bleeding. She had been kept in police custody for 22 days after her arrest and gangraped every day. Under acute psychiatric trauma from this experience, she was then handed over to the jail authorities.[29]

Several cases have addressed the deeply inhumane conditions of many institutions established to provide care for persons with psychiatric disabilities. In *Dr. Upendra Baxi vs. State of Uttar Pradesh*[30] the Supreme Court ordered a medical panel to evaluate the inmates at the Agra Home. The report demonstrated that though a majority of inmates had varying degrees of mental disability, some had been released by the superintendent without being evaluated and had not been provided any means by which to travel to their home towns. The Court recommended that psychiatric treatment be provided. In *Rakesh Chandra Narayan vs*

---

[27] *Sheela Barse vs. Union of India* 1986 3 SCC 632, Vide order dated 15.4.1986.

[28] *Khatri (I) and Others v. State of Bihar*, 1981 (1) SCC 623; *Anil Yadav and Others v. State of Bihar and Others*, 1981 (1) SCC 622 and *Khatri (II) and Others v. State of Bihar and Others*, 1981 AIR (SC) 1068.

[29] R. Nanda, 'PUCL Bulletin', November 1981, http://www.pucl.org/from-archives/81nov/jails.htm, accessed 17 August 2011.

[30] *Dr. Upendra Baxi vs. State of Uttar Pradesh* (1983) 2 SCC 308. The cases referred to in this section are only indicative, not exhaustive.

State of Bihar[31] the Supreme Court found the conditions in the mental hospital near Ranchi to be inhumane, and appointed a committee to visit the site and submit a report about the establishment's operations and standards of care. In the case of *S.P. Sathe vs. State of Maharashtra*,[32] Bombay High Court regulated the administration of electroconvulsive therapy (ECT) to mentally ill persons after hearing of the conditions at the Institute of Psychiatry and Human Behaviour (IPHB) in Panaji, Goa. Patients at the IPHB were reportedly given ECT without anaesthesia, a practice which could lead to general discomfort as well as bone fractures and dislocations. In addition, the IPHB neglected to obtain informed consent from the patients before administering the treatment. In *Chandan Kumar Banik vs. State of West Bengal*,[33] the Supreme Court criticised the inhumane conditions at the Mankundu Mental Hospital in the District of Hooghly, banned the practice of restricting patients with iron chains, and instead ordered drug treatment for them. In Tamil Nadu, in the asylum fire case,[34] the Supreme Court ordered each state to undertake a survey of every institution offering psychiatric care to ensure that all were following the prescribed standards set out in the *Mental Health Act* of 1987.

Whether persons with psychiatric disabilities are accused of an offence or not, the denial of personal liberty and the general denial of legal capacity takes aggravated forms that do not depend necessarily on the specific capabilities of the person concerned in each case. The idea of care for the profoundly affected falls back on a contractarian approach to the enjoyment of social goods, where the assumption is that a person with psychiatric or intellectual disability is a social burden, incapable of any positive contribution to the social order. The only element measured is the capacity to cause injury to self or others — this injury could

---

[31] *Rakesh Chandra Narayan vs State of Bihar* (1989) SUPP 1 SCC 644.

[32] Writ Petition No 1537 of 1984, Bombay, www.cehat.org/humanrights/caselaws.pdf, accessed 3 December 2008.

[33] *Chandan Kumar Banik vs. State of West Bengal* (1995) Supp. 4 SCC 505.

[34] *Death of 25 Chained Inmates in Asylum Fire in Tamil Nadu v Union of India and others*, 2002 AIR (SC) 979. This is also perhaps the first case that uses the term 'mentally challenged persons' in place of mentally ill, lunatic, insane persons — while drawing a distinction between mental illness and mental retardation, as set out in the Mental Health Act, 1987.

be physical, it could even be the disruption of a placid social exterior by mere presence.

What is left out of the account completely is an interpretation of injury or harm to the person concerned by public authorities and communities through degrading treatment, confinement, and segregation. Also left out of the account, and this to my mind is the most significant aspect, is the injury or harm caused to the social fabric by the routinisation and legitimation of practices of brutal and degrading treatment of persons — discursive and physical — through the medium of the government, legislature, and judiciary.

This is the first point at which norms of constitutional morality are traded for public morality, which then becomes the lens through which public authorities and community alike comprehend the realities of persons of 'unsound mind'. The fact of a dominant consensus that incarceration is the most feasible way of dealing with mental illness and intellectual disabilities is a demonstration of the pervasiveness of discrimination under Article 15. Further, this easy slippage into the realms of public morality in the case of persons with disabilities enables the interlocking of discrimination with the derogation of personal liberty on a more general level along other indices as well.

Conclusion

I have attempted in this article to map the construction of disability in judicial discourse and its consequences for our understanding of non-discrimination and liberty. The fact of *discrimination* against persons with disabilities continues to present a problem because of the deep entrenchment of able-bodied norms in the conceptualisation of rights and the articulation of non-discrimination and liberty by courts, and in the constitution itself. The double negation of disability in the constitution has disabled the possibility of engaging in constitutional communication on disability-based discrimination and its intersection with the right to liberty for persons with disabilities. This negation has also resulted, importantly, in the denial of abilities and disabilities as measures of diversity in a plural society, thus curtailing the possibilities for plural politics. While it may be argued that the Persons with Disabilities Act, 1995 does address the problem of discrimination against persons with disabilities and is read effectively with Article 14, we find on close examination that the definition of disability is wanting and that it still does not enable a constitutional formulation on non-discrimination.

However, what provides an edge to possibilities of the articulation of disability rights is the idea of a *constitutional articulation* — which has the effect of moving disability from an inarticulate, depoliticised category to an articulate, political category on which non-discrimination is to be guaranteed. How may we get around the double negation, working with the idea of constitutional morality and finding ways of 'wheeling', 'covering', and 'encircling'[35] the negation, finding new constitutional languages in the process?

---

[35] I borrow these words from the poem by Lois Keith, 'Tomorrow I'm Going to Rewrite the English Language', in idem (ed.) *Mustn't Grumble: Writing by Disabled Women*, London: The Women's Press, [1994] 1995, p. 57. Cf Minae Inahara, 'This Body which is Not One, p. 58.

6

Whose Security, Whose Development?: Lessons from Campaigns against Female Infanticide in Tamil Nadu

Swarna Rajagopalan

Introduction

I was born in 1964 to a family whose origins are in what used to be called North Arcot district in Tamil Nadu. In the decade between 1961 and 1971, the sex ratio in Tamil Nadu registered its sharpest decline, from 992 to 978.[1] In North Arcot, it slipped from 998 to 988.[2] I am always struck by the good fortune that kept me from being one of the infants killed for being female or abandoned for all practical purposes to a life of negligence and malnutrition for the reason. The right to life — to survive past infancy and childhood; the right to live well and with the freedom to choose what that should mean — we experience these as indivisible and prize them as inalienable. In each of our lives, security, development, and democracy are first experienced at the individual level through this right to life.

There could be few better issues through which to reflect on the relationship between security, development, and democratic governance than the baby girl's fragile enjoyment of the right to life. Female infanticide and foeticide (or sex-selective abortions)

---

[1] Tamil Nadu Peoples' Forum for Social Development, 'Social Development in Tamil Nadu — Serious Concerns, A Peoples' Memorandum to the Govt. of Tamil Nadu on the State Budget 2000–2001', http://www.swtn. org/publications/social_development_in_tamilnadu%e2%80%93serious_ concerns_2001.pdf, p. 10, accessed 13 August 2010.

[2] Sheela Rani Chunkath and V. B. Athreya, 'Female Infanticide in Tamil Nadu: Some Evidence' *Economic and Political Weekly*, 32 (17), April 1997, p. 3, http://www.cwds.ac.in/Library/collection/elib/sex_selection/ss_female_ infanticide.pdf, accessed 20 January 2010.

are a security issue, a development challenge and a human rights violation. A preliminary exploration of this tripartite relationship, which is simultaneously mutually reinforcing and mutually inimical, is the object of this case study.

This article is structured inductively. It begins with a descriptive account of the case study: the campaign against female infanticide in Tamil Nadu. The next section uses gender violence as a lens through which to reflect on security, development, and democratic governance. This is the launch pad for the discussion of the interface between security, development, and democratic governance in the final section of the article.

Curbing Female Infanticide

In this case study, campaigns and interventions to eliminate female infanticide serve as a lens to illustrate the synergies and tensions inherent in the interface between security, development, and democratic governance. There has not been a comparable effort to tackle female foeticide, a variation of the same male child preference, and therefore, infanticide alone forms the subject of this case study.

The Setting: Tamil Nadu

About 62.5 million people live in Tamil Nadu, India's southernmost state. They pride themselves on still speaking a classical language that they describe as 'older than sticks and stones'. Their history encompasses two imperial ages, three classical literary congresses, and an egalitarian impulse whose early expression was in the poetry of Bhakti saints and whose contemporary expression has been in the rationalist movement articulated best by E. V. Ramasami 'Periyar'. While by and large women are safe in Tamil Nadu and enjoy mobility and freedom in a way their northern sisters may not, they also live with a culture in which a classical and popular ethos prizes qualities associated with machismo. Violence is one dialect of that machismo.

The modern political history of Tamil Nadu is traced to elite organisations that sought to limit the early Brahmin domination of government jobs and what they saw as the 'Brahmin–Bania' coalition of the Gandhian Congress. By the 1930s, the elitist moment had passed, and Periyar's 'Self-Respect Movement' had swept over Tamil Nadu. Protesting the imposition of Hindi, speaking up for Tamil, decrying caste, ritualism, and religiosity, Periyar offered the people of Madras Presidency an alternative social vision. This rationalist, modernist vision remains the official ideology of the state whose politics has been dominated by parties from Periyar's movement.

There are two reasons why Tamil Nadu is a good location for the study of the interface between security, development, and democratic governance. First, the state has not known the upheaval of war or partition in modern times. The conditions for governance have therefore been extraordinarily stable. The tsunami had horrendous consequences but it was not a problem that bled the state over a period of time. Second, the rationalist ideology of the dominant parties in the state hold policy-making promise, especially in combination with the populist bent of the state's leadership. Gender equality would seem to be a corollary of the modernising element in Periyarist thought.

Female Infanticide in Tamil Nadu

In the late 1980s, alarmed by the declining sex ratio in the state, the Tamil Nadu government began partnering with NGOs to campaign against female infanticide. In general, the sex ratio in India has been in freefall through the 20th century.

Table 6.1: Sex Ratio and Child Sex Ratios in India and Tamil Nadu, 1901–2001

Year	Sex Ratio		Sex Ratio (0–6 Years)	
	Tamil Nadu	*India*	*Tamil Nadu*	*India*
1901	1,044	972	–	–
1951	1,007	946	999	983
1961	992	941	995	976
1971	978	930	984	964
1981	977	934	974	962
1991	974	927	948	945
2001	987	933	942	927

Sources: Table 1, in Sheela Rani Chunkath and V. B. Athreya, 'Female Infanticide in Tamil Nadu: Some Evidence' *Economic and Political Weekly*, 32 (1), April 1997, p. 3, http://www.cwds.ac.in/Library/collection/elib/sex_selection/ss_female_infanticide.pdf, accessed 20 January 2010; Census of India, http://www.censusindia.net/data/ppt_t10.PDF, accessed 12 February 2004.

A declining sex ratio is arguably the most fundamental indicator of the status of women in a society; especially where their chance of survival is diminished through conscious agency, there can hardly be another interpretation. The growing difference between the general sex ratio and the child sex ratio suggests that something began early on to make a difference to the survival prospects of girl children. The most basic kind of physical security — the right to life, the web of social, economic, and cultural factors that fall into the developmental realm, and the state's ability and willingness to act as well as the nature of state actions, contribute interesting insights for our broader study.

In 1992, Amartya Sen published an article in *British Medical Journal* in which he wrote that there were more than 100 million 'missing women' worldwide.[3] But a few years before that, in 1986, activists from the Society for Integrated Rural Development took journalists from a Tamil magazine to Usilampatti to report on the high incidence of female infanticide in that district. The *Junior Vikatan* article shook Tamil Nadu with its headline: 'Fearing Dowry they Kill Girl Babies'. *India Today* picked up the story, investigated it, and female infanticide in Tamil Nadu made national headlines.[4]

Until the press broke these stories in the late 1980s, it was largely assumed that female infanticide was uncommon in the modern age, a relic of the past, and found mostly in rural areas. Sabu George wrote in 1999 that as late as 1989 demographers claimed this did not happen in South India, although there were British accounts from the 19th century and he himself had heard from people in North Arcot, Madurai, and Salem that it had been practised for generations.[5] George's research between 1986 and 1990 in northern Tamil Nadu led him to conclude that 10 per cent of newborn girls in villages he was studying were victims of female infanticide, a finding reinforced by other researchers. Athreya and Chunkath, an economist–administrator team, stated that 'the practice is widespread in a contiguous belt of districts

---

[3] Amartya Sen, 'Missing Women', *British Medical Journal*, 304, 1992, pp. 587–88.
[4] Gita Aravamudan, *Disappearing Daughters: The Tragedy of Female Foeticide*, New Delhi: Penguin Books India, 2007, pp. 1–5.
[5] Sabu M. George, *Female Infanticide in Tamil Nadu, India: From Recognition to Denial?* http://www.hsph.harvard.edu/Organizations/healthnet/SAsia/suchana/0225/george.html, accessed 4 April 2001.

running south to north along a western corridor of the state. The belt runs from Madurai to Theni in the south through Dindigul, Karur, Namakkal, and Salem to Dharmapuri and Vellore in the north.[6] Primary health centres (PHCs) have been cited to suggest that from a high of around 3,000 cases of infanticide a year in the 1990s, there has been a sharp decline to just 225 in 2003.[7]

What is female infanticide? Female infanticide is the intentional killing of girl children on account of the preference for sons. Methods of killing abound: poisoning the infant's milk with oleander; feeding the infant castor oil mixed with paddy husk; stifling the baby with a pillow; drowning her in milk; burying the infant in sealed mud pots; feeding the infant crushed sleeping pills or pesticide.[8] The killing is usually done by a female elder and very occasionally by the midwife or other birth attendant at the family's behest. Girls born further down the birth order are more likely to be killed or neglected and left with poor survival chances.

In the last 30 years, sex-selective abortion — also referred to as female foeticide — has also been practised across India, and is more common than female infanticide. Female foeticide has spread to urban and semi-urban areas, and is also prevalent in Indian diaspora communities. The numbers on sex-selective abortion vary from '3 million a year' to '10 million between 1981 and 2005' — either way they are shocking. The spread of sex-selective abortions belies the faith that people place in education and economic wellbeing.[9]

Why do people kill their girl babies? Male child preference is the simple answer, and male child preference is explained in terms of agrarian labour requirements, custom (such as sons

---

[6] Venkatesh Athreya and Sheela Rani Chunkath, 'Tackling Female Infanticide: Social Mobilisation in Dharmapuri, 1997–99', *Economic and Political Weekly*, 2 December 2000, pp. 43–45.

[7] 'Human Development and Health', presentation by Health Secretary, Tamil Nadu State Government to the State Planning Commission, 18–19 May 2005, http://www.tn.gov.in/spc/workshop/6-HD%20and%20Health-SEC.PPT, accessed 15 March 2010.

[8] Drawn from across Gita Aravamudan, *Disappearing Daughters*.

[9] Foeticide is not the subject of this article simply because efforts to end it have been relatively ineffective, and perhaps a little half-hearted; we will, however, return to that challenge briefly in the last section of this article.

being needed for funeral rites), and patriarchal inheritance laws. Researchers have identified several factors that make this a lethal preference. First, as people choose to have fewer children, they are more likely to select the gender of those children. Second, Sabu George points to the Green Revolution and the spread of cash or commercial crop cultivation. The way that credit, warehousing, markets, and technology now work coupled with patriarchal restrictions on women's mobility marginalised their role in the new economy. Third, with some farmers becoming affluent, conspicuous consumption has become common in both rural and urban India. Lavish weddings and wedding gifts are ways to show off the new affluence, and giving and taking dowry have spread not just to new regions and communities but also well beyond the occasion of the wedding to a lifetime of demands.[10] Fourth, advances in reproductive health technologies are being used to act on male child preference.[11] Regulatory and punitive legal mechanisms have not served as a deterrent, and we read that with relatively liberal abortion laws, India is also emerging as a destination for diaspora Indians to return to have these tests and abortions done.

Campaigns and Interventions

To their credit, state and civil society in Tamil Nadu have acted with enthusiasm (if not alacrity) against the practice of female infanticide. In fact, one scholar states that this is the 'first and only state in India to officially acknowledge female infanticide as a problem'.[12]

PHCs have been the focal point of state interventions and invaluable partners in the campaign against female infanticide

---

[10] 'Expanding Dimensions of Dowry', All-India Democratic Women's Association, 2003, discussed in Jagori, *Marching Together: Resisting Dowry in India*, New Delhi, 2009, www.jagori.org/wp-content/uploads/2009/07/dowry_infopack.pdf, accessed 22 August 2010. The actual document could not be found on the Internet.

[11] Sabu M. George, *Female Infanticide in Tamil Nadu, India*. See also M. Gandhimathi Jeeva and Phavalam, 'Female Infanticide: Philosophy, Perspective and Concern of SIRD', *Search Bulletin*, 13 (3), July–September 1998, pp. 9–17. http://www.cwds.ac.in/Library/collection/elib/sex_selection/ss_female_infanticide_philosophy.pdf, accessed February 2010.

[12] Sharada Srinivasan, 'Gender Bias in Child Mortality', *Economic and Political Weekly*, 22 December 2001, p. 4768.

thanks to their presence on the ground across districts. They have also housed the reception centres for the Cradle Baby Scheme (CBS), with the existing staff of the PHC serving to care for the abandoned baby girls. PHC records are a critical component of the studies that have underpinned policy planning in this sphere. Tamil Nadu's Directorate of Public Health has also pioneered district-wise Vital Events Survey (VES) from 1996–99 and in 2003, creating a database on births and infant deaths. PHC records and the VES data together have enabled the administration and social sector to tackle female infanticide more effectively.[13]

In 1992, the Tamil Nadu government launched two schemes intended to address the problem of female infanticide, among other things: the CBS and the Girl Child Protection Scheme (GCPS). Their impact is still being assessed and debated, but they have caught the attention of the central government and other state governments and the GCPS has been adopted with or without changes across the country.

The CBS offered parents an alternative to killing female infants. They could now leave their unwanted daughters at baby reception centres, from where they would presumably be offered up for reception. The scheme was first introduced in Salem district and in 2001 was extended to Madurai, Theni, Dindigul, and Dharmapuri. The numbers vary, but with the scheme in operation since 1992, the first abandoned girls would be 18 years old by now. One report estimated that, 'Till March 2008, this programme has saved the life of 3,044 children.'[14] A 2007 Right to Information (RTI) petition revealed that as on 1 June that year, 2,589 girls were received at government centres, but most arrivals had occurred after 2000. The same response stated 1,545 babies were surrendered and 950 were abandoned.[15]

---

[13] Sheela Rani Chunkath and V. B. Athreya describe data collection on female infanticide in their 1997 article 'Female Infanticide in Tamil Nadu: Some Evidence', *Economic and Political Weekly*, 32 (17), April 1997, http://www.hsph.harvard.edu/Organizations/healthnet/SAsia/suchana/1210/chunkath.html, accessed 13 April 2001.

[14] 'Positive Bias for Girls', *The Hindu*, 24 January 2009, http://www.thehindu.com/2009/01/24/stories/2009012454430700.htm, accessed 20 March 2010.

[15] P. C. Vinoj Kumar, 'Where do Rejected Little girls Go ...', *Tehelka Magazine*, 5 (12), 29 March 2008, http://www.tehelka.com/story_main38.asp?filenam e = Ne290308where_rejected.asp, accessed 4 January 2010. This article was an important resource for the critique of the Cradle Baby Scheme.

Critics of the CBS appear to outnumber its supporters, and there are many reasons for this. First of all, while parents believe that they are giving up children to the care of the government, in reality, the government passes them on to adoption agencies on an average two months after they are received. At this point, the government ceases to keep track of them or their welfare. Agencies are forbidden to speak about the cradle babies received, and direct investigators to the government for answers. The fate of the babies received is uncertain and undocumented. From around the time the CBS was extended across the state, the number of adoption agencies in Tamil Nadu has doubled, according to reports.[16] Reports of irregularities and corruption in the adoption process have also brought the CBS under scrutiny. Some would go so far as to say that the scheme has promoted trafficking in infants.[17]

Second, although since 1992 successive governments have pledged support to this cause, and to the CBS, the outlay available to the scheme has been to the order of ₹ 6–12 lakh a year.[18] Obviously, this pittance does not allow for special staff, leave alone specially trained staff. A *Tehelka* special report quoted P. Phavalam of the Society for Integrated Rural Development (SIRD) (which first brought female infanticide in Tamil Nadu to light) as saying that while the infant mortality rate in Tamil Nadu was 31, it was 162 for the cradle babies.[19]

An Usilampatti mother said to Gita Aravamudan:

> "Better to send my daughter to her maker than to leave her to the mercy of an *anadhashram* [orphanage] ... Even if this one is a daughter, I will never leave her in the cradle. Today she may be a baby but tomorrow she will grow up into a young woman and who knows how the orphanage will use her?" [20]

---

[16] Ibid.

[17] Arjun Bedi, 'Bare Branches and Drifting Kites: Tackling Female Infanticide and Feticide in India', *ISS Public Lecture Series 2008*, no. 5, The Hague, Netherlands, 16 October 2008, p. 26, http://campus.iss.nl/~bedi/inaugural_Bedi.pdf, accessed 10 March 2010.

[18] P. C. Vinoj Kumar, 'Where do Rejected Little Girls Go ...'

[19] Ibid.

[20] Gita Aravamudan, *Disappearing Daughters*, p. 18.

For activists, the fundamental issue is that the CBS seems to implicitly endorse male child preference. The message sent out is, 'Fair enough, you don't want this daughter, but don't kill her, leave her with us.' Placing the cradles in districts where female infanticide is not known seems to encourage the abandonment of daughters.[21] Moreover, it sanctions the violation of the daughter's right to live with her natural family.

The GCPS offers parents who only have daughters a financial incentive. Also introduced in 1992, the scheme was based on the premise that girls are considered a financial burden for parents and it reached out to poor families with small daughters where at least one of the parents had undergone sterilisation before reaching 35 years. A small sum of money would be placed in a deposit account in the girl's name and, in addition, educational and other assistance would be made available. Few took advantage of this scheme in the first five years of its working, but it was still adopted at the national level in 1997. The GCPS was restructured in 2001–2002 to increase the financial emoluments offered and the number of beneficiaries increased 50-fold.[22]

Less controversial than the CBS, there are still some concerns about the GCPS.[23] One is that the scheme targets poorer families, but the practice of female foeticide is growing faster in affluent sectors. The second is that those who have now enlisted in the scheme are not from the female infanticide 'belt' districts of Dharmapuri, Madurai, Salem, Theni, and Namakkal but Chennai, Coimbatore, Kancheepuram, Kanyakumari, the Nilgiris, Thanjavur, and Thiruvarur, where this practice is limited. Moreover, the GCPS requires one parent to have undergone sterilisation, and ends up appealing more to those who lack a strong preference for sons, rather than changing the attitudes of those who do. Sharada Srinivasan and Arjun S. Bedi see this

---

[21] Lalitha Sridhar, 'Treating Infanticide as Homicide is Inhuman', *InfoChange News & Features*, August 2004, http://infochangeindia.org/20040817165/Women/Features/-Treating-infanticide-as-homicide-is-inhuman.html, accessed 7 January 2010.

[22] Sharada Srinivasan and Arjun S. Bedi, 'Girl Child Protection Scheme in Tamil Nadu: An Appraisal', *Economic and Political Weekly*, XLIV (48), 28 November 2009, p. 11.

[23] Ibid., pp. 11–12.

requirement as a strong disincentive for parents who might otherwise enlist in this scheme. The coercive aspect of this requirement has also drawn criticism.[24]

Both the CBS and GCPS address the symptoms of male child preference — the willingness to eliminate or abandon a female child — rather than to transform that preference itself. This limits their value as tools of social change.

In 1997–99, the Tamil Nadu Area Health Care project adopted street theatre as a strategy in Dharmapuri to both conscientise the community against female infanticide and involve people in broader public health issues.[25] The project mobilised 350 social activists and volunteers to work together in troupes of 16 to perform specially developed plays around Dharmapuri district. They were first trained in a fortnight-long camp, which was in itself a transformative experience for many of them. The troupes stayed in the community, necessitating communication and negotiation with panchayat leaders. This created a local leadership including panchayat representatives, activists, and health functionaries for the fight against female infanticide. Over just 40 days, 18 troupes gave almost 3,000 performances, and directly or indirectly, they reached more than a third of Dharmapuri's population. A follow-up programme was held of eight panchayat union-level conferences made up of elected panchayat presidents, healthcare workers, and activists, where the panchayat presidents committed themselves to rooting out female infanticide. Venkatesh Athreya and Sheela Rani Chunkath, writing about this project, are very cautious about claiming instant success; however they point to the decline in female infanticides in Dharmapuri from 1,244 in 1997 to 997 in 1999, contrasting these figures with a contrary upward trend not just in female infanticide belt districts like Salem and Namakkal, suggesting the impact of this experiment is worth monitoring.[26]

Civil society has played an important role in spreading awareness and spearheading change. The first media reports in

---

[24] Sabu M. George, *Female Infanticide in Tamil Nadu, India.*

[25] Venkatesh Athreya and Sheela Rani Chunkath, 'Tackling Female Infanticide: Social Mobilisation in Dharmapuri, 1997–99', *Economic and Political Weekly,* 2 December 2000, pp. 4345–4348.

[26] Ibid., pp. 4347–4348.

1986 followed from the SIRD's initiative. In 1998, a coalition of civil society organisations, research institutions, and activists formed the Campaign against Sex Selective Abortion (CASSA). The objective of the campaign is to prevent the misuse of reproductive health technologies, promote reproductive health rights of women, and halt the decline of the sex ratio. CASSA uses educational programmes, monitoring exercises, and research publications to promote this objective. CASSA has been a vocal critic of the CBS and CASSA activists have also challenged the conviction of mothers in female infanticide cases on the grounds that they themselves are victims of the system.

The Indian Council for Child Welfare (ICCW) was another leader in this work, but it began by establishing créches and recruiting local women to run them.[27] They built trust by facilitating self-help groups and helping with income-generation activities. They also organised health and hygiene training programmes for adolescents. After several months, the topic of female infanticide was broached and despite initial resistance, ICCW volunteers began to monitor high-risk families discreetly. This combination of education, persuasion, and social policing resulted in a decline in the practice in the Usilampatti villages where ICCW worked. 'The ICCW's success in Usilempetti is mainly because it never told the villagers that it was there to prevent or end female infanticide.'[28]

The M. S. Swaminathan Research Foundation launched the 'Voicing Silence' project in 1992, with a view to bringing together culture and social activism as a catalyst to women's empowerment and creating awareness of gender issues. The project has developed plays, organised theatre festivals around these issues, and organised training workshops to support women to use theatre to express themselves on these matters. 'Voicing Silence'

---

[27] Shobha Warrier, 'Again a Girl! Are You Not Ashamed of Yourself?', 'The Rediff Special: A Special Report on Female Infanticide', Rediff.com, 8 March 1999,http://www.rediff.com/news/1999/mar/08woman.htm, accessed 4 April 2001; Shobha Warrier, 'The Girls take an Oath that They Will Not be Involved in Female Infanticide either Directly or Indirectly', interview with Andal Damodaran, 'The Rediff Special: A Special Report on Female Infanticide'.

[28] Shobha Warrier, 'Again a Girl! Are You Not Ashamed of Yourself?' 'The Rediff Special: A Special Report on Female Infanticide'.

served to facilitate dialogue, networking, and follow-up at the grassroots level in affected districts like Salem and Madurai.[29]

A very important factor in the success of these initiatives was perhaps that government and civil society worked together. NGOs partnered on specific programmes and also collaborated with government projects. A sense of shared purpose has clearly made a difference on the ground. More recently, the collective reach of the Self-Help Group movement, National Cadet Corps. and National Service Scheme have been harnessed to further this campaign.[30]

Interventions against Female Infanticide have also included Arrests and Convictions

Karupayee was arrested in January 1994 in Usilampatti on charges of killing her infant daughter. She already had two living daughters and two other daughters had died soon after birth, so the ICCW's local team had been monitoring her pregnancy. Karupayee went home early with her daughter from the hospital and when the ICCW social worker visited their home, the daughter was missing. A complaint was filed and prompt police action followed. Karupayee and her husband Karuthakannan confessed; they had strangled the baby and buried her in front of their house. Karupayee was arrested (not her husband because he was not present when this was done).[31] Female infanticide is usually charged as culpable homicide and the sentence is life imprisonment. P. Phavalam from SIRD and CASSA told a journalist:

---

[29] Mina Swaminathan, A. Mangai, and S. Raja Samuel, 'Confronting Discrimination: Some Approaches to the Issue of Female Infanticide', *Search Bulletin*, 13 (3), July–September 1998, pp. 64–74, http://www.hsph.harvard. edu/Organizations/healthnet/SAsia/suchana/0110/swaminathan_etc.html, accessed 13 April 2001.

[30] See, for instance, Ramya Kannan, 'SHG Launches Aggressive Campaign against Infanticide', *The Hindu*, 7 December 2003, at http://www.hindu. com/2003/12/07/stories/2003120705190100.htm,accessed 13 October 2010; Amutha Kannan, 'NCC Cadets Join Hands to Fight Female Infanticide, *The Hindu*, 31 August 2009, http://www.hindu.com/edu/2009/08/31/ stories/2009083150470200.htm, accessed 13 October 2010.

[31] Gita Aravamudan, *Disappearing Daughters*, pp. 4–7.

Karuppayee made big news because she was the first woman in Tamil Nadu to be convicted of female infanticide. She was interviewed umpteen times and attained the status of a "notorious celebrity". Her case is pending before the high court and she is out on bail. The impact of all this on her life has been terrible. She no longer wishes to meet the media and has become a recluse. She prefers not to interact at all. We have interviewed over 25 women who have been convicted. Many have been badly scarred by their experiences.[32]

Social activists have questioned how appropriate it is to single out women, especially mothers, for punishment. In their view women are also victims — they face untenable pressure from families and the community to bear male children. Women who kill their children have not learnt to value themselves, a lack of self-worth they transfer to their female newborns. They are dependent on their families for identity and survival, and when threatened with desertion or worse for bearing a girl child, have nothing to draw upon for resistance. The Tamil Nadu State Commission for Women, however, recommended after a public hearing that other women complicit in the killing should not be spared. The mother may be a victim, but she is also part of the pressure group that encourages the crime.[33] The men usually find an alibi and escape arrest, leading to a tragic miscarriage of justice.[34]

In addition, judicial custody shatters the family, punishing the other children for crimes their parents committed. Schooling, poverty, homelessness, even being orphaned if either of the parents dies or commits suicide — they pay a disproportionate price. While female infanticide is hardly a secret or uncommon practice

---

[32] Lalitha Sridhar, 'Treating Infanticide as Homicide is Inhuman', *InfoChange News & Features*, August 2004, http://infochangeindia.org/20040817165/ Women/Features/-Treating-infanticide-as-homicide-is-inhuman.html, accessed 7 January 2010. Mythily Sivaraman describes such cases in 'Female Infanticide — Who Bears the Cross?' *People's Democracy*, XXV (25), 24 June 2001, http://pd.cpim.org/2001/june24/june24_infanticide.htm, accessed 7 on January 2010.

[33] Feroze Ahmed, 'Panel Recommends Milder Punishment for Female Infanticide', *The Hindu*, 9 June 2003.

[34] Venkatesh Athreya and Sheela Rani Chunkath, 'Tackling Female Infanticide', p. 4345.

in certain areas, being apprehended by the police results in the community (the same community that may have reinforced male child preference) ostracising them. The children lose every source of support they might have.

There is also concern that treating female infanticide as a law-and-order problem and punishing it as a crime has the effect of simply driving the practice underground.[35] Threatening to register cases offers opportunities for extortion and bribes are collected to cover up infanticide cases.[36] Corruption in the police and administration makes it possible to misreport both the cause of death and gender of a child, to say nothing of falsified death certificates. State officials come from the same society where these horrendous practices are valorised; collusion between local officers and guilty families makes it possible to obfuscate the crime and hinder the law from taking its course.

Amid all the campaigning and the scheme-making, there have also been attempts to stop reporting beginning with the false charges faced by the SIRD when it first took journalists to Usilampatti to accounts of ministers cautioning NGOs not to report cases to the media.[37] Parallel to the wish to tackle the problem seems to run a wish to cover up and save face.

A recent attempt to assess the impact of interventions classified them in terms of reach and intensity into three groups: heavily treated districts, lightly treated districts, and minimally treated districts.[38] It found that large-scale, district-wide interventions backed by the district administration made a positive impact. Moreover, 'the district-wide monitoring and counseling of high-risk mothers at the grassroots (by NGOs/women's self-help groups/village health nurses), linked to the credible threat of police and legal action and the possibility of economic support via schemes such as the GCPS comprise an intervention model' which has shown results and may be replicated.[39] A multi-pronged approach is more likely to work than each or any of these schemes in isolation. Most important, the greatest success

---

[35] Ibid.
[36] Sabu M. George, *Female Infanticide in Tamil Nadu, India*.
[37] Ibid.
[38] Arjun Bedi, 'Bare Branches and Drifting Kites'.
[39] Ibid., p. 26.

has been seen where the district administration and NGOs have worked together. Social change, it seems, requires public–private partnership!

What the Fight against Infanticide Tells Us

Since the first reports in 1986 about female infanticide in parts of Tamil Nadu, state and civil society have attempted to turn back the tide on this practice.

An unusual response, but critical to successful policy making and intervention, was the commissioning of the district-level Vital Events Survey (VES). The Department of Public Health administrators had the foresight to run this survey for a few years at a stretch, creating a baseline, and then it was run once more a few years later. However, the true utility of data is when it is collected regularly over a period of time. Given that the problem — female infanticide — was not random or episodic, there could hardly have been a justification for not running the survey regularly. It was just a change of team and a reordering of priorities.

The Danish International Development Agency-funded project and Madras School of Social Work project are examples of interventions that seek to change the thinking of the community. Both projects used theatre to convey a particular message as well as to encourage people to express themselves. Effectively communicating the idea that female infanticide is wrong, project leaders were able to persuade members of the affected communities to volunteer to be advocates, monitor at-risk families, and thereby become change agents. Both projects also created networks of women with leadership skills. Both seem to have run their course, raising questions about follow-up. Moreover, while female infanticide may have been a localised problem, male child preference is not, but it has apparently not been possible to expand the reach of these programmes.

Over the years, civil society groups have formed a coalition to coordinate their advocacy efforts for greater effect. CASSA brings together some of the first groups to take on this issue as well as newer, smaller organisations across Tamil Nadu. Such a coalition brings together a wealth of experience which can be useful to both state and civil society's efforts.

The GCPS provides an incentive to those who choose to have and keep their daughters. What is implicit in this, however, is the idea that having a daughter is not its own incentive,. reinforcing the very prejudice that creates the problem of female infanticide in the first place. Moreover, the requirement that one of the parents have undergone some form of sterilisation means that the scheme appeals to those who have no particular preference, rather than 'converts' those who do. It also lends a coercive dimension to the scheme.

The arrest and subsequent conviction of mothers for killing of their girl babies has also been controversial. Exemplary punishment has its uses, but the argument that these convictions have punished victims has some degree of truth in this case. The other members of the family and community who might share and might have reinforced these beliefs go unpunished, but the women and other children are disproportionately affected.

The most high-profile 'solution' to the female infanticide problem, the CBS, is the most problematic. First, it locates the problem in the killing of the girl child and not in male child preference. Second, poor record keeping, lack of transparency, and abdication of responsibility characterise the operation of the scheme. Third, it is underfunded so even while an infant is at the PHC, there may be no one to take care of its special needs. Finally, the way the scheme has worked has spawned adoption rackets around Tamil Nadu.

Female infanticide rates have indeed come down in Tamil Nadu, but grassroots groups say it is because parents are opting for sex-selective abortions instead.[40] This is established by contrasting changes in the Infant Mortality Rate with the Sex Ratio at Birth.

The campaign against female infanticide has shown some good instincts and has been successful in some ways. However, lack of sustained effort and follow-up beleaguer the better interventions. The more problematic ones have sustained, but so have the reasons that were problematic in the first place. In addition to data collection not continuing, it appears as if neither evaluation

---

[40] Campaign against Sex Selective Abortion, *Position Note on Cradle Baby Scheme*, May 2007, http://cassa.in/pdf/Position%20paper%20on%20%20 Cradle%20baby%20scheme%20English.doc accessed 4 January 2010.

exercises nor dialogues with those on the ground have informed decisions to initiate or continue the state-run interventions.

The Challenge of Gender Violence

Gender violence is

> violence that is directed at an individual based on her or his specific gender role in a society. It can affect females or males; however, gender-based violence affects women and girls disproportionately. It is violence intended to establish or reinforce gender hierarchies and perpetuate gender inequalities.[41]

Gender violence is experienced across class, community, culture, life stage, and age. It begins with foeticide and ends with elder abuse. It is the power play of patriarchy — male privilege and male child preference are manifestations of patriarchal values. Gender violence offers an opening to reflect on security, development, and democratic governance in multiple ways that will be explored in this section.

Gender Violence and Security

The connection between gender violence and security is self-evident, even facile, until we consider that traditionally, security studies focused on states and their challenges of war and peace. After all, the simplest meaning of the word 'security' is safety, and being safe from physical harm is undoubtedly a way of being secure.[42]

---

[41] Judy A. Benjamin and Lynn Murchison, *Gender-Based Violence: Care & Protection of Children in Emergencies: A Field Guide*, Save the Children, 2004, p. 3, http://resourcecentre.savethechildren.se/content/library/documents/gender-based-violence-care-protection-children-emergencies-field-guide, accessed 17 August 2011.

[42] Swarna Rajagopalan, 'Violence against Women and Security', InfoChange India, November 2008, http://infochangeindia.org/Governance/Security-for-All/Violence-against-women-and-security.html accessed 24 September 2010. See also Swarna Rajagopalan, 'Women and Security: In Search of a New Paradigm', in Farah Faizal and Swarna Rajagopalan (eds), *Women, Security, South Asia: A Clearing in the Thicket*, New Delhi: Sage Publications, 2005, pp. 11–88; 'Research, Policy, Reality: Women, Security, South Asia', in *Sustainable Development: Bridging the Research/Policy Gaps in Southern Contexts.*

In the traditional view, the state is the primary referent of security, and security is about keeping states safe from threats — mainly external but also internal. However, the threshold of the home and the workplace and the realm of interpersonal interactions are firmly outside the purview of 'security'. In the last 20 years, scholars and practitioners have begun to prise open the sealed box of the private sphere to admit that the private or personal are also political and that perhaps there is some relationship between violence in the private and public spheres. The willingness to impose one's will through the use of force is the same whether it is interpersonal and takes place within a home or workplace or whether it takes place in a military context. However, the idea that gender violence is a security issue is still not mainstream unless the violence occurs in the public sphere of state institutions or during a conflict.

Gender violence is insecurity; the perpetrators are individuals and the victims are individuals but the context is social. Although data collection in this area is far from perfect, the statistics available still point unmistakably to acute insecurity.

(a) A commonly cited statistic of unknown provenance states that one in three women has experienced physical violence. Applied to the population of India, that means that out of 496,514,346 Indian women,[43] around 165,504,782 have experienced violence in some way. This is a larger number than the projected population of Australia: 22,444,581.[44]

Volume 2: Social Policy, Sustainable Development Policy Institute, Oxford: Oxford University Press, pp. 80-97, 2005, http://www.swarnar.com/sdc03.pdf, accessed 15 September 2010; 'Conceptualizing Security, Securing Women', 'National Seminar on Challenges to Peace and Security in South Asia: Emerging Trends', Chennai: Department of Defence Studies, University of Madras, 19 February 2004, http://www.swarnar.com/securingwomen0204. pdf, accessed 15 September 2010.

[43] Census of India, India at a Glance: Population, http://www.censusindia.gov. in/Census_Data_2001/India_at_glance/popu1.aspx, accessed 1 September 2010. These are 2001 census figures.

[44] Australian Bureau of Statistics, Australian Population Clock, http://www. abs.gov.au/, accessed 1 September 2010.

(b) Amartya Sen wrote in 1992 about 37 million missing women.[45] By this time in 2010, we may safely and conservatively assume the number is closer to 45 million, especially because we are told that 3 million female foetuses are aborted every year in India. This is the rough equivalent of the population of countries like Ukraine and Colombia.[46]

(c) 56.5 per cent of Indian women between 20–49 years were married by the age of 18;[47] of these, 66.9 per cent experienced domestic violence.[48] The experience of violence by 67 per cent of any other population group would be an unacceptable state of affairs.

The first argument for regarding gender violence as a security issue is that the most basic component of insecurity is the threat of physical harm. As Kalpana Kannabiran writes:

> It is within the realm of the normal, the routine, that violence against women is deeply embedded, and it is because the greatest part of violence against women is the violence of normal times that it carries with it the guarantee of impunity irrespective of penal, punitive or constitutional safeguards.[49]

Writing about a strong correlation between female deficit and crime — not just crimes against women — Jean Drèze and Reetika Khera suggest that 'low female-male ratios and high murder rates are simply two manifestations of a patriarchal environment:

---

[45] Amartya Sen, 'Missing Women—Revisited: Reduction in Female Mortality has been Counterbalanced by Sex Selective Abortions', *British Medical Journal*, 327, December 2003, pp. 1297–1298.

[46] Population—Country Comparison, Index Mundi, http://www.indexmundi.com/g/r.aspx, accessed 1 September 2010.

[47] UNICEF, 'Table 7: Child Marriage, Domestic Violence and Choice of Partner, Early Marriage: A Harmful Traditional Practice', 2005, p. 40, http://www.unicef.org/publications/files/Early_Marriage_12.lo.pdf, accessed 1 September 2010.

[48] UNICEF, 'Early Marriage: A Harmful Traditional Practice', 2005, p. 22, http://www.unicef.org/publications/files/Early_Marriage_12.lo.pdf, accessed 1 September 2010.

[49] Kalpana Kannabiran, 'Introduction', in Kalpana Kannabiran (ed.), *The Violence of Normal Times*, New Delhi: Women Unlimited, 2005, p. 3.

patriarchal values and practices manifest themselves both in high levels of violence and in a strong preference for male children (leading, in turn, to low female-male ratios)'.[50]

Unbalanced sex ratios have disastrous long-term security consequences. Valerie M. Hudson and Andrea Den Boer's comparative historical research has showed that in periods when males far outnumber females in a society, levels of violence rise dramatically. Skewed sex ratios are their focus, but when they talk about passive and active killing of girl children, we could extend that to include lifelong negligence and vulnerability to violence.[51] We know already from demographic changes in the last two decades that violence against women rises as the number of women declines; low sex ratio states in India have seen forced polyandry, trafficking, sale and purchase of women, honour killings, and declining safety in public spaces. Hudson and Den Boer estimate that there will be around 30 million 'surplus men' (those for whom wives cannot be found because of the female deficit) each in India and China by 2020.[52] Young men, unable to afford a bride in a situation where women are scarce, unable to marry, having poor ritual and social status in societies structured around marriage and matrimonial kinship, are easily drawn to what in India is termed 'anti-social' activities. In our time, they could be easy prey for gangs and militant groups.

Research has shown that children who witness violence in the home accept it as normal; boys grow up to be violent[53] and girls grow up expecting violence.[54] When we overlay the impact of an imbalanced sex ratio on this research insight, it is evident

---

[50] Jean Drèze and Reetika Khera, 'Crime, Gender, and Society in India: Insights from Homicide Data', *Population and Development Review*, 26 (2), June 2000, pp. 345–46 http://www.jstor.org/stable/172520 accessed 16 November 2009.

[51] Valerie M. Hudson and Andrea Den Boer, 'A Surplus of Men, A Deficit of Peace', *International Security*, 26 (4), Spring 2002, p. 5.

[52] Ibid., p. 11.

[53] National Coalition against Domestic Violence, Factsheet on Domestic Violence, 2007, http://www.ncadv.org/files/DomesticViolenceFactSheet%28National%29.pdf, accessed 2 September 2010.

[54] UNICEF Innocenti Research Centre, Domestic Violence against Women and Girls, Innocenti Digest No. 6, June 2000, p. 12, http://www.unicef-irc.org/publications/pdf/digest6e.pdf, accessed 2 September 2010.

the deliberate killing of female infants and female foetuses is harbinger of a society desensitised to the pathology that is violence.

Gender violence has unmistakable consequences for the livelihood security of individuals. For women, across time and place, the threat of gender violence has been met with restrictions on the mobility of women and girls. Schooling stops with puberty, women are not allowed to leave the house to seek employment, and every night brings them curfew. Without access to education, those women who must earn their living are doomed to unskilled, low-paid, and usually informal labour. Those who cannot go out to earn their living are doomed to dependence on men, and greater vulnerability within the so-called safe haven that is the home. Economic independence does not guarantee immunity from violence; but economic dependence definitely increases vulnerability to it.

The discourse of 'protection' arises from the threat of violence, but this protective blanket can have a jagged inner lining. Protector turns predator; child sexual abuse, domestic violence, rape (including date rape, marital rape, and custodial rape), and elder abuse are violence perpetrated by someone the victim knows and trusts, often someone expected to protect them. The culture of protection is also the culture of silence. Depending economically and materially on the abuser who is regarded as protector by the community makes it impossible for those who are powerless to openly say they have been abused. The threat of gender violence becomes a self-fulfilling prophecy.

'Protection' of women comes to be equated with 'protection' of community, especially community honour. This, in turn, exposes individuals to two dangers. First, individuals, male or female, are killed in order to avenge perceived slights to the honour of a community. Contentiously labelled 'honour killings', practices in the name of honour go beyond execution to abduction, rape, public humiliation, and battery. The second danger is that of sexual violence in times of conflict, especially inter-communal conflict. By the logic that creates violent 'protection' practices for women's bodies because the honour of a community is identified with them, sexual violence becomes the weapon that cuts deepest when a community is to be dishonoured and disgraced. Like the 'violence of normal times', sexual violence in times of communal conflict has also mostly gone unpunished — although it is good to note that it is no longer overlooked.[55]

Gender Violence, Development, and Modernity

One of the most common responses in a discussion of gender violence is that the education and economic empowerment of women will eliminate or at least dramatically reduce the threat of gender-based violence against them. Tragically, this is not true. NFHS 3 showed that the prevalence of domestic violence is not very different between couples in which the husband is better educated than the wife (36 per cent) and couples in which the wife is better educated (32 per cent).[56] The same research found that women who go out to work were more likely to have experienced violence (39–40 per cent) than those who did not go out to work (29 per cent).[57]

Male child preference is one of the most commonplace expressions of patriarchy. The reasons for male child preference are many.[58] Hindus, for instance, express the desire to have at least one son in terms of funeral rituals: 'I need someone to light my funeral pyre.' More common in academics are materialist explanations that typically have three aspects. The first is that sons fulfil the need for a particular kind of labour.[59] For instance, among communities with fighting traditions, sons were needed to defend the community's honour and properties. Similarly, agricultural communities have always seen sons as labour assets.

---

[55] For a stomach-churning account of gender violence, especially sexual violence, during the 2002 Gujarat riots, read Syeda S. Hameed, 'Sexual Abuse in Revenge: Women as Targets of Communal Hatred', in Kalpana Kannabiran (ed.), *The Violence of Normal Times*, New Delhi: Women Unlimited, 2005, pp. 312–31.

[56] National Family Health Survey 3, 'Chapter 15: Domestic Violence', 2006, p. 512, http://www.nfhsindia.org/NFHS-3%20Data/VOL-1/Chapter%2015% 20-%20Domestic%20Violence%20(468K).pdf, accessed 24 September 2010.

[57] Ibid., p. 499.

[58] For an overview of commonly cited explanations, see Veena Talwar Oldenburg, *Dowry Murder: The Imperial Origins of a Cultural Crime*, Oxford: Oxford University Press, 2002.

[59] Madhu Gurung, 'Female Foeticide', 1999, pp. 13–14, http://www. cwds.ac.in/Library/.../elib/foeticide/fo_female_foeticide.pdf, accessed 25 September 2010.

The second aspect relates to inheritance and property rights.[60] Muslim women have always had the right to inherit familial property, but other Indian women have won that right through law only recently. Gifts or legacies to women are seen in the context of patrilineal families as alienating family property; daughters thus shrink the family estate, such as it might be.

The spread of the practice of giving and taking dowry constitutes the third aspect of the materialist analysis of male child preference. Indeed, the most common explanation for female infanticide and sex-selective abortion is that daughters are an economic drain and dowry is the most important factor for the spread of infanticide. Dowry is now demanded and given even in communities which gave bride price or followed other wedding traditions, and it is given on more occasions than the wedding; festivals and other life-cycle rituals are also opportunities for making dowry demands. In 2003, the All-India Democratic Women's Association published a report, 'Expanding Dimensions of Dowry', according to which dowry demands are not expanding to new communities and regions but across the lifespan of a marriage.[61]

> 'Look at her,' one of the young men interjected. 'If she has one more girl what will she do? Think of all the expenses. Think of the clothes she will have to buy, the jewellery she will have to make. Think of the coming of age ceremony she will have to perform, the *varadatchinai* and *seer varisai* she will have to give. Where do you think the money will come from? One girl is bad enough ...'[62]

---

[60] V. Geetha, *Patriarchy*, Calcutta: Stree, 2007, pp. 83–84; papers by Nirmala Banerjee, Padmini Swaminathan, and Karin Kapadia in Karin Kapadia, (ed.), *The Violence of Development: The Politics of Identity, Gender & Social Inequalities in India*, New Delhi: Kali for Women (2002)/Zubaan (2006), New Delhi.

[61] The AIDWA report is not available in the public domain on the Internet. See 'New Report Shows Rise in Dowry Cases in India's Progressive States', InfoChange India, 2 August 2003, http://infochangeindia.org/200309062894/Women/News/New-report-shows-rise-in-dowry-cases-in-India-s-progressive-states.html, accessed 26 September 2010; Jagori, 'Marching Together ... Resisting Dowry in India', July 2009, p. 3, http://www.jagori.org/wp-content/uploads/2009/07/dowry_infopack.pdf, accessed 26 September 2010.

[62] Gita Aravamudan, *Disappearing Daughters*, p. 10.

The value of a woman goes down every time the value of gold
goes up...Who does this gold benefit?[63]

The policy-relevant questions here are what the nature of
the modernisation process and development choices have been
that facilitate or perpetuate these material conditions.

Studies of the Kallar community whose practice of female
infanticide first brought to light the recent southward spread of
this practice, relate this spread to the changed political economic
circumstances in which the community finds itself.[64] Living in
the arid zone, the Kallars have a history of working as mercenary
soldiers and highway robbers. Early studies described the community as matrilineal, practising cross-cousin marriages and
bride price. Women controlled the economic resources of the
household and the community. In the 1950s–1960s, both dowry
and bride price came to be practised,[65] and by the late 1980s, the
transformation had taken root.

With the construction of Vaigai dam, the community's for-
tunes changed in the same ways that the Green Revolution
changed Punjab. The gap between those positioned to benefit
from the dam and those who were rendered landless grew, as
the former diversified their activities and moved out of the area.
Correspondingly, the status of women was diminished. Those
who were displaced from their land ended up working as wage
labour. Moreover, migration and upward mobility introduced
new practices like dowry and ostentatious wedding ceremonies
into the community. It has been held that there is 'a correlation
between the rise of this practice [dowry] and women's loss of
traditional rights in land, their displacement and discrimination
in the labour market, the destruction of traditional handicrafts
that employed women, and their marginalisation in the new
economy'.[66] A strengthening of male child preference followed,
and female infanticide became commonplace.

---

[63] Ibid., p. 17.

[64] For a summary of several key studies see Vina Mazumdar, 'Amniocentesis
and Sex Selection', Occasional Paper, Centre for Women's Development
Studies, 1994, pp. 12–13, http://www.cwds.ac.in/OCPaper/Amniocentesis
VM.pdf, accessed 26 September 2010.

[65] Ibid.

[66] Ibid. Mazumdar is actually quoting a mimeographed study by V. Vasanthi
Devi which could not be found in the public domain on the Internet.

Feminist economists have documented how Indian women have fared in the decades of planned development. Nirmala Banerjee points out that they enter the wage-labour market with many disadvantages.[67] Literacy among Indian women is very low, notwithstanding nationwide literacy missions. This means they are not competitive in the better-paid sectors of the economy, and are confined to the low-paying, low-skill jobs. Second, Banerjee says that the reluctance to let unmarried girls enter the labour market means that most Indian women enter the labour force in their 20s. The pressure to get girls married early means that by the time they are in their 20s, most of these women are married and likely have children. Attendant responsibilities limit their hours of work and their mobility. Ironically, women's diminished livelihood prospects make marriage more important to their parents' planning of their future, even as the same prospects weaken their prospects in the marriage market.

Men too face challenges in this changed, mostly unstable, livelihood environment. Banerjee states bluntly: '... since marriage is the one career where men are in demand and in a position to dictate terms, they have started to use it to improve their lifetime income prospects by demanding a dowry'.[68] Marriage and dowry improve men's life chances, but diminish those of women and of families with many daughters. Gender differences are overlaid with class differences; women with access to education and women whose parents can afford a match with men who have stable livelihood prospects do considerably better than their counterparts who have neither. But the assumption that education and wage labour will emancipate women is misplaced, as Padmini Swaminathan shows.[69] They do not compensate for the structural disadvantages of caste and gender which, in fact, limit access to both and undermine their potential.

---

[67] Nirmala Banerjee, 'Between the Devil and the Deep Sea: Shrinking Options for Women in Contemporary India', in Karin Kapadia (ed.), *The Violence of Development: The Politics of Identity, Gender & Social Inequalities in India*, New Delhi: Kali for Women (2002)/Zubaan (2006), pp. 52–54.

[68] Ibid., p. 57.

[69] Padmini Swaminathan, 'The Violence of Gender-Biased Development: Going Beyond Social and Demographic Indicators', in Karin Kapadia (ed.), *The Violence of Development: The Politics of Identity, Gender & Social Inequalities in India*, New Delhi: Kali for Women (2002)/Zubaan (2006), pp. 69–141.

Even if more women go out to work, it is not necessarily intrinsically a positive thing. Research among workers in the Madras Export Processing Zone suggested that the strain of work at home, getting to their workplace, working conditions (from harassment to lack of toilets to exposure to dust and chemicals), and the ever present threat of violence and humiliation in fact may mitigate the empowering impact of having an income. Moreover, women are hired for short periods, without a contract and not retained beyond that point. The way these enterprises function, not only are workers not able to mobilise and act collectively for better conditions, their existence is barely registered in the companies' books.[70]

The gendered impact of development as it has unfolded has largely elevated the status and expanded the opportunities of men and diminished the status of women and shrunk the universe that is open to women. Upward mobility. for men has led to the imitation of customs like dowry and consumption practices that have traditionally contributed to women's vulnerabilities.[71] A very small number of privileged women benefit from development and economic growth, but they too benefit less than men in their class.

Devotion to the idea of modernity may actually be one reason why there have been concerted efforts to act against female infanticide while the campaign against sex-selective abortion has barely made a dent against the practice. Female infanticide is easily labelled as primitive, traditional, primeval, and anachronistic. The crude methods used to kill female infants underscore this portrayal. To document female infanticide has, in fact, been to contrast it with the standpoint and objective of 'civilisation', modernity, and development. Female foeticide, on the other hand, is the offspring of development and the advancement

---

[70] Padmini Swaminathan, 'The Trauma of "Wage Employment" and the "Burden of Work" for Women in India', in Kalpana Kannabiran (ed.), *The Violence of Normal Times*, New Delhi: Women Unlimited, 2005, pp. 83–121.

[71] Karin Kapadia, 'Translocal Modernities and Transformations of Gender and Caste', in idem (ed.), *The Violence of Development: The Politics of Identity, Gender & Social Inequalities in India*, New Delhi: Kali for Women (2002)/ Zubaan (2006), pp. 142–82.

of diagnostic technology. The ability to access sex-selective conception and abortion and the accessibility of the technology even in India's rural hinterland are signs of prosperity and development even though their impact is anything but positive or progressive.

Both female infanticide and sex-selective abortion are gender violence and murder. The practice of female infanticide has been localised, and this is one reason why organised campaigning and action against it have been possible. Sex-selective abortion is admittedly harder to detect; but difficult is not impossible. The muted, somewhat scattered mobilisation against the latter may have to do more with the coding of the technology, the practitioner, and the conditions of access with 'modernity'. Machines, doctors (as opposed to village midwives), clinics (as opposed to home births and executions), and travelling clinics are appurtenances of 'modernity'. The lethal patriarchal preference for male children is at the root of killing of infants and abortion of foetuses, but it is not patriarchy that is offensive to state and society — it is the absence of 'modernity'. That is what one must conclude.

The well-intentioned 'costs-of-domestic-violence' approach seems to equate development with growth. The American Centre for Disease Control identifies two components to this cost — direct and indirect. Direct costs are actual healthcare, and judicial and social service costs incurred by society. Indirect costs include productivity losses from both paid and unpaid work and lost lifetime savings for women who succumb to violence.[72] The challenge is to take into account the social costs of gender violence. In fact, a World Bank paper on the subject concludes:

> ... there is a need for more studies on the economic costs of regionally-specific types of GBV such as female genital mutilation, dowry violence and incest, in order to position this issue as what it is: not only a woman's issue, a public health issue and a human

---

[72] Andrew R. Morrison and Maria Beatriz Orlando, 'The Costs and Impacts of Gender-based Violence in Developing Countries: Methodological Considerations and New Evidence', Working Paper 36151, World Bank, November 2004, p. 7, http://siteresources.worldbank.org/INTGENDER/Resources/costsandimpactsofgbv.pdf, accessed 25 September 2010.

rights issue, but also as an issue affecting poverty, development and economic growth.[73]

The 'costs-of-domestic-violence' approach may be characterised as being to the development discourse as securitisation is to the security discourse — a way of framing the issue so that it becomes a policy priority.

Gender Violence and Democratic Governance

The word 'governance' gained currency in the 1980s and 1990s, mainly in development, technocratic, donor, and policy discourse. Its usage was promoted, among other things, by the guidelines and grant-making priorities of international donor organisations which supported 'governance'-related projects around the world.[74] Governance is the work of government — making and implementing policy and creating conditions for constitutional and policy objectives to be reached. Governance refers both to the state as it carries out its mandate in response to the changing world around it and to a 'conceptual or theoretical representation of co-ordination of social systems, and for the most part, the role of the state in that process'.[75]

Good governance consisted in efficiency and efficacy, or being able to plan and deliver as promised. While a World Bank study defined good governance in terms of 'sound development management',[76] the UNDP understanding of governance was

---

[73] Ibid.

[74] For instance, the Ford Foundation funded an important multi-country project in South Asia called 'Problems of Governance in South Asia' in the late 1980s–early 1990s. The studies were undertaken by country scholars and reflected their individual disciplinary and political concerns rather than using a single framework.

[75] Jon Pierre, 'Understanding Governance', in Jon Pierre (ed.), *Debating Governance*, Oxford and New York: Oxford University Press, 2000, p. 3, http://books.google.co.in/, accessed 3 April 2010.

[76] World Bank, *Governance and Development*, 1992, page 1, http://books.google.co.in/books?id = he3-MVQqsqwC&printsec = frontcover&dq = World + Bank + (1992) + Governance + and + Development.&source = bl&ots = rUCYGRwj vc&sig = 69AX0VGnryck-TU7vArkU7VpRbE&hl = en&ei = bVqxTLPFLcXJcY SumYYH&sa = X&oi = book_result&ct = result&resnum = 8&ved = 0CC0Q6A EwBw#v = onepage&q = World%20Bank%20(1992)%20Governance%20and %20Development.&f = false accessed 10 October 2010.

mediated by the concept of human development that was first articulated and applied in its annual reports. An oft quoted UNDP paper identifies state, private sector and civil society as three domains of governance, which it defines thus: '... the exercise of political, economic and administrative authority to manage a nation's affairs. It is the complex mechanisms, processes, relationships and institutions through which citizens and groups articulate their interests, exercise their rights and mediate their differences'.[77]

From 'good governance', the emphasis has now shifted to 'democratic governance', whose twin emphases are identified as participation and accountability.[78] What is democratic governance? The idea of democratic governance is a hybrid of rule of law and rationality, inclusivity and efficacy, responsiveness and efficiency. The 2002 UNDP Human Development Report identified nine normative elements of democratic governance:

> People's human rights and fundamental freedoms are respected, allowing them to live with dignity.

- People have a say in decisions that affect their lives.
- People can hold decision-makers accountable.

---

[77] United Nations Development Programme, 'Preface', *Reconceptualising Governance,* Discussion Paper 2, New York: Management Development and Governance Division, Bureau for Policy and Programme Support, January 1997, p. x, http://mirror.undp.org/magnet/Docs/!UN98-21.PDF/!RECONCE. PTU/!front.pdf accessed 10 October 2010.

[78] UNDP, 'A Guide to UNDP Democratic Governance Practice', p. 16, http://content.undp.org/go/cms-service/download/publication/?version=live&id=2551865, accessed 10 October 2010. On pp. 14–15, the guide offers the following definitions: '... governance is defined as comprising the mechanisms, processes and institutions that determine how power is exercised, how decisions are made on issues of public concern, and how citizens articulate their interests, exercise their legal rights, meet their obligations and mediate their differences ...' (And democratic governance ...) 'requires efficient institutions and an economic and political environment that renders public services effective and makes economic growth possible; at the same time, DG for human development must be concerned with whether institutions and rules are fair and accountable, whether they protect human rights and political freedoms, and whether all people have a say in how they operate.'

- Inclusive and fair rules, institutions and practices govern social interactions.
- Women are equal partners with men in private and public spheres of life and decision-making.
- People are free from discrimination based on race, ethnicity, class, gender or any other attribute.
- The needs of future generations are reflected in current policies.
- Economic and social policies are responsive to people's needs and aspirations.
- Economic and social policies aim at eradicating poverty and expanding the choices that all people have in their lives.[79]

Constitutive elements of the *process* of democratic governance as well: participatory decision making; accountability; inclusivity; fair play; gender equality; non-discrimination; sustainability; and responsiveness. While the onus of democratic governance primarily rests with the state apparatus, democratic governance by definition depends on the participation of society at large.[80]

The third Millennium Development Goal is 'Gender Equality and Women's Empowerment', and it offers the point of entry

---

[79] UNDP, 'Human Development Report: Deepening Democracy in a Fragmented World', 2002, p. 51, http://hdr.undp.org/en/media/HDR_2002_EN_Complete.pdf, accessed 4 April 2010.

[80] The influence of Amartya Sen's definition of development in terms of freedom, where freedom is both means and ends, is clear in the UNDP view, which in turn has been extremely influential. But the legacy of the 1960s thinking about political development is also there in the idea that democratic institutions must be strengthened 'so that they keep pace with the changing distribution of economic and political power' (UNDP, Human Development Report: Deepening Democracy in a Fragmented World', p. 61). Samuel P. Huntington's *Political Order in Changing Societies* (New Haven: Yale University Press, 1968), for instance, argued that it was the lag between economic development and subsequent political mobilisation around rising expectations on the one hand and institutional capacity to absorb and respond to this mobilisation and these expectations that led to what for him was the worst outcome: political instability. In fact, two key lessons identified by recent research on democratic governance in Latin America is that 'effective states' and 'institutionalized party systems' make a positive difference to the ability to consolidate democratic governance (Scott Mainwaring and Timothy R. Scully, 'Latin America: Eight Lessons for Governance', *Journal of Democracy*, 19 (3), July 2008, pp. 116–20.

for engendering development and governance.[81] Much of the work relating gender to governance is focused on the issue of participation: how much women participate in the democratic process, how responsive governance is to women's needs, and what the barriers are to participation as full citizens.[82] This reflects an assumption that the greater inclusion of women in politics and policy making is not just an intrinsic good but also instrumental one; more women will make for more gender-sensitive policy. Seema Kazi writes:

> If *democratic* governance is to be realised in *practice*, it should combine institutional accountability and transparency with the incorporation of policy measures that address the empirical fact of gender inequality. Gender equality is an integral aspect of struggles for social justice. States' record of governance must accordingly be assessed in terms of advancing *in practice* the inter-related goals of social justice and gender equality.[83] (Emphasis in original)

Any consideration of democratic governance that focuses on participation and justice but not on the pervasive reality of gender violence is incomplete. Gender violence puts a ceiling on full citizenship and enjoyment of inalienable human rights. The experience of gender violence transcends the threshold that stands between women's full engagement with the public sphere on the one hand and the public sphere's engagement with the politics of the home and relationships. The threat of gender violence stops women, in particular, from being active in the public sphere.

---

[81] Noeleen Heyzer, 'Globalization and Democratic Governance: A Gender Perspective', background paper for '4th Global Forum on Reinventing Government', 2002, unpan1.un.org/intradoc/groups/public/documents/un/unpan006228.pdf, accessed 10 October 2010.

[82] See, for instance, Yasmin Tambiah (ed.), *Women & Governance in South Asia: Re-imagining the State*, Colombo: International Centre for Ethnic Studies, 2002. Also, IDRC, 'Democratic Governance, Women's Rights and Gender Equality: Synthesis Report', 2010, draws on eight commissioned papers to focus on inclusivity and participation.

[83] Seema Kazi, 'Democratic Governance and Women's Rights in South Asia', IDRC, 2010, p. 10.

The reach of state and society stop short of the threshold of the home, declaring violence within the home beyond the jurisdiction of the state and the interventions of society. Martha Nussbaum points out that where the attempt to gain and press advantage is considered 'dangerous and inappropriate' in the public sphere, the head of the household is granted privilege and authority that is unavailable to other members.[84] She points out that while law in fact dictates and regulates private matters — from age of marriage to sexuality to adoption — it also perpetuates the 'public–private' distinction in other ways, such as recognising rape outside the home as sexual violence but often treating marital rape as beyond its jurisdiction.[85]

If gender equality is a defining concern of democratic governance, then a gender audit of governance practices must prioritise responses to the prevalence of violence — against women, men, girls, boys, and sexual/sexuality minorities. To what extent does 'gender violence' figure in the actual programmes and projects of a government? And if we extend the domains of governance to include civil society and the private sector, then to what extent does it figure in the collective conscience of a society?

The modern history of the state–society interface in India may actually be said to begin with the colonial state's attempt to legally abolish sati and child marriage.[86] Independent India built the idea of gender justice into its constitution in the form of Article 15 which prohibits discrimination on many grounds, including sex. Post-independence India has tried to legislate away many iniquitous practices from dowry to rape.[87] A controversial

---

[84] Martha Nussbaum, 'Gender and Governance: An Introduction', in Martha Nussbaum, Amrita Basu, Yasmin Tambiah, and Niraja Gopal Jayal, *Essays on Gender and Governance*, Human Development Resource Centre UNDP, 2003, p. 6.

[85] Ibid., pp. 8–10.

[86] The abolition of sati, 1829; the Child Marriage Restraint Act, 1929 (also known as the Sarda Act).

[87] Dowry Prohibition Act, 1961; Dowry Prohibition (Maintenance of Lists of Presents to the Bride and Bridegroom) Rules, 1985; Indecent Representation of Women (Prohibition) Act, 1986; Commission of Sati (Prevention) Act, 1987; Pre-Natal Diagnostic Techniques (Regulation and Prevention of Misuse) Act, 1994; Pre-Natal Diagnostic Techniques (Regulation and Prevention of Misuse) Rules, 1996; Protection of Women from Domestic Violence Act, 2005; Protection of Women against Sexual Harassment at Work Place Bill, 2007.

attempt to reform through codification the secular practices of the Hindu community was made in the early years after independence. This culminated in the passage of four bills: the Hindu Marriage Act, 1955; Hindu Succession Act, 1956; Hindu Adoptions and Maintenance Act, 1956; and Hindu Minority and Guardianship Act, 1956.

The reform by law of Hindu practices reflects the contrary impulses of liberalism in general — on the one hand, there is a commitment to reform whether the motivation is modernity or human rights or justice; on the other hand, there is a hesitation to intervene in the practices of the 'other' born of cultural relativism. Reform is most contentious — we might even say only — when it involves women, their bodies, family relationships, and the household. This means that of all the areas in which a state might intervene, these are the most difficult — red herrings, even, distracting attention from the problem this is an attempt to address. In 2005, when Imrana was raped by her father-in-law, many aspects of her case became controversial — who would see that she got justice, what the basis of that justice would be, and the response of the larger community.[88] Imrana's gender, communal and, arguably, class identity undermined her right to justice in the first instance.

The other problem is that laws need enforcement. While the community might agree in principle that gender violence, especially sexual violence, is undesirable, this agreement is based on two assumptions: that violence happens to others and that which one experiences (as perpetrator or victim) is not violence. The reach of the state stops here; the best-intentioned police personnel, lawyers, or social workers cannot act unless victims identify abuse as violence and unjustified. This is where the other domain of governance becomes important — civil society.

Furthermore, those who are tasked with law enforcement often share the very values that make violence seem acceptable to its perpetrators and victims. The inclination to counsel patience, 'adjustment', and conciliation follow from these values, where

---

Links to the text of many of these laws can be accessed at http://wcd.nic.in/wcdact.htm, accessed 15 September 2010.

[88] For more information on this case, see 'Chaitanya Guide 3: Imrana's Gauntlet', August 2005, http://www.chaitanyaconsult.in/chaitanya/guide/cg3gauntlet.htm, accessed 15 September 2010.

the victim of violence is also given some responsibility for their condition. In Imrana's case and countless other cases, it is a value system that suggests the victim marry the rapist as compensation for having suffered violence. The loss of chastity and honour and destroyed matrimonial prospects are more important than the victim's trauma after violence. Similarly, domestic violence victims are counselled to think of the family.

Moreover, because the line between victim and offender, immediate perpetrator and structural injustice is murky in instances of gender violence like female infanticide, it is hard to identify a course of action that will yield the immediate return of saving lives as well as the long-term consequence of social justice without miscarriage of justice, as well as meet the standards of transparency and accountability that democracy requires. Arrests made on charges of female infanticide ended up victimising the person with the least decision-making autonomy — usually, the mother of the dead infant. Whether it is the CBS or GCPS or the workings of the law-and-order system, the way it works ends up discriminating against the most defenceless.

In India, violence has been an important issue for the women's movement from the 1980s onwards. Unjust decisions in rape cases, spiralling reports of dowry-related deaths, and the use of diagnostic techniques for sex-selective abortions were rallying points for women across the political spectrum. Faith in the foundations of the political system lent a legalistic orientation to the demands made by women's organisations for new laws and prohibitions. Less attention has generally been paid to creating support systems for survivors and to raising social consciousness against the underlying causes of gender violence.

The Tamil Nadu campaign against female infanticide holds interesting insights into the relationship between gender violence and democratic governance. First of all, it is clear that on the part of the state, notwithstanding a sympathetic statutory and ideological climate, swift, creative action depended on the initiative of individual administrators. Second, when the state did introduce measures it imagined were remedial, there seems to have been no anticipation of consequences. The implicit endorsement of male child preference in the CBS illustrates this.

In fact, the various interventions that made up the campaign against female infanticide did not necessarily reflect the ideal of gender equality. The DANIDA, ICCW, and MSSW interventions tried to create an attitudinal shift, but the CBS and the GCPS inadvertently reinforced male child preference. There is no public education programme that addresses discrimination or prejudice. There does not seem to have been any official evaluation of the scheme either. From this, it is tempting to speculate that the motivation for the introduction of such schemes arose from impulses closer to populism or a wish to be seen doing the right thing, than a profound commitment to gender justice.

The government has also been unresponsive to the changing nature of the problem: that infanticide is being replaced by foeticide as the 'weapon' of choice. All of these interventions have barely made a dent in the patriarchal preference for male children. With a battery of laws in place, there are still few arrests or prosecutions and virtually no reliable data.

The role that civil society has played has been more consistent, if less effective. Organisations and individuals who first got involved with the campaign against infanticide have remained engaged with this issue for the most part. Their effectiveness is limited though without the infrastructural power of the state. Apart from the CASSA, most civil society programmes were most active during the 1990s when concerned district administrations were looking for entry points for lasting change.

The DANIDA, ICCW, and MSSW interventions were designed to engage members of the community in a conversation about their lives. They did not directly take on the practice but placed it in a broader context of outreach to the community. Their work had a ripple effect, engaging more and more people. It was also inclusive, and to be fair, so is the GCPS — it has two fairly generic requirements. However, it is a fact that the CBS and GCPS were not the product of a consultative process, nor were consultations held to consider their effectiveness before extending them. Lack of resources, lack of commitment, and lack of imagination have variously limited the ability to follow up, to follow through, and to sustain any of these efforts beyond a point. The DANIDA and MSSW projects were well-documented but seem to be short-lived. The CBS was created without an adequate budget for special child-care providers.

The governance gap also manifests as a data gap. Indeed, documentation and data collection are in general low priorities, locking programming into decision-making based on anecdotal evidence or popular pressure in the moment. The VES plugged this gap briefly but seems to have become infrequent, and it is possible it has even been abandoned. NGOs do not have the funding, but the state government could have sustained the district-level VES. The quality of data collection is a reflection of the effectiveness of monitoring and documentation in a given situation. Almost a quarter century after the first *India Today* story broke, the fact that documentation on female infanticide is still limited might point to apathy, callousness, or both underlying the rhetoric on saving the girl child.

The government could also have made it mandatory both to keep records about babies abandoned in the receiving centres, as well as to keep track of adoptions. Right now, thousands of girl children have more or less disappeared without a trace into the abyss of an uncaring system. Without trained and committed staff or any record keeping, there is no question of accountability. Parents have had a change of heart or wanted to ask about their children, but where is the information to give them?

Looking at democratic governance through the lens of gender violence, especially female infanticide, points to under-researched questions: Why has a rationalist, ostensibly progressive political elite not backed the campaign against infanticide and sex-selective abortion more firmly, consistently, and thoughtfully? In other words, does patriarchy trump other ideological concerns? Why have civil society organisations not networked even more effectively over a 25-year period, and why have existing networks not made a stronger impact? What would a gender violence audit, qualitative and quantitative, suggest about the gender sensitivity of governance mechanisms in Tamil Nadu?

Human Security + Human Development + Human Rights = Democratic Governance?

The discursive journeys in recent decades around 'security,' 'development', and 'democracy' have each culminated in a variation of that concept and an operationalisation of that value that places human beings at the centre of attention. The shift displaces the state but only enough to accommodate a wider variety of actors, and introduces a greater plurality of aspirations, resources, and strategies. The intersecting interface between human security, human development, and human rights opens up new, yet very old, intellectual agendas, and the laws, agents, and actions of states offer up texts for our consideration. A brief review of definitions is a useful point of departure for the analytical discussion to follow.

A summary definition of human security states that it is 'the idea that the individual is at the receiving end of all security concerns, whereby security is understood as freedom from want and/or freedom from fear'.[89] 'To protect the vital core of all human lives in ways that enhance human freedoms and human fulfilment' is how the Commission on Human Security defines it, adding detail that embraces virtually every aspect of life: 'protecting people from critical (severe) and pervasive (widespread) threats and situations'; 'using processes that build on people's strengths and aspirations'; 'creating political, social, environmental, economic, military and cultural systems that together give people the building blocks of survival, livelihood and dignity'.[90] Should there be any doubt on our part, the Commission states: 'Human security thus brings together the human elements of security, of rights, of development.'[91]

Anticipating this as early as 1994, the UNDP Human Development Report (HDR) cautioned against conflating human security with human development. Human development, it stated, was a broader concept, 'a process of widening the range of people's choices', while human security meant that 'people can exercise these choices safely and freely, and that they can be relatively confident that the opportunities they have today are not totally lost tomorrow'.[92]

If human development was going to widen people's choices, as we were told in successive HDRs, starting from 1990, then

[89] Rita Floyd, 'Human Security and the Copenhagen School's Securitization Approach: Conceptualizing Human Security as a Securitizing Move', *Human Security Journal*, 5, Winter 2007, p. 40.
[90] Commission on Human Security, *Human Security Now*, 2003, http://www.humansecurity-chs.org/finalreport/English/chapter1.pdf, accessed 3 January 2010, p. 4.
[91] Ibid.
[92] UNDP, 'Human Development Report: New Dimensions of Human Security', 1994, http://hdr.undp.org/en/media/hdr_1994_en_chap2.pdf, p. 23, accessed 10 February 2010.

the right to health and longevity, the right to education, and the right to a 'decent standard of living' were the three most essential areas for those choices.[93] As income is not the sole focus of people's lives, the first HDR argues, nor should it be that of development. Higher incomes do not lead automatically to the betterment of people's lives, and development should focus on making that connection stronger. The report acknowledges that 'political freedom, guaranteed human rights and self-respect' are also desirable choices, taking us into political territory.

Though the Millennium Development Goals (MDGs) list of more or less traditional socio-economic goals, there is a clear correlation between each of the MDG and human rights standards.[94] Achievement of the MDGs enables the enjoyment of human rights. Human rights guarantees also facilitate the achievement of the MDGs.

Although the Universal Declaration of Human Rights (UDHR) is 'universal' in its vision and in speaking to all UN member states, human rights violations continue to occur at the hands of state agents, non-state political actors, corporates, communities, families, and individuals. We have internalised the language of rights but hardly the behaviour. To states goes the major responsibility of guaranteeing human rights and protecting citizens from human rights violations. States are often the most egregious violators of citizens' rights, although far from being the only ones. Moreover, as we have seen, human rights guarantees extend well beyond political rights to economic, social, and cultural rights. The scope of this mandate is almost coterminous with the whole of the state's working agenda.

What is the 'human-rights approach'? A 2003 consultation of UN agencies arrived at three features of a human rights-based approach to programming.[95] First, all programmes should further

---

[93] UNDP, 'Human Development Report', 'Defining and Measuring Human Development', 1990, p. 10. http://hdr.undp.org/en/media/hdr_1990_en_chap1.pdf, accessed 10 February 2010.

[94] Oslo Governance Centre, UNDP, 'Human Rights and the MDGs: Making the Link', 2007, hurilink.org/Primer-HR-MDGs.pdf, accessed 3 April 2010, p. 11.

[95] United Nations Population Fund, The Human Rights-Based Approach http://www.unfpa.org/rights/approaches.htm, accessed 10 February 2010; United Nations, The Human Rights-Based Approach to Development

the UDHR. Second, human rights standards and principle should guide and inform all sectors and stages of programming and all development cooperation. These principles include: universality and inalienability; indivisibility; interdependence and inter-relatedness; equality and non-discrimination; participation and inclusion; accountability and rule of law. Finally, 'Development cooperation contributes to the development of the capacities of "duty-bearers" to meet their obligations and/or of "rights-holders" to claim their rights.'[96] In formulating this agreement, the UN system was following rather than leading global civil society organisations (and many academics), many of whom had long advocated human rights approaches to political and socio-economic problems.

So, 'Human Security + Human Development + Human rights = Democratic Governance'?

Atul Kohli, writing on the crisis of governance in India, states that '... a democratic developing country is well-governed if its government can simultaneously sustain legitimacy, promote socio-economic development, and maintain order without coercion'.[97] This foreshadows the idea of 'human security', which is generally attributed to the authors of the 1994 UNDP Human Development Report. '... not just security of their nations', '... not just security of territory', and '... not in the weapons of our country', wrote Mahbub Ul-Haq in 1994 of a new concept of human security whose referent would be 'people'.[98] The UNDP Report stated,

---

Cooperation: Towards a Common Understanding among the UN Agencies, 05/02/1969 http://www.crin.org/docs/resources/publications/hrbap/HR_common_understanding.doc, accessed 17 August 2011.

[96] http://www.crin.org/docs/resources/publications/hrbap/HR_common understanding.doc.

[97] Atul Kohli, 'Political Change in a Democratic Developing Country', in Niraja Gopal Jayal (ed.), *Democracy in India*, New Delhi: Oxford India Paperbacks, 2001, p. 129.

[98] Mahbub ul Haq, 'New Imperatives of Human Security', RGICS Paper No. 17, New Delhi: Rajiv Gandhi Institute for Contemporary Studies (RGICS), Rajiv Gandhi Foundation, 1994, p. 1, cited in Kanti Bajpai, *Human Security: Concept and Measurement*, Kroc Institute Occasional Paper #19:OP:1, August 2000, p. 11.

In the final analysis, human security is a child who did not die, a disease that did not spread, a job that was not cut, an ethnic tension that did not explode in violence, a dissident who was not silenced. Human security is not a concern with weapons — it is a concern with human life and dignity.[99]

Freedom from fear and freedom from want — phrases that entered this discourse from the despatch of the US representative at the San Francisco Conference — were identified as the two major components of human security.[100] The big distinction made both by the UNDP and by Canadian and Norwegian officials who took up the concept was that human security put people at the centre. Much of the early effort was to list all the threats that could be classified as 'human security' and they included drugs, HIV/AIDS, environmental degradation, and state repression.[101] The new idea of security thus extends to embrace many issues that were hitherto classified as 'development' or 'politics'. Democratic governance would seem to refer to the authoritative structures that enable human security.

The Security–Development–Democratic Governance Interface: Lessons Learnt

Gender violence is physical insecurity. Even where violence takes the form of verbal/psychological abuse or economic exploitation, the loss of human dignity is tantamount to physical harm. It has a complex relationship with material conditions. Power is at its root and economic difference is an important element of power; workplace sexual harassment exemplifies this but where dowry is seen as a substitute for inheritance, it is again the relationship between economics and power that is at play. Some kinds of gender violence become more common with economic growth

---

[99] UNDP, 'New Dimensions of Human Security', Human Development Report 1994, http://hdr.undp.org/en/media/hdr_1994_en_chap2.pdf, p. 22, accessed 10 February 2010.

[100] Ibid., p. 24.

[101] Kanti Bajpai's paper records all the various lists that were generated as a prelude to suggesting a way to conduct a human security audit.

and expansion of resources, income, and access to technology. The misuse of diagnostic technologies to opt for sex selection, for instance, has become more common as family incomes have risen; people prefer to leave cruder ways behind. The epidemic scale of gender violence also results in a loss of productivity across the economy, expenditure on medical treatment and, finally, loss of livelihood for victims. Gender violence concerns both state and society, but the state is limited by convention to responding to things that happen in public spaces and hard-pressed to actually intervene even when laws address private space and relationship violence. Civil society has no enforcement capability and is too resource-strapped to make its support available in a consistent way. Thus through this one lens, we gain insights on the ways in which security, development, and democratic governance are mutually intertwined.

Absolute positions are heard in debates on security, development, and democratic governance. Gender violence shows them to be impossible, and nothing illustrates this better than the challenge of punishing the perpetrators of female infanticide. The problem is security. The motivation is said to be dowry, expectation of which has come with development. It falls to the government to enforce the law and provide justice to the killed infant. But who should it arrest and prosecute: the mother, who cannot independently choose to use contraceptives, but stifles her daughter's birth; the family, whose values reflect those of society, but will prevail upon a mother to give up her daughter; society, as in neighbours, relatives, and the larger community, including people in law enforcement and public healthcare, who say: 'One more girl? How unfortunate!'? To not arrest the perpetrator would be a travesty of democratic governance, but to arrest a mother or a midwife could be a travesty of justice, if justice cannot take cognisance of their circumstances.

There is a symbiotic, if non-linear, relationship between security, development, and democratic governance. Insecurity is caused by the absence of change, the process of change, and also the consequences of change. Development is intended to remove some sources of insecurity and provide a better life for individuals and groups. It is the work of governance to promote development and create security. Development debates create their own challenges for governance which become security challenges. What is happening with the allocation of land for special economic zones everywhere illustrates this. The zones create jobs for a large number of people but they also displace farmers who must seek alternative livelihoods. The battle over Nandigram was one instance of this conflict; likewise, the construction of large irrigation projects. Governance failure is, therefore, development failure and a source of insecurity. By appending 'democratic' to governance, we add the expectation that the state will be responsive to emerging needs and demands. With each new shift in the socio-economic environment, new challenges and new sources of insecurity are born, and government agencies must read anew, interpret afresh, and review their responses and plans. There is nothing static about the security, development, and democratic governance interface, either conceptually or in practice.

This is amply illustrated by our case. Female infanticide existed in small pockets even a couple of hundred years ago. However, modernisation facilitated the spread of the practice in many ways — the loss of livelihood, the introduction of dowry, the reduced status of women. The right to life of baby girls was endangered even as sections of society were beginning to enjoy a more comfortable life. That governance was blind to the spread of this practice and did not notice the changes recorded in child sex ratio were signs of failure. But the state administration's willingness to act, in creative and collaborative ways, would mitigate its failure except for the fact that its commitment had not been sustained and that its policies and programmes had a hasty, populist, half-baked quality to them. It would seem that the GCPS and CBS were both introduced in a hurry and that the government has not felt the need to review and reform them. The absence of records underscores this impression, as does the superficiality of the government effort. The result is that civil society–state interventions against female infanticide have not had the impact they could have had.

At the end of this meandering exploration, we can say three things for certain. First, security, development, and democratic governance are indivisibly interlinked today, both by the ways in which we conceptualise them and the ways in which we experience them. Second, the agenda of democratic governance — engaging state and civil society — is security and sustainable development. Finally, both state and civil society are important for this agenda — creating security and insecurity, creating a better life for everyone. When the state acts alone, its impact is superficial and not sustained. When civil society groups act alone, their impact goes this far and no further; they cannot enforce change.

7

Rules of Governance in Developing Rural India*

Ratan Khasnabis

Introduction

The orientation of the pre-liberalised Indian economy was distinctly different from the present-day economy of India. The pre-liberalised Indian economy was a state-directed mixed economy. It is well known that the Indian Republic, under the leadership of Jawaharlal Nehru, adopted a policy in which the state was to play the pivotal role in the economy. The emphasis was on achieving economic growth by accelerating public investment in a mixed economy framework. This policy became more pronounced following the adoption of the Nehru–Mahalanobis heavy industry-oriented planning strategy. Parliamentary commitment to a socialistic pattern of society (1954) which was followed by the Industrial Policy Resolutions of 1956 largely shaped the course of development during the next three decades. As Indira Gandhi came to power, more radical steps including bank nationalisation were taken. That the state was to maintain the leading role was reinforced by adopting 'socialism' in the Directive Principles of State Policy in the Constitution of the Republic. In India, private right to property was no longer considered as a fundamental right.

Distributive justice was also a much talked about subject in this era. Economic development was expected to cover the poor and the underprivileged who had already been endowed with the right to choose the government in a federal setting. However, economic exclusion and marginalisation still ruled the roost. Poverty, particularly rural poverty, continued to have its sway. In the absence of adequate land reforms, rural inequality in asset

---

* The research assistance provided me by Abira Roy and Anusri Mahato is gratefully acknowledged. The usual disclaimer applies.

distribution could hardly be reduced. In urban India also, access to economic opportunities remained perversely distributed. No wonder that class conflict, which often appeared in the form of caste- and community-based contradictions, sharpened over time. Again, in course of time, privation-induced regionalism emerged as an important political force to reckon with.

The Indian state, which was basically the continuity of the British Indian state, did perform well in managing this complex situation. Apparently, the political authority was successful in formulating such rules of governance that would adapt to the emerging needs of the society. This was quite a challenging task particularly in a society in which the contradiction between economic democracy (market democracy) based on exclusion and inequity (in entitlement to market) and political democracy based on universal adult suffrage (i.e., no exclusion) was becoming sharper over time and there was a growing expectation that the state would play the role of a mitigator in resolving this contradiction. In hindsight, it appears that the Indian state performed remarkably well in meeting this challenge. How could it be achieved? The article plans to address this question.

The course of development that India has adopted since the introduction of the New Economic Policy is radically different from what had been there during Nehru–Indira era. State initiative has now been replaced with the initiative of private capital and the market which, with its twin features of exclusion and inequality, is being accepted as omnipotent in the economic life of the people. The rules of governance that the state used to follow, by carefully working out targeted policy measures so that the underprivileged could be included in the development process, are being undermined in the new dispensation as the factory and labour laws are being revised in favour of capital and protective measures for the small enterprises, agriculture, and unorganised workers are being withdrawn systematically. It appears that the notion of governance itself is changing under the new dispensation. What the state can do and cannot do is being renegotiated.

Issues related to governance are to be discussed in this general perspective. What were the rules of governance when India was following the state-centric development strategy? What was the role of the non-state (social) institutions in the scenario where state was assuming a bigger role in the economy and the expectation that the state can deliver was growing over time? How did the non-state institutions adjust with this changing scenario? Admittedly, the role of the state in economic development is being renegotiated in the post Nehru–Indira era. The market and not the state is gradually being accepted as the pivot of the economic life of the citizens of India. What then is the possible fall out of this renegotiation on state and non-state institutions of governance? The article seeks to answer these questions as well.

The focus of this study is, however, rural India. To be precise, our emphasis is on studying the process of evolution of the rules of governance with respect to rural India. This is so because, even if the importance of agriculture in the Gross Domestic Product (GDP) of the country is declining, about 70 per cent of Indians still earn their livelihood from agriculture and other informal sector activities in rural India.

Governance in Early Nehru Era

Rural India on the Eve of Independence

At the time of independence, rural India was basically peasants' India. Nearly 85 per cent of Indians lived in villages and agriculture and allied agricultural activities provided livelihood for about 67 per cent of the gainfully employed persons in India at that time.[1] Agricultural productivity was poor because the technology was poor and only about 16 per cent of the cropped area was then under irrigation. Rural India was poor; illiteracy was widespread and life expectancy at birth was very low even in late colonial India.[2]

Rural power at the time of independence was largely based on economic power wielded from land, the most important asset

---

[1] Census 1931. There was another census before independence. Held in 1941, the coverage of this census was not as wide as of Census 1931. The 1931 Census data is therefore considered to be more dependable for a study on the livelihood scenario in India on the eve of independence.

[2] A. Vaidyanathan, 'The Indian Economy since Independence (1947–70)', in Dharma Kumar (ed.), *Cambridge Economic History of India*, vol. II, Cambridge: Cambridge University Press, 1982, pp. 947–48.

in the then rural India. As Daniel Thorner points out,[3] there had been three broad social classes in rural India based on land at that time, namely, *malik*, *kishan*, and *mazdoor*. The difference among these social classes, as Thorner argues, was based on (a) type of income obtained from the soil (rent, fruits of own cultivation or wage); (b) nature of rights over soil (proprietary, tenancy with security, unsecured tenancy, or no legal rights at all); and (c) extent of work performed (owner operator, wage labour). Rent receivers were identified by Thorner as *malik*s. The operators were *kishan*s and the wage labourers were *majdoor*s. Such categorisation does not, however, help us understand the social reality of internal differences among the *kishan*s. In fact, Thorner's *kishan*s were further differentiated into three different categories, namely, 'rich', 'middle', and 'poor'. Based on types of income, nature of right, and extent of work performed, the agrarian classes in rural India were therefore broadly divided into five classes. With Indian specificities and wide regional variations, these five agrarian classes can be identified as landlord, rich peasant, middle peasant, poor peasant, and landless labourer.[4]

Among the gainfully employed persons who were engaged in agriculture, about 3 per cent had been rent receivers. Agricultural labourers accounted for 31 per cent of 10.2 crore of persons engaged in agriculture at that time. The rest, about two-thirds of the agrarian population in India, had been what Thorner identified as *kishan*s — a social class which was internally differentiated to a great extent. For example, on the basis of nature of right, about 45 per cent of the *kishan*s were owner cultivators and the rest were tenant cultivators. Again, there had been a large number of share croppers who were not registered as tenants in the 1931 Census.

Rural India was also differentiated in terms of caste. Caste describes a birth-based non-economic[5] social identity which divides

---

[3] Daniel Thorner, *The Agrarian Prospect of India*, Mumbai: Asia Publishing House, 1956.

[4] Such classification follows Lenin's methodology in rural class differentiation and contribution of Mao-Tse Tung on Lenin's methodology. For references see V. I. Lenin, *Development of Capitalism in Russia*, Firebird Publications, 1977 and Mao-Tse Tung, *Chinese Revolution and Chinese Communist Party*, Foreign Languages Press, 1965.

[5] Initially caste was based on division of labour in social production. Hence caste had a correspondence with economic identity of a person. In course of

the society in terms of various status groups. Status based on caste which provides non-economic sentiments or identity should not have a relation with social power. But then, in India, status-backed social power derived from a superior caste position often served to sustain subjugation and exploitation of those in the lower status. It is true that social power cannot exist without economic power, land-based economic power, to be specific, in the context of rural India in the pre-independence period. Indeed, caste-based social power had a correspondence with class-based economic power. However, the correspondence between 'class' and 'caste' was rather complex. In many cases 'caste' did correspond with a 'class'; in some cases, it did not. This was so because with the progress of British rule, the traditional division of labour which was the original basis of the caste system ceased to exist in many areas of India. Nevertheless, certain broad patterns can be identified. For example, landlords usually belonged to the upper caste (Brahmin, Kamma, Reddy, Okkalinga, Lingayat, Deshmukh, Patidar). Landless labourers were usually from untouchable castes (*chamar*) and the *kishan*s, who were differentiated as rich, middle, and poor peasants, were usually from various intermediate castes.[6] Subjugation and exploitation of the economically weaker castes had often been performed by exploiting caste sentiments and by exercising control over informal village panchayats. The age-old Brahminical ideology also had a great role to play in maintaining the social order. In fact, the village society was ruled by consent and the consent was manufactured by the upper caste people with the help of the Brahminical ideology.

At the time of independence rural India, which was basically peasants' India, was thus a class-differentiated and caste-differentiated society. The vast majority of these peasants were landless and marginal farmers mostly belonging to the lower castes. Land was mostly owned by the landed gentry who wielded enormous social and political power to rule the countryside. This was possible first, because the British state did not need any

---

time, economic identity-based status divided the society in terms of various status groups identified as caste groups. So long as the social division of labour remains unchanged (which was largely a reality during pre-British days), status based on caste did correspond with class status.

[6] D. Thorner and A. Thorner, *Land and Labour in India*, London: Asia Publishing House, 1962.

radical realignment of social and economic power in rural India for maintaining its rule in the countryside. The other reason was that whatever reforms in governance might have been done by the British, the age-old institutions of higher caste-dominated panchayats usurped them because such institutions still ruled to roost in rural India. Even the institutions of self-governance, as introduced by the British, were ruled by the rich upper-caste (and upper-class) village gentry.[7]

The Peasant Question

Because India became independent through a peaceful transfer of power to the Indian elite, there was no revolutionary change in the social order. The legacy of caste- and class-based rule that rural India bore was only transferred to the new rulers. This being so, we would expect that the rural society would still continue to be ruled by consent that had been manufactured by the upper-caste people with the help of Brahminical ideology, the rule which was continuing from pre-British days, with marginal changes that the British rule had inserted in the system. While this was largely true, we should not ignore the fact that the scenario at the grassroots level was fast changing in the late colonial period. In spite of the domination of the Brahminical ideology, the peasant question was now becoming important and the authority of the rural elite was being undermined. This was evidenced by the fact that the peasant struggle developed rapidly in rural India during the late colonial period. Sometimes such struggles developed spontaneously; sometimes these were organised by the local Congress and socialist (also communist, in later period) leaders. The material basis of such struggle was land-based inequality, rack renting, and socio-economic privation reflected in class (and caste) oppression.

---

[7] The British of course introduced a new principle of justice that was supposed to ensure equal treatment for everybody in the court of law. But as M. N. Srinivas pointed out ('Caste in Modern India', *The Journal of Asian Studies*, 16 (4), Association of Asian Studies, August 1957, pp. 529–48), rural India made use of both the systems of justice. The traditional panchayats, caste as well as village, were still functioning and the British rule did not upset the traditional hierarchy as maintained in Indian villages even when it introduced the institution of local government which were typically ruled by the upper caste gentry. In most cases, issues related to justice were settled outside the British introduced judicial system.

Because of historical reasons which we need not elaborate on here, such contradictions have been so sharp in the late colonial period that there had been periodic eruptions of peasants' movements which often took violent forms. One such example is the peasant upsurge in Oudh. As D. N. Dhanagare writes:

> The agrarian disturbance in Oudh, which began as demonstrations in Pratapgarh district in late 1920 became more widespread with rioting in Rae Bareli and Faizadabad districts in 1921. These followed the stereotype of pre-political outbreaks of peasants violence. Sizeable groups of *kishans* — ranging between 3000 and 10000 in number — were engaged in disturbances: they attacked *Talukdars'* crops and property and looted bazaars, particularly the shops owned by notorious merchants and money lenders. At some places they attempted to force the release of their arrested leaders and fellow *kishans*.[8]

The Oudh rebellion which took place in the 1920s was not an isolated phenomenon. There had been many such cases of rebellion before and after Oudh insurgency. In fact, on the eve of independence, rural India reeled under peasant unrest.[9] No wonder that at the time of independence:

> Indeed things seem to be heading towards a showdown. For a time it appeared as though nothing would stop a bloody and violent conflict in the country side. In the months preceding India's independence on August 15, 1947, and in the period following it, the entire countryside in India witnessed ceaseless agrarian conflicts.[10]

The Indian National Congress which came to power had to set the rules of governance under the given dispensation. The task

---

[8] D. N. Dhanagare, *Peasant Movements in India 1920–1950*, New Delhi: Oxford University Press, 1983, p. 118.

[9] By 1936, All India Kishan Sava (AIKS), a platform for the peasants, was formed. By early 1940s, AIKS was largely taken over by the Communist Party of India. Between 1941 and 1944 membership of AIKS increased from 225,781 to 553,427. AIKS had initiated two left-wing peasant struggles in Telangana (1946–51) and Tebhaga (1946–47), the impact of which had been widespread.

[10] K. Malaviya, 'Agrarian India', in A. R. Desai (ed.), *Rural Sociology in India*, Bombay: Popular Prakashan, 1969.

was formidable because the Congress came to power without any radical movement that might change the balance of power in favour of the underprivileged. The task was formidable also because, with the unchanged social order, the new Indian state adopted the parliamentary form of government on the basis of universal adult franchise which adheres to the principle of equity (nobody can be excluded from the voting process). Under a parliamentary regime, the rules of governance are usually based on a combination of force and consent. The ruling class has to develop its hegemony by forming a historical bloc which garners the support of the majority by developing consent. In India, it was quite difficult to develop such a hegemonistic rule. The reality was that there was a sharp contradiction between the landed gentry and the peasants because inequality in the distribution of ownership holding was quite high and a large section of the toiling people in rural India did not have any right on agricultural land. Finding a basis of consent for a certain social order to be backed by a Gramscian 'historical bloc' was difficult, if not impossible, under such a situation. It appears that in the early Nehruvian era, the Indian state could hardly address this problem successfully.

We will elaborate this point. Gramsci's 'historical bloc' works under the hegemony of the ruling class. As Gramsci writes,

> the normal exercise of hegemony in the area which has become classical, that of the parliamentary regime, is characterized by the combination of force and consent (consensus) which vary in their balance with each other without force exceeding consent too much. Thus it tries to achieve that force should appear to be supported by the agreement of the majority.[11]

But then, as Gramsci writes, 'the fact of hegemony undoubtedly presupposes that the interests and tendencies of the groups over which hegemony is to be exercised are taken into account, there is a certain equilibrium of compromise'.[12] As the equilibrium is

---

[11] James Joll, *Gramsci*, London: Fontana, 1977, p. 99. Joll quotes this passage as translated by him from Gramsci's original essay '*Quaderni del Carcere*'.
[12] A. Gramsci, *Prison Notebook*, London: Fontana, 1971, p. 161.

achieved, the Gramscian 'historical bloc' is formed and the rules of governance are formed accordingly.

Nehru's India was ruled by parliamentary democracy based on universal adult suffrage. Universal adult suffrage should ensure equity in right to cast vote across class, caste, creed, and community. Under such a political system, the hegemony of the ruling classes which had to be exercised under the parliamentary regime could be developed, as pointed out by Gramsci, by taking into account the 'interest and tendencies of the groups over which the hegemony is to be exercised'. But then, in the context of rural India, the ground reality was that there had been sharp contradictions in 'interest and tendencies of the groups' because there had been sharp contradiction between landed gentry and *kishans*. Contradiction was also discernible among various strata of *kishans* (rich, middle, and poor) as also between landless agricultural labour and the *kishans*. Finding the equilibrium of compromise and forming a historical bloc under such a dispensation was rather difficult.

The new rulers had to take this factor into account. The vast majority of the Indian peasants badly needed land reforms. Framing the rules of governance in a parliamentary regime by taking into account 'the interests and tendencies of the groups over which the hegemony is to be exercised' appeared to be impossible without taking up agrarian reforms in the agenda of the state.

Agrarian reforms had been in the agenda of the Congress Party since the Karachi Congress (1931). Following independence, the Congress set up a committee (Agrarian Reform Committee) which recommended that land should belong to the tillers and therefore intermediaries should be abolished. The tillers should get security of tenure; continuous cultivation for six years should automatically lead to full occupancy right. It also recommended that after getting occupancy rights, the tenants should also get the proprietary right on land and therefore they should have the right to purchase land at reasonable price. Redistribution of land by introducing a ceiling on land for personal cultivation was also suggested.

In effect, the land reforms measure following the Congress Agrarian Reform Committee's recommendations, as implemented by various provincial governments,[13] targeted only the intermediaries in the form of *zamindari, jaigirdari,* and *malguzari,* which were abolished. The power of the princes in the erstwhile princely states was also curtailed (and ultimately abolished). However, the intermediary interests on land enjoyed by the landlords by retaining land under their 'personal cultivation' was not touched upon in vast areas of the heartland of India. Only in Assam, Kashmir, Himachal Pradesh, West Bengal, and Sourashtra (Gujarat), ceiling on land that could be retained for 'personal cultivation' was introduced at this stage. As a result, rent-seeking interest still prevailed in vast areas of agrarian India. The land reforms legislations also facilitated this because 'personal cultivation' was generally defined in such a way that the owner was not required to cultivate personally for keeping the land under 'personal cultivation'. The poor and the landless peasants would have benefited had there been provisions for redistribution of holdings — a measure which would have adversely affected the upper section of *kishan*s as well. The upper section of the *kishan*s who were the main beneficiaries of Estate Acquisition Acts that abolished intermediaries in the form of *zamindari* or *jaigirdari,* did not definitely want to stretch the act of abolition of intermediaries further; the erstwhile landlords who retained a substantive part of their estates for 'personal cultivation' even after their estates were acquired also did not want this. The state legislative assemblies which were now dominated by the erstwhile landlords and the rich *kishan*s did enact land reform laws because of growing pressure from the landless peasants but 'since there is no historical precedent for a social class willingly expropriating itself, we find that land reform legislation was passed grudgingly, was riddled with loopholes and was indifferently implemented'.[14]

We would therefore conclude that the new rulers did not take into account 'the interest and tendencies of the groups over which the hegemony is to be exercised'. In fact, the landlords and the upper sections of the *kishan*s (the rich peasants) formed a joint front against the poor and the landless peasants 'in order

---

[13] According to the Indian Constitution, agriculture including land reforms is a state subject.

[14] B. Davey, *The Economic Development of India: A Marxist Analysis,* Nottingham, Spokesman Books, 1975, p. 168.

to oppose any intervention of land reforms which might mean redistribution of land in favour of the rural poor'.[15] The incipient revolt in rural India which had been discernible during the transfer of power was

> bought off by making concessions to the top layers of the peasantry at the expense of the biggest landlords and the remnants of the aristocratic classes. These latter had been loyal props to British rule; but now that the British had left, their economic, social and political power was curtailed (Davey, B. 1975; p. 166).

Under the changed scenario, the erstwhile landlords now retained landed interest by keeping a huge amount of land for 'personal cultivation'. Thus they developed an area of common interest with the upper section of the *kishan*s against any move for redistribution of land. Consequently, in the early Nehru era, there developed an alliance between the landlord and the rich peasants (upper section of the *kishan*s) against the poor and landless peasants. This alliance now wielded social and economic power in rural India by skilfully utilising the caste issues.

Rules of Governance

What, then, were the rules of governance in the early Nehru era? The 'equilibrium of compromise' that provides the basis of a hegemonistic rule in a parliamentary regime had not been there in the early Nehru era when the (reformed) landlords and rich peasants formed a bloc against the rural poor on land question and land redistribution in favour of the rural poor was largely stalled. Parliamentary democracy based on universal adult suffrage was, however, introduced. Ideally, this was bound to intensify the conflict between the landlord and the rich peasants on the one hand and the poor and landless peasants on the other — a conflict that would be reflected in formation of separate electoral blocs in the parliamentary regime. However, this did not take place in India. In rural India, this issue was addressed by the ruling class not by thwarting the democratic process itself but by subverting it in such a way that they could utilise their economic and extra

---

[15] P. C. Josi, 'Land Reforms in India and Pakistan', *Economic and Political Weekly*, December 1970.

economic power to mobilise other social classes in their favour. This went on for quite a long time even though the formal rules of governance were based on parliamentary democracy. The rule was definitely against the landless and poor peasants. But then, there was hardly any challenge to this rule even though the franchise was universal. The rulers usually belonged to the Congress party and they used to oppose pro-people reforms, notwithstanding the fact that Nehru's India was for socialism and land reforms had been in the political manifesto of the National Congress.

To follow textbook logic, under such a dispensation the rules of governance should be based on a coercive tactic, and not on an 'agreement of the majority', to follow Gramsci. Such a rule should be characterised by excessive dependence on force. A 'balance between force and consensus', which is required for the 'normal exercise of hegemony' in a parliamentary regime, would not exist in such a situation. But then, the contemporary history of rural India does not bear out that society was indeed moving in that direction. Given that the peasantry had been restive and 'things seemed to be heading towards a showdown'[16] at the time of transfer of power, rules of governance based on excessive dependence on force should have resulted in much bloodshed. The reality, however, was that rural India did not experience much peasant conflict during the first 15 years of independence. Elections were held at regular intervals and the rural power remained with the landlord and the rich peasants. In sum, the ruling elite did not face much challenge even when India adopted parliamentary democracy based on universal adult suffrage and the rulers had to earn the mandate of the people.

We would argue that this was so because the political scenario was fast changing in post-independent India. The basic fact was that the peasant movement could be bought off by making concession to the top layer of the peasantry. Since the *kishan sabha* was historically dominated by the upper *kishan*s, such a negotiation was possible even though the communists tried to oppose it. The concession that the state offered to the upper peasantry was enough to attain an 'equilibrium of compromise' which was needed to run a parliamentary democracy. The concession that

---

[16] K. Malaviya, op. cit.

the upper peasantry and the (reform) landlords received was immediately translated to social and economic power that would empower them to rule the countryside without taking into account the 'interest and tendencies' of the poor and landless peasants over which the hegemony has to be exercised.

At the material level, the consequence was that instead of the *zamindars* and *jaigirdars*, the upper *kishans* and the (reform) landlords now ruled the village society. The distinct advantage that this alliance enjoyed was that the members of this alliance knew the villages better — better than the erstwhile *zamindars* or *jaigirdars* and they had control over age-old social institutions, many of which were caste-based institutions. They could garner support in favour of their rule even when the political power was formally vested to a new institution called the Bidhan Sabha or Lok Sabha. Because of this advantage, the classical model of the parliamentary system could be distorted here. It was not necessary that the rules of governance in rural India were to be based on a 'normal exercise of hegemony' in a typical parliamentary regime, as theorised by Gramsci. As in the colonial era, governing the countryside could still be largely left to the non-state (social) organisations. With the landed gentry wielding power over these organisations, consent could be manufactured in favour of the existing rules of governance without taking into account the 'interest and tendencies of the groups over which hegemony is to be exercised'. Rural India was not, therefore, under a classical parliamentary regime, where the rules of governance should follow Gramscian logic. Alternative rules of governance typical to a classical parliamentary regime based on universal adult suffrage had the potentiality of replacing the existing rules of governance by a set that adheres to a normal exercise of hegemony which 'presupposes that the interest and tendencies of the groups over which hegemony is to be exercised are taken into account'. The rural elite in early Nehru era pre-empted this by denying the political democracy to function properly.[17] There was thus no necessity of forming a 'historical bloc' which would work under the

---

[17] See A. R. Desai (ed.), *Rural Sociology in India*, Mumbai, Popular Prakashan, 2006 for two narrations, one by Kathleen Gough and the other by B. Cohn on how the rural elite subverted the parliamentary election in the early Nehru era.

hegemony of the ruling class(es) as it should have been in a classical parliamentary regime. Neither was there any compulsion that 'the interest and tendencies of the groups over which hegemony is to be exercised are taken into account'. The application of force could be kept at minimum because rural India was still semi-feudal in nature: it could be ruled by the landlords (of the post-Estate Acquisition era) and the rich peasants (who were now endowed with proprietary right over land) without taking recourse to violence. They could do so by wielding power over non-state (social) organisations which were still very powerful in the Indian countryside. Their rule earned legitimacy mainly through these institutions that honoured feudal, hierarchy-based relations. The government was still viewed by the subaltern as *ma–baap sarkar* and in their vision, this *sarkar* has to be formed by the upper-class (and upper-caste) people.

Many such non-state organisations were caste-based organisations. Caste did play an important role for the rural elite in garnering power to rule the countryside. Landlords and rich peasants mostly belonged to the upper caste which had exercised enormous social and political power at the grassroots level since the British days. They exercised such power through informal institutions such as traditional village panchayats, which were usually constituted by heads of leading lineages of important caste groups. Because of economic (and educational) superiority, the upper-caste leaders largely dominated these panchayats. The elaborate political machinery linking members of the elected bodies, party leaders, and village leaders which we experience nowadays was yet to develop at that time. This, however, did not create any problem in exercising caste-based hegemony in the village society. As India adopted party-based democracy, the importance of political parties did increase. However, this had very little impact on rules of governance in rural India at that time because the ruling political party (Congress) was still being dominated by people from upper caste[18] and the rules were framed accordingly.

---

[18] In 1947, the upper caste formed 78 per cent of the membership of Bihar Pradesh Congress Executive Committee (R. Ahuja, *Indian Social System*, New Delhi: Rawat Publications, 1993, p. 344).

In sum, the rules of governance in rural India in the early Nehru era were not based on a 'normal exercise of hegemony', as it should be in a typical parliamentary regime. Although governance was formally based on universal adult franchise, the rural elite could successfully make it work in their favour not by forming a historical bloc but by exercising the economic and extra economic power over the subaltern. The subaltern could hardly retaliate because the tempo of the peasant movement subsided with the abolition of intermediaries and the promise of land redistribution. This was so because the peasant movement at that time could be bought off by making concessions to the top layer of peasantry.

Governing Rural India: State, Development, and Governance

Changing Rural Scenario

With the passage of time, political democracy based on universal adult suffrage found a stronger footing in rural India. Consequently, governance based on economic and extra economic power of the landed gentry faced severe challenges in many parts of India, even though the peasant movement remained weak. This was so because the importance of government-run institutions increased as the state now entered into the economic life of the people in a bigger way, thanks to the Nehruvian policy of state-led development programme. As the state-sponsored economic programme started reaching rural India, the importance of the rules framed by democratically elected governments at the provincial and at local levels gradually increased. The power to exercise control over the formal bodies that can be captured by utilising the instrument of universal adult suffrage thus became important. A consequent change in ideological space, as described by A. Béteille in the context of a typical South Indian (Tamil) village, was as follows:

> The introduction of democratic forms of government, and more particularly of adult franchise has created in the minds of the people a new consciousness of their own political importance, irrespective of caste, class and other social factors. Villagers, however low their social and economic positions, have by now had

the experience of being courted during elections by important political personalities from towns and cities. The support of the masses can no longer be taken for granted. And in this matter the new political leaders, the contact men, have an edge over *mirasdars* of the older type.[19]

Béteille observed this with respect to the village Sripuram in 1967. Not that this was true with respect to every village in rural India in the late 1960s. But this description typically identifies a trend which would grow over time and the consequent changes in the rules of governance that it would bring in. To continue from Béteille, the new-generation leadership in villages was not from the old landlord class. The popular leaders of the village Sripuram were not necessarily big landowners.

The panchayat president who is a key figure in village politics owns some land, but this is not his principal source of power. We have seen how his power depends on a plurality of factors among which his contacts with politicians and party bosses outside the village and his position in an elaborate system of patronage are important ones.[20]

We shall soon discuss the theoretical implication of such a development. We should, however, add at this point that the incidence of growing awareness of individual about his own political importance, as noted in Béteille,[21] does in no way indicate that the social identity of an individual in terms of his caste-based status was gradually being replaced with bourgeoisie individualism or a class-based identity. In fact, with the growing importance of adult franchise and the elected form of government, the importance of caste-based organisation also increased in rural India. This was largely due to the reservation policy of the state which started with reservation for Scheduled Castes and Scheduled Tribes and gradually encompassed the other backward castes as well. Nobody was willing to forego caste-based identity in the social milieu — because caste, a non-economic social identity which one acquires by birth, was found to be a source of economic power,

---

[19] A. Béteille, 'Caste, Class and Power', in Dipankar Gupta (ed.), *Social Stratification*, New Delhi: Oxford University Press, 1991, p. 341.

[20] Ibid., p. 339.

[21] A. Béteille, 'Caste, Class and Power'.

but this time not for the upper castes but for the backward castes which would now enjoy the benefit of reservation. In India, the importance of caste-based identity therefore did not decline with the development of parliamentary form of government. Caste was, in fact, reinforced in India. Individuals became aware that caste-based identity could be utilised for getting a better share of power in the changed political caste scenario.

The theoretical implications of the growing importance of the institutions of parliamentary democracy, particularly the institutions of elected local self governments (panchayats), can now be discussed. As we have argued in the second section of this article, the hegemony of the ruling class(es) in the parliamentary regime could work in the early Nehru era without seeking the agreement of the majority. This was possible because the ruling elite could still enjoy the control over the masses by exercising economic and extra economic power through their sway over social institutions. With the passage of time this became difficult. With growing importance of parliamentary democracy, governance through new (democratic) institutions of state became important. But such governance should imply a change in the context. Typically, this should be characterised by 'the combination of force and consent (consensus) which varied in their balance with each other without force exceeding consent too much'. However, this can work only if the ruling class(es) can develop its (their) hegemony by taking into account the interest and tendencies of the groups over which hegemony is to be exercised. The scenario should be such that the parliamentary regime run by the ruling classes again receives the consent of the poor and the underprivileged in the changed context.

Did the scenario of rural India change in this direction? Did the landlords and the rich peasants try to maintain their authority over these new institutions by earning the consent of the rural poor (small and marginal farmers and landless labourers) which requires them to take into account the interest of these marginalised people? The interest of the marginalised villagers could best be addressed by taking up the unfinished part of the land reforms measure. It appeared that in the vast countryside of India things did not change in this direction. New institutions of governance were definitely coming up. The participation of the rural poor in the democratic process was gradually increasing. The rural elite had to renegotiate with the changed scenario. We submit that they could do this successfully without losing their power to rule the countryside. They were now trying to exercise control over the new political machinery that linked members of the elected bodies, party leaders, and village leaders in a network of relations different from the old feudal hierarchy-based relations. They realised that this was necessary because in a Westminster-type democracy, political power is exercised through a political party-based democracy. In the Indian context, caste equations were also to be taken care of. Admittedly, many of the old rulers failed to cope with the changed scenario. A new breed of village leaders, mostly from non-*mirasdar* (backward caste) households, did emerge (as noted by Béteille) in rural India. But the fact of the matter was that in the absence of radical land reforms there was no basic change in production relations. Rural India remained semi-feudal and the new political institutions functioned with this backward economic setting as its base. As institutions, these elected bodies were still run on the basis of the ideology of the old hierarchical system. Even if a new breed of village leaders from backward castes were inducted in the process, the system essentially remained the same and the new political leaders, in fact, reproduced the old order.

This indeed was the scenario in rural India in the late Nehru and early Indira Gandhi era when the old Congress rule was challenged. A new breed of village leaders emerged in rural India. Many of them were not with the Congress but very few were for radical reforms in agriculture. It appeared that rural India was gradually brought under a new political order that would function on party-based democracy which does not exclude the poor from the electoral process although the system does not target any fundamental change in agrarian relations. To put the statement in Gramscian framework, rural India was now brought under the parliamentary regime which does not exclude the village poor and would function under the hegemony of the ruling classes; but at the same time the regime would work without meeting the basic interests of the poor and the landless peasants. The hegemony might be maintained even by inducting leaders from the poor families. But the economic system would essentially remain semi-feudal; the land question would not be addressed.

Equilibrium of Compromise?

How could this be achieved? We submit that the Indian state tried to achieve this by introducing a concept of development which does not need any radical change in economic relations. The essence of the concept of economic development through state investment in a mixed economy setting, the hallmark of Nehruvian policy of economic development, was precisely this. Essentially it is a policy that can be implemented without any radical change in production relations — neither in industry nor in agriculture. At the same time, it attempts to attain a Pareto superior situation, i.e., a situation in which someone's economic position need not worsen for betterment of the other. This orientation of the state was set by Nehru when at the early stage of the Republic, it was decided that India would be a mixed economy in which state was to play a major role. The state would exercise regulation and control over the private sector and also take the major responsibility of accelerating investment. This implied that India would follow a policy of planned economic development in which state would mobilise funds for public investment in order to achieve 'self sustained growth' and 'reduction in inequality'.[22] As perceived by the policy makers, this would take place in a society where property relations would largely remain unchanged, and along with the private sector there would develop a public sector under the control of the state. Development would thus take place in a mixed economy framework in which the state would play the pivotal role. In policy papers, this strategy of development was mentioned as socialistic patterns of development.[23] The Indian state took up this course of economic development right from the early Nehru era. For executing this policy, the emphasis was mainly on accelerating public expenditure on development. Public expenditure on development rose from ₹ 1,960 crore in the First Five Year Plan to ₹ 8,628 crore during the Third Five Year

---

[22] Government of India, 'Second Five Year Plan', New Delhi: Planning Commission, Government of India, 1956, Chapter 2.

[23] Over and above interfering in the running of the economy in various ways 'what it meant in effect was that the Government was to take an active part in certain kind of economic activity; it meant the setting up of public sector industries' (Pramit Chaudhuri, *The Indian Economy: Poverty and Development*, Delhi: Vikas, 1978).

Plan (1961–66). The orientation did not change as Indira Gandhi came to power. In fact, Indira Gandhi accelerated it further. Her first plan (the 4th Five Year Plan) had public investment worth ₹ 14,398 crore — much higher than that of the third plan, even if we consider the inflation adjusted data on plan allocation. Regulation and control became more severe during Indira Gandhi's regime. At one stage, 'socialism' was included in the Directive Principles of the State Policy of the Constitution of India.

With increasing public expenditure and a carefully designed state policy on regulation and control, the Indian state tried to build up the much needed consent to rule 'without force exceeding consent too much', under the hegemony of the ruling classes — the big bourgeoisie and the big landlord (which included the upper section of the *kishan*s as well). That the interests of the ruling classes were carefully honoured is revealed by the fact that the Indian state, even in the heyday of 'socialism', never failed to serve the interests of these two classes. It is not true that the so-called socialistic policy that introduced state activism in the industrial sector was antagonistic to private capital. In fact it helped the private industry by introducing systematic under pricing of some inputs produced by the public sector, for which there had been high public investment. Private capital benefited from the high rates of protection and import restrictions. The policy of encouraging import substitution technology also helped private capital. Public expenditure on Green Revolution technology benefited the large farmers (and the landlords) who now invested in agriculture because agriculture had become remunerative thanks to subsidised inputs and high procurement prices.[24] But then, the state also tried to establish its legitimacy among the poor and underprivileged. Thus the state took up some livelihood-related relief and development programmes for the poor as well, under the slogan of '*Garibi Hatao*'. It was as if the country was heading towards a 'win–win' situation for every social class.

---

[24] W. Frankel observed that the Green Revolution had a pro-rich farmer bias (*India's Green Revolution: Economic Growth and Political Costs*, Berkeley, California University Press, 1971). This observation was based on a field study covering four states of India.

As the state adopted such a policy, gradually the ruling classes could develop the consent to rule over the poor without addressing the basic issue — the issue of land reforms. India thus entered an era in which the countryside could be ruled without denying the entry of the poor in the democratic institutions. The orientation was built by Indira Gandhi who tried to meet the rural challenge by taking up Green Revolution technology on the one hand[25] and a few state-sponsored relief and development programmes for the rural poor on the other.

There had been a crisis of governance — particularly during late 1960s — due to the food crisis on the one hand and the failure of the state to achieve the promised 'win–win' situation for every social class through the policy of planned economic development. But Indira Gandhi's policy helped the ruling classes overcome the crisis. Gradually it appeared that the state could now develop the much needed 'equilibrium of compromise' so that the new institution of democracy could function on the basis of consent so that the application of force which the state needed to exercise as and when necessary 'would appear to be supported by the agreement of the majority'.[26] Indira Gandhi was the chief architect of this order and achieved it by eliminating the resistance within the Congress against her economic policy of state-centric development.

Rural Economy and Rural Governance: Continuity and Change

Rural Economy: Continuity and Change

The basis of this equilibrium was, however, weak. With increasing state investment, there had been economic growth. But the rate

---

[25] The introduction of Green Revolution technology was also necessary for meeting the wage goods constraints on industrial development. Since there was no agrarian reform, India was facing a periodic food crisis which increased price of food articles. As the price of food articles increased, the wage rate increased which reduced profit rate in the industry and thus the rate of investment declined. The answer to this problem was sought initially by depending on PL 480 wheat. After the crisis 1967 the ruling class adopted the Ford Foundation recommended the programme of Green Revolution.

[26] A. Gramsci, as in James Joll, *Gramsci*, p. 99.

of growth was rather poor, particularly in rural India. Between 1950–51 and 1979–80, India's GDP increased by only 3.5 per cent per year. The annual growth rate of agriculture and the allied sector was still lower (2.2 per cent). During this period the secondary and tertiary sectors grew at 5.3 per cent and 4.5 per cent respectively.[27] Since secondary- and tertiary-sector activities were largely concentrated in urban India, the data implicitly indicates that the GDP growth rate had an urban tilt. The per capita growth rate of GDP was 1.4 per cent (urban and rural combined) during this period. We may infer that the per capita growth rate of GDP in rural India was still lower, because the growth rate in agriculture and allied agricultural activities, the main plank of the rural economy at that time, had been much lower.[28]

The basis of the equilibrium of compromise was weak also because poverty remained widespread in rural India. On the basis of the poverty line fixed at a monthly per capita expenditure of ₹ 15 in 1960–61 prices, an expenditure level that represented an 'extremely low level of living' and one which had been widely accepted as 'minimum level' in the policy debate,[29] M. Ahluwalia estimated that 54.1 per cent of the rural population in India lived in poverty in 1956–57. In 1967–68, the year of the massive food crisis, the percentage increased to 56.5. After accelerated state intervention in rural livelihood related issues, the percentage did decline (which possibly was the basis of apparent consent that Indira Gandhi earned from the poor). But in terms of absolute number, poverty was still widespread in India. According to the *World Bank Report* (1989), 23.68 crore of persons in rural India were living below the poverty line in 1970. By 1983, the number increased to 29.2 crore. At the end of the Nehru–Indira era (i.e., just before India introduced the new economic policy), the number of poor villagers was still as high as 25.22 crore.

---

[27] Deepak Nair, 'Economic Growth in Independent India: Lumbering Elephant or Running Tiger?'*Economic and Political Weekly*, 41 (15), 15–21 April 2006, p. 115.

[28] This is also reflected in the declining share of agriculture in GDP. The share of agriculture in GDP was 55.3 per cent in 1950–51. By 1980–81, it declined to 38.1 per cent.

[29] M. Ahluwalia, 'Rural Poverty and Agricultural Performance in India', *Journal of Development Studies*, 13 (3), 1977, pp. 298–323.

Poverty was widespread because rural livelihood at that time mostly depended on agriculture and allied agricultural activities and a large number of families in rural India had no access to land. According to the official data, in 1951 17.8 per cent of total agricultural population was classified as agricultural labourers or their dependents. Roughly 50 per cent of agricultural labour households owned no land.[30] Among the landowning households, the distribution of holdings was extremely skewed in favour of the big landowners. Analysing the National Sample Survey data (17th Round, 1961–67) Chaudhuri observes that the

> top 3 per cent of the households owned 28 per cent of the land; the top 8 per cent owned roughly 45 per cent. Lowest third owned less than 1 per cent. The bottom 80 per cent of the households owned less than one third of the total area.[31]

Over time, the incidence of landlessness among the rural population also increased severely. Analysing the NSSO (59th Round) data, Vikas Rawal observes that by 2003–2004, the scenario was such that

> about 41.6 per cent of the households in rural India did not own any land (of these, about 10 per cent did not own even homestead land). About 31.2 per cent of the households did not own any land other than homestead and did not do any cultivation on their homestead (2008, p. 45).[32]

For the landowning classes, the distribution of holdings remained skewed in favour of the big landowners in spite of land reform legislations enacted during Nehru–Indira regime. Analysing the NSSO (59th Round) household level data, Rawal observes that 'in 2003, the Gini coefficient of ownership holding of land (land other than homestead) in India was about 0.76'[33] which indicates that inequality in the distribution of ownership

---

[30] Pramit Choudhuri, *The Indian Economy: Poverty and Development*, New Delhi: Vikas, 1978, p. 271.

[31] Ibid., p. 28.

[32] Vikas Rawal, 'Ownership Holdings of Land in Rural India: Putting the Record Straight', *Economic and Political Weekly*, 43 (10), 8–14 March 2008, pp. 45.

[33] Ibid., p. 47.

holding was very high in India. Rawal also observes that 'the inequality in ownership of land was the highest in Tamil Nadu, Punjab, Haryana and Andhra Pradesh, the states that were (earlier) noted for the highest levels of landlessness'.[34]

This was so because the much needed 'equilibrium of compromise' was sought without addressing the land question, the land redistribution question, to be precise. In the early Nehru era, there was no ceiling on land for 'personal cultivation' in major states of India (see the second section of this article). Due to growing pressure from below, all Indian states adopted legislations on land ceiling.

> The ceiling laws were enacted in two phases (1) period from 1960 to 1972 when no specific policy guidelines were present; and (2) the period since 1972, after the adoption of national policy guidelines. As of 2002, states have re-distributed approximately 5.4 million of acres of land to 5.6 million beneficiary households (West Bengal accounts for 20 per cent of the re-distributed land and 47 per cent of the ceiling surplus land).[35]

Needless to say, the land redistribution programme benefited only a tiny section of the rural poor.

With growing landlessness, extreme inequality in the distribution of holding and low productivity in agriculture in spite of huge subsidy from the state, agriculture could hardly sustain the growing population pressure in rural India. There had been migration to urban India, but urban pull was not very strong, so much so that more than 70 per cent of Indians still had to earn their livelihood from rural economic activities. As a result, the rural livelihood pattern also changed in India.

According to NSSO estimates, agriculture, which accounted for 72.1 per cent of total employment generated in the country in 1971, registered a sharp decline in growth rate of employment from 2.32 per cent during 1972–77 to 0.65 per cent during 1983–87. Between 1972–73 and 1987–88, the growth rate of employment in agriculture was just 1.37 per cent — lower than the growth rate of rural population during this period.[36] Agriculture still remained

---

[34] Ibid.
[35] T. Hanstad, T. Haque, and R. Neilson, 'Improving Land Access for India's Rural Poor', *Economic and Political Weekly*, 43 (10), 8–14 March 2008, p. 52.
[36] NSSO, Employment and Unemployment Situation in India, Various Rounds.

the principal source of livelihood for the rural workforce in India. But slowly, there were developing other sources of livelihood — mostly informal in nature — in the villages of India. By the end of the last century, the rural employment scenario, as revealed in NSSO data (55 Round) was such that agriculture accounted for 71.4 per cent of the employed (usual plus subsidiary) rural males in India. Rural (informal) manufacturing was the source of livelihood for 7.3 per cent of employed rural males. 4.5 per cent were employed in construction. Trade, hotel and restaurant, transport, storage, and communication had been the source of livelihood for 10 per cent of rural male workers. 5.7 per cent were now engaged in social, community, and personal services. The declining importance of agriculture as the source of livelihood was further recorded in the next NSSO Round (61st) survey, which revealed that agriculture now provided livelihood for only 66.5 per cent of the rural male workers.

With declining employment opportunities in agriculture and slow growth of other non-formal jobs, there was rising unemployment and underemployment in rural India. In 1973, an Expert Committee on Unemployment (Bhagwati Committee) estimated on the basis of NSSO 28th Round data on the employment situation in India that in 1971, the number of unemployed was 1.87 crore and out of this 1.61 crore (86 per cent of the total) unemployed lived in rural India.[37] Along with this, there were 2.35 crore of rural workers who worked less than 28 hours a week. The latter were described as underemployed. The comparable data on unemployed for more recent years is not available because in subsequent NSSO surveys the time use was considered on a person–day basis, in terms of half days rather than clock time. Based on the revised basis of time use, unemployment has now four different measures. The most useful in our context is Current Daily Status (CDS) unemployment (no work for 14 half days of the reference week). In the NSSO survey of 1993–94 the survey, which was undertaken immediately after the introduction of the new economic policy, the percentage of CDS unemployment among the rural male workers was found to be 5.34. With estimated workforce at 185,105, the estimated number of CDS

---

[37] This included 85 lakh rural workers who were working less than 14 hours a week.

unemployed among the male workforce was 97.84 lakh. In the next two quinquennial surveys (1999–2000 and 2004–2005) the CDS unemployment among rural male increased to 7.2 per cent and 8 per cent respectively. For data on underemployed rural males we have the NSSO data on 'persons reporting 0.5 or more days of unemployed with work for 0.5 to 3 days in a week'. 54.9 per cent of the Current Weekly Status (CWS) workers (549 out of 1,000 persons) in rural India faced underemployment of this nature during 1993–94. The percentage was marginally lower in the next quinquennial survey.[38]

Thus, as the institutions of democratic governance were strengthened and as the state tried to develop 'equilibrium of compromise' by taking up public expenditure to accommodate 'interest and tendencies of the groups over which hegemony is to be exercised',[39] the economic reality in rural India was moving in a different direction. In the absence of structural reforms that would have served the poor, the Nehru–Indira orientation of the state policy essentially strengthened the existing order, which, inter alia, indicated that the basis for 'normal exercise of hegemony' remained extremely weak. In fact, this is what India was up to the end of 1990s. The economic basis of exercising the rule by consent was extremely fragile in this country.

Political Parties and Rule by Consent

The Indian state could still survive. Not only could the state survive, over time it also earned legitimacy of its rule and therefore in its governance, force did not exceed consent too much. Except for a short spell of emergency, governance did not have to undermine the democratic institutions. This was possible because of a few specific factors which need to be discussed. Ordinarily, rising economic contradictions should intensify class contradictions and consequently the legitimacy of the existing order should face challenges from the working class and the peasantry. There should develop popular resistance within the democratic system and

---

[38] J. Krishnamurthy and G. Raveendran, *Measures of Labour Force Participation and Utilisation*, Delhi: National Commission for Enterprise in the Unorganised Sector, 2008.

[39] James Joll, *Gramsci*, London: Fontana, 1977.

through political mobilisation, from resistance there should develop counter hegemony which would undermine the hegemony of the ruling bourgeois landlord classes. As we have discussed, in the vast countryside of India the Indian state failed to address the problem of unemployment and mass poverty. This must have intensified class contradictions. As a result, the legitimacy of the existing rule should have faced challenges and consequently political mobilisation for a counter hegemony should have gathered momentum. For several historical reasons, the course of development that took place in India was different. The basic prerequisite for the ascendance of counter hegemony through political mobilisation is the consolidation of the working-class movement. Except Bengal and Kerala, the strength of the working-class movement in fact declined as the model of party-based political rule got a firm footing in India.

Crisis, however, mounted, particularly in the heartland of rural India where there had been mass poverty. As expected, the political authority of the Congress was challenged as early as 1967 when there was massive political mobilisation against the Congress in the general election and the party was defeated in many provinces of India. Indira Gandhi tried to regain the mass base of the party by accelerating public expenditure and exercising regulation and control over the economy. In order to accelerate public investment and also in order to serve the weaker section by 'priority sector lending', 14 scheduled commercial banks were nationalised in 1969. The aim was to please the poor so that her Congress party could rule India.

For some time, it appeared that India was under Bonapartism[40] where the state becomes quasi-autonomous and speaks for all classes in the society. Bonapartism is the product of a situation where the hegemony of the ruling bourgeois (and landlord) classes cannot be maintained, but the working class cannot affirm its hegemony either. In the late 1960s, India possibly passed through that phase of governance. Indian state appeared now as a supra class state which placed itself above the interest of the propertied classes. But as Marx pointed out, the real task of the Bonapartist state was to guarantee the safety and stability

---

[40] See Hal Draper, *Karl Marx's Theory of Revolution*, vol. 1, New York: Monthly Review Press, 1977.

of the bourgeois society. This indeed was the situation in India where the state maintained the framework of 'mixed economy' that does not aim at changing the existing production relations in spite of the rhetoric of 'socialism'. In fact, this was Indira Gandhi's answer to crisis and she was remarkably successful in consolidating the state without changing its basic orientation. As the Indian state consolidated, the democratic institutions also consolidated.

In spite of whatever Indira Gandhi had done, economic contradictions sharpened over time. But the threat of political mobilisation for establishing a counter hegemony of the working class (and the poor peasants) over the democratic institutions with a view to undermining the hegemony of the ruling classes, the real threat to the existing order, gradually became weak. Political mobiliations had of course been there. But these were not for working-class hegemony. These were based on non-class ideology and were designed to operate within the general hegemony of the ruling classes. The burgeoning contradiction in the economic sphere had been utilised for these mobilisations. Such mobilisations succeeded in gathering popular support so much so that the hegemony of the single party was over in this country. The republic gained in two ways. First, political mobilisations could thus be contained within the ruling-class hegemony and therefore the democratic institutions could further be strengthened without facing the threat of counter hegemony to the existing order. Second, the Republic no longer needed Bonapartism for its survival and therefore it could function as a typical state based on consent of the majority without taking care of the 'tendencies and interests' of the majority. Such a state could even take up neoliberal economic reforms without facing any threat from the subaltern because there would be no political mobilisation to reckon with that would strive to establish a counter hegemony.

How was this achieved? This was achieved by accommodating various non-class political trends within the hegemony of the ruling classes. As governance by a single party (Congress) became impossible because of the changing pattern of social cleavage and as the Republic stuck to a Westminster-type democracy, the changing pattern of social cleavage was captured by various other parties that would enter in the parliamentary process. With success in political mobilisation they would share power at the state and the central levels in the federal form of governance because the system operates on party-based democracy. The basic rule of the game, however, was that these parties would operate as the Congress had been operating, within the hegemony of the ruling classes. As political mobilisation would be carried out mainly by these (and Congress) parties, voices of protest would also be confined to the hegemony of the ruling classes and the country would be ruled by consent. Application of force, if any, would thus appear to be supported by the agreement of the majority. The political scenario gradually changed in this direction particularly after the fall of the Janata government. There emerged several political parties which would operate within the general hegemony of the ruling classes and claim a share in governance. Many of these political parties were region-/ caste-based parties operating on narrow political bases and focusing on specific sections and interests. Many of them utilised traditional non-state organisations to consolidate their support base in parliamentary politics. In ideological space, some were for 'social justice' (RJD, SP, BSP), some for regional identity (National Conference, Akali, AGP, DMK, AIDMK), and some for 'development' (BJD, TDP). But no party except the left was for a division on class line and hardly would they take any stance against neoliberal economic policy. They would share power with the big parties (BJP, Congress) on the basis of their strength in political mobilisation but would operate within the hegemony of the ruling classes.

In the absence of a formidable challenge from the left, India could therefore be ruled within a democratic framework. The rules of governance would be based on consent even though privation and hunger would go on increasing.

Neoliberalism and Crisis of the Parliamentary Political Parties

This arrangement can really work as evidenced in the parliamentary politics of India. One issue, however, still needs to be addressed. With the ascendance of neoliberalism, political parties will face difficulty in mobilising political support from the masses, because the neoliberal economic policy is renegotiating the role of the state in economic development. The strength of the Indian state, right from the early Nehru era, was that it played a major role in the economy by carefully designing the policy of regulation and control so that the poor and underprivileged would always consider the state as a buffer against the attack from capital; state activism had also been taken to have welfare implications for the poor. The expectation from the political parties was that they would utilise state power for the benefit of their supporters, benefit that they could deliver by utilising the power to regulate and control, as also by designing the state policy for the welfare of the electorate. This was, in fact, the reason why these parties were successful in political mobilisation. This was true with respect to national-level parties like the Congress and the BJP; this was also true with respect to region-/caste-based parties operating on narrow political basis and focusing on specific sections and interests. When neoliberalism renegotiates the role of the state, all these parties should face difficulty in garnering support because even if 'class' is blurred by 'caste', 'region', or 'justice', privation and mass poverty remain as the grim reality and people still seek relief from the state via the political parties which are supposed to run the state.

'Against this backdrop, two interrelated developments need mention: parties are fast losing their role in setting the agenda and secondly, core issues of contestation are rapidly getting de-politicised'.[41] In the era of neoliberalism, the paradigm has changed. Not only is the role of the state in economic development being renegotiated, the role of political parties in the business of the state is also being renegotiated. In the context of state policy, neoliberal view is that political parties would no longer set the agenda. The agenda would be set by the national and international advisors and the bureaucracy. The issues would then be placed in the so-called public domain where civil society organisations would debate and media would form opinion. Political parties are not engaged in this task. The implication is that policy would be formulated by the agencies which are not accountable to the people.

As a consequence many issues are quietly being driven away from the arena of contestation. In fact, the process started with the

---

[41] Suhas Palishkar, 'Revisiting State Level Parties', *Economic and Political Weekly*, 39 (14), 3–10 April 2004, p. 1470.

surreptitious introduction of changes of economic policy at the beginning of 1990s. Since then, changes in defense and foreign policies, trade policy and the very direction of the Indian State have taken place outside the party political domains.[42]

Under the new dispensation, the arena of public policy would be set separately and 'the political parties are reduced to going through the motion of political competition which involve very few substantive issues. So much so that party political arena would look more and more consensual and party competition would be reduced to something like a "sports event"'.[43] If the major policy issues are thus taken out of the arena of the political parties, the political parties will have to concentrate on minor issues for political mobilisation. The democratic institutions will function on a chartered course and seeking consent for governance will become a non-issue. A parliamentary regime can function without addressing the issue of deriving 'equilibrium of compromise' — an issue that rulers during the Nehru–Indira regime had to ponder. We submit that this is how neoliberalism rules. Major policy issues are systematically being taken out of 'politics'. As a result, the democratic institutions need not at all address the issue of seeking consent for earning legitimacy of rule. The political parties are to adhere to this rule of the game. In order to share power they are to accept this as the given order under which they are to function.

We should, however, add that the neoliberals also need these political parties in order to legitimise the new rules of governance where the state initiative has to be replaced with the initiatives of the private capital and the market, with its twin features of exclusion and inequality, which have to be accepted as omnipotent in the economic life of the people. The rules of governance that the state under the Nehru–Indira regime used to follow, by carefully working out the areas of the intervention of the state, have to be undermined in the regime of neoliberalism. The role of the state, particularly what the people should expect from the state, will have to be renegotiated. The neoliberals would need the political parties in order to propagate that there is no other alternative to this policy. The remarkable consensus among the

---

[42] Suhas Palishkar, op. cit, p. 1478.
[43] Ibid.

political parties about the very orientation of the neoliberal state indicates that this goal has largely been achieved.

Mobilisation from Below

Even though political parties are fast losing their importance in setting the agenda with respect to major policy issues, the importance of seeking mobilisation from below still exists for the state and the political parties do play an important role in this domain. This is because the neoliberal policy does not deny the role of the state as service provider at the grassroots level with respect to issues related to social sector (health and education) where market-mitigated solutions are typically inefficient. Promoting the empowerment of 'weaker sections', ensuring entitlement to employment for the unskilled rural workers (Rozgar Yojana) and the like and stepping up public investment to facilitate private investment-led growth are also in the agenda of the state under neoliberal dispensation. Many of these need the involvement of the people at the grassroots level. The rationale in the language of neoliberal economics is that in the social sector and in livelihood-related state-sponsored projects, there is a principal-agent problem. The citizens, the villagers in these cases which are to benefit from the state-sponsored projects, are the principals and the persons in the delivery system (the bureaucracy) are the agents. If the principal delegates decision-making power to the agent 'then there is a possibility that the agents will act, not in principal's interest but their own. And if there is asymmetry in availability of information between principal and the agent, the problem becomes much worse'.[44] In order to minimise this problem, as the argument goes, it is better to decentralise decision making, as far as practicable.[45] The neoliberals are therefore retaining (and strengthening) the Panchayati Raj Institutions (PRIs) that may ensure the participation of the people at the grassroots level, thus minimising the problem of moral hazards.

The neoliberals are not the first to discover the virtue of the PRIs. The absence of elected local bodies was first identified as

---

[44] V. Vyasuhu, 'Transformation in Governance since 1990s: Some Reflections', *Economic and Political Weekly*, 5 June 2004.

[45] P. Bardhan, 'Decentralisation of Governance and Development', *Journal of Economic Perspectives*, 16 (4), 2002, pp. 185–205.

a major impediment to rural development during the days of Community Development Project when it was observed that 'the tendency of the government's village level workers and other agricultural extension services is to go to the "natural leaders" of the village (i.e., the rural rich) and concentrate their energies there',[46] a tendency that defeats the very purpose of these projects. In terms of neoliberal economics, the problem at that stage was with identifying the principal itself. The Indian state decided to meet this challenge by revitalising the PRI system and assigning a role for the PRIs in the development process. This was because there was no initiative from below and because, due to the domination of the rural elite in provincial government, the state governments also bypassed the PRIs in executing various rural development projects (such as the Integrated Agricultural District Programme) during the 1960s and early 1970s. Consequently, the first-generation PRIs soon became defunct. Following the recommendations of the Ashok Mehta Committee (1978) a second generation of PRIs came into being in a few states including West Bengal. But then, in many of the states, PRIs still remained defunct largely because the politicians at the state level were still unwilling to transfer a part of the power they enjoyed to the local bodies.

After a long political battle with state governments (not the West Bengal government), it was decided that the central government would amend the Constitution so that the formation of PRIs would become mandatory for the state governments. In 1993, with the 73rd amendment to the Constitution, the PRI was introduced as the third tier of the government in Indian Republic. All the states had to pass confirmatory acts as the PRI system became an organ of the state. Following the constitutional provision, in all the major states, the PRI now runs under a uniform three-tier system: district, *taluk*/bloc, and village levels. PRIs are to function under the leadership of the elected bodies and the elected bodies are to have a uniform five-year term according to all confirmatory acts. The constitution has now a list of 29 items in its 11th schedule that function with respect to which might be delegated to the local bodies. Funds and functionaries are also to devolve to the local bodies.

---

[46] B. Davey, *The Economic Development of India*, p. 183.

In the context of rural governance, the importance of PRIs is increasing over time as many social sector- and livelihood-related state-sponsored schemes are being executed through PRIs nowadays. Political mobilisation at the level of the local bodies has therefore become important. As the authority of the elected local bodies is increasing, the traditional seats of rural power are to negotiate with the changing reality. Activism at the PRI level is increasing. However, the power still remains with the local elite. Ordinarily, what happens is that the panchayats are 'captured' by the local elite by exercising control over the political machinery that link members of the elected bodies, party leaders, and village leaders in a network of relations. They are the 'politicians' operating at various tiers of government including the village panchayats. Based on a study of 500 villages in four southern Indian states, Timothy Besley, S. Narayanan, and K. Murthy have observed that 'politicians on an average own five acres of land, which is more than twice the average land ownership of non-political households ... where both politicians and non-politicians households tend to rely on agriculture, politicians are significantly more likely to be cultivators than agricultural labourers'.[47] Another important finding of this study is that 'politicians who belong to SC/ST also tend to be elites compared to their comparison group (non-politician SC/ST households)'.[48] The scenario is unlikely to be different in north Indian states.

It is true that after a series of amendments of the Panchayati Raj legislations, some devolution has really taken place. Even then, the delivery system for rural development largely failed to mobilise the rural poor in the decision-making process, because the systems retains an elite bias; the inequality in the distribution of rural assets in general and land in particular acts as a powerful deterrent to the empowerment of the underprivileged in rural India. The elite bias is often reflected in the caste bias of the panchayat bodies. The elite who rule the panchayats usually belong to the upper caste. As a result, the panchayats often fail to mobilise the lower-caste people in the decision-making process.

---

[47] Timothy Besley, Rohini Pande, and Vijayendra Rao, 'Political Economy of Panchayats in South India', *Economic and Political Weekly*, 24 February 2007, p. 665.
[48] Ibid.

Even when the decision-making process is formally decentralised, seldom does it deliver the fruits of decentralisation to the weaker section of the society. Consequently, the panchayat system fails to ensure people's participation. As a result, it remains inefficient. A formally decentralised delivery system thus becomes ineffective and the pace of rural development remains poor. If neoliberals attempt to meet the principal agent problem by strengthening the PRI without addressing the problem of asymmetry in asset distribution, rural India will have the continuity of old rules of governance, only with a change in rhetoric.

Rural Governance and the Left

Parliamentary Left

In West Bengal and Kerala, the rules of rural governance were likely to be different, because these two states could address the issue of land reforms and within the limits set by the constitution of India, they could try to establish rules of rural governance largely on the basis of changed production relations. This was so because in these states the parliamentary left could come to power through popular mandate under the Indian parliamentary system. Since land reforms had been a state subject, in both the states, the leftist rules tried to implement the provisions of the land reforms acts, the provisions which, if implemented, might tilt the balance of rural power in favour of the landless and poor peasants.

Thanks to the left rule, West Bengal, which has only 3.5 per cent of the agricultural land of India, now accounts for 18 per cent of the vested land of the country. The state also accounts for 20 per cent of the total redistributed land of India. As expected, with success in land reforms, the rural balance of power in West Bengal was tilted in favour of the small and marginal farmers. The state has a strong presence of the PRI and the PRI is largely controlled by the poor in this state. This is reflected in the class nature of the PRI leaders. By 1993, the West Bengal PRI was largely under the leadership of small artisans, poor peasants, and small traders.[49] That the lower-caste people increased their numerical strength

---

[49] Government of West Bengal, 'Human Development Report', Development and Planning Department, 2004.

in the village panchayats was also observed in a village study.[50] West Bengal introduced the new PRI system in 1978, well before the 73rd Amendment of the constitution. Elections to the local bodies were held at regular five-year intervals. It is true that the extent of devolution was not satisfactory in the state — well below what Kerala could achieve. But then the PRIs did perform well even within the limited power that had been devolved to them. On the basis of a field study covering 89 representative villages under four successive left-ruled panchayat administrations, P. Bardhan and D. Mukherjee observed that the average levels of poverty alleviation efforts were high in these villages. The authors concluded that 'the West Bengal Panchayats directed a significant portion of benefits of different developmental and poverty alleviation programmes to the poor'.[51]

However, we should not conclude that the domination of the rural rich is over in the villages of West Bengal. This is not true and this was not expected either. There was no revolutionary change in the property relations in the countryside of Bengal. The only change which is visible in rural Bengal is that economic domination is no longer land-based domination. The other point to be noted is that West Bengal agriculture is now in the main the agriculture of small and marginal farmers. This has had an impact on the nature of governance in rural Bengal. The rural rich had to come into an alliance with the small and marginal farmers for enjoying rural power, a fact which is reflected in the body politics of West Bengal.

The basic problem with the PRI in West Bengal is that in spite of the introduction of a fourth tier to the PRI (the village-level *sansad*), the PRI in this state is now failing to ensure the participation of the people. This might be due to the fact that the initiative of the people has gradually been replaced with the initiative of the ruling party. As the initiative of the party replaces the initiative of the people at the PRI level, the PRI itself suffers from the principal agent problem; there develops the problem of adverse selection. At the popular level, in the absence of proper forum, the discontent due to adverse selection by the PRI is

---

[50] S. Bhattacharya, 'Caste, Class and Politics in West Bengal', *Economic and Political Weekly*, 38 (3), 18 January 2003.
[51] P. Bardhan and D. Mukherjee, 'Poverty Alleviation Efforts of Panchayats in West Bengal', *Economic and Political Weekly*, 2004, p. 972.

often expressed by politicising the issues. The rural unrest that West Bengal is facing now, the unrest that assumes a political character every now and then, is largely due to this course of development in the PRI democracy in West Bengal.

The course of development in Kerala had been different. The state was never under the continuous hegemony of the left. As a result, replacing the initiative of the people by the initiative of the ruling party did not develop as an accepted practice in Kerala PRI. At the same time, Kerala had the imprint of the left in setting the orientation of the PRI, as it had been in the case of West Bengal. Kerala also went through the process of land reforms, thanks to the success of the left in the state legislative politics as early as in 1957. In 1957, the CPI contested 100 of the 126 assembly seats in the election, winning 60 which, together with five assembly seats won by party-supported independents, gave it an overall majority to form the first communist government in a province of India. The communist government, headed by E. M. S. Nambudiripad, introduced a land reform bill 'whose main aim would be to safeguard the tenants' interest. The bill also proposed to introduce a ceiling on land holding, fixed fare rent, and created provision for redistribution of the surplus land to the landless'.[52]

The CPI government also appointed a commission for suggesting administrative reforms. The report published in July 1958 suggested that 'the basic unit of administration at village level was to be the panchayat. An elected body, it was to act both as an advisor to and an agent of government in the area of development and welfare'.[53] The short-lived CPI ministry could neither enact the land reforms bill nor could it introduce the PRI (following the recommendations of the administrative reforms committee). However, the 1959 Land Reforms Bill was enacted in revised form without many of the pro-tenant provisions in the original bill by the Congress–PSP ministry and this became law in 1961. The 1966 UF government re-revised it and set the orientation of land reforms that would abolish landlordism by

---

[52] T. J. Nassiter, *Communism in Kerala*, New Delhi: Oxford University Press, 1982, p. 149.
[53] Ibid., p. 167.

the compulsory vesting of their proprietary rights to the government and their subsequent assignment to the cultivating tenants. Hutment dwellers were also granted security of tenure under this act. The ceiling on personal cultivation set by this act was the lowest in the subcontinent (6–7.5 acre for a single adult and maximum 20 acres for a family with three minor children). Since the act received enormous popular support, the subsequent government did never try to alter it and the orientation of the village economy of Kerala was set accordingly. Today, Kerala's agriculture is the agriculture of small and marginal farmers. Like many other states in India, Kerala society has caste- and community-based divisions. But unlike in other states, these divisions have largely lost the linkage with land-based property relations.

The PRI in Kerala did not, however, get greater power before the 73rd Amendment of the constitution. The 1966 UF government did introduce a bill to devolve greater authority to PRIs. But the bill failed to get the legislative approval because the government did not pursue it.[54] There was no election in the PRI since 1963 and the PRI could not function properly, as it had been in case of other states of India. Major initiative towards activating the PRI came only in 1991 when the Left Democratic Front government took serious steps towards setting up district councils in the state and overhauling the local self-government system. Since then the state has decentralised much of the funds, functions, and functionaries to the grassroots level. Kerala's peoples' plan,[55] the plan which is based on the initiative from below, has received attention from the experts in the field of decentralised planning, nationally and internationally.

Kerala has developed an alternative model of development based on decentralised planning in which mass mobilisation through PRIs plays a very important role. PRIs in Kerala are endowed with funds, functions, and functionaries for planning and executing local area development with the involvement of the people. Since all the political parties get involved in this exercise and since no political party or front can ignore the opposition, in Kerala the initiative of the people is never replaced with the

---

[54] Ibid., op. cit, p. 290.
[55] See T. N. Thomas Isaac, *Local Democracy and Development*, New Delhi: Leftword Books, 2000.

initiative of the political parties. Kerala could thus minimise the principal agent problem which persists in PRIs of all the states, including West Bengal.

The problem that Kerala is facing nowadays is that the areas in which Kerala PRIs engage a considerable part of their initiative are gradually being reduced thanks to the neoliberal policy of promoting private healthcare and education services. The niche area of Kerala's PRIs had been the social sector. Thanks to state initiative from the pre-independence days, Kerala has performed very well in the area of public health and elementary education. As PRIs were revamped, the responsibilities of the state in public health and elementary education were largely devolved to the PRIs. Much of what came about as people's participation was in maintaining and improving the state sponsored delivery system related to healthcare and elementary education. What happened after the introduction of the neoliberal policy at the central level is that private service providers are now entering these areas in a big way. As a result, the area of operation of the public health-care and educational services is getting reduced in Kerala. There are indications that Kerala's once powerful social sector is now severely being undermined.[56]

Governance and Extra-Parliamentary Left

As neoliberalism resets the agenda of the state and the major policy decisions are taken by the agencies which are not accountable to the people, thereby leading the Republic to a situation in which a parliamentary regime can function without addressing the issue of deriving 'equilibrium of compromise', a space is gradually being created outside parliamentary politics where the extra-parliamentary left finds a support base. In the vast country-side of India, covering more than 200 districts (out of 607) there has emerged a politics of governance under the leadership of CPI (ML) Maoists which challenges the hegemony of the Republic itself. This was only expected, as the Republic was hijacked by neoliberals and the issue of finding the 'equilibrium of compromise', the issue that bothered all the rulers in the Nehru-Indira regime, has simply been reduced to the problem of 'inclusive growth'.

---

[56] See T. K. Oomman, 'Kerala's Social Sector under Neo-liberalism', *Economic and Political Weekly*, 43 (9), 7 March 2007.

In the name of 'inclusive growth', what India is encountering today is private capital-led 'development terrorism'. Neoliberalism aims to achieve growth not by pursuing the old policy of promoting a Pareto superior position for every social class but by emphasising on growth that would exclude the people in the margin from the growth process itself. This is being achieved by terrorising the poor and underprivileged who are systematically being robbed of whatever means they had. As A. Bhaduri describes:

> massive land grab by large corporations is going on in various guises, aided and abetted by the land acquisition policies of both the federal and state governments. Destruction of livelihoods and displacement of the poor in the name of industrialization, big dams for power generation and irrigation, corporatisation of agriculture despite farmer's suicides, and modernization and beautification of our cities by demolishing slums are showing everyday how development can turn perverse.[57]

Jharkhand is now a stronghold of the Maoists. In the era of so-called 'inclusive growth', in Jharkhand there are:

> periodic reports of starvation deaths from Palamau, Santhal Parganas and Kolhan, the tardy implementation of Supreme Court orders on mid-day meals to school children, the absence of basic infrastructure of schools, primary health centres and anganwardis; and the increasing repression against people, which was manifested in the large number of POTA cases that were filed even against minors and seniors citizens.[58]

In the era of neoliberalism, when the state is not bothered with the issue of finding 'equilibrium of compromise', there have developed two Indias:

> The India that shines with its fancy apartments and houses in rich neighborhoods, corporate houses of breathtaking size, glittering shopping malls, and hi-tech flyovers over which flows a procession of new model cars. These are the images from a globalised India on the verge of entering the first world. And then there is the

---

[57] A. Bhaduri, 'Development or Development Terrorism?', *Economic and Political Weekly*, 42 (7), 17–23 February 2007, p. 552.
[58] Nandini Sundar, 'Laws, Policies and Practices in Jharkhand', *Economic and Political Weekly*, 40 (41), 8 October 2005, p. 4461.

other India. The India of helpless peasants committing suicides, dalits lynched regularly in not-so-distant villages, tribals dispossessed of their forest land and livelihood, and children too small to walk properly, yet begging on the streets of shining cities.[59]

In the name of 'inclusive growth', the neoliberals in fact are excluding a vast part of India from the growth process. Consequently, the Republic is losing its authority in these areas. The state cannot rule over these areas by a normal exercise of hegemony (where force does not exceed consent too much). Thus a space has been created where the Maoists can operate by challenging the hegemony of the Indian state itself.

Whether the Maoists can survive depends on a crucial issue, namely, whether they can earn the consent of the people of the 'other India' for a Maoist rule. It is too early to comment on the prospect of a Maoist rule in the 'other India'. One point, however, may be mentioned even at this stage. Unless the Indian state resets its agenda in which achieving 'equilibrium of compromise' reappears, a strong case for a Maoist rule would definitely exist at least in the vast countryside of India.

---

[59] A. Bhaduri, 'Development or Development Terrorism?', p. 552.

Bibliography

Primary Sources

AICC Circular to all PCCs. 1947. AICC (1), File no. G 3 of 1946–47. New Delhi: Nehru Memorial Museum and Library (NMML). 2 February.

AICC Circular to all PCCs and constructive organizations. 1947. AICC (1), G 3 of 1946–47. New Delhi: NMML. 9 July.

AICC Circular to all PCC Secretaries. 1947. AICC (1), File no. PI (Pt. III) of 1946. New Delhi: NMML. 15 April.

'Anil Yadav and Others v. State of Bihar and Others'. 1981 (1). SCC 622.

Bansgopal's letter to Purushottamdas Tandon. 1947. *Purushottamdas Tandon Papers (Correspondence)*. New Delhi: National Archives of India (NAI).

'Chandan Kumar Banik vs. State of West Bengal'. 1995. SUPP 4 SCC 505.

Circular from Provincial Constructive Committee, UP to all DCCs and TCCs. 1947. AICC (I), File no. G 41 (KW I) of 1946. New Delhi: NMML. 20 July.

Confidential note to the working committee. 1948. *Patel Papers (Correspondence)*, 6 December, Microfilm Reel no. 1. New Delhi: NAI.

Constituent Assembly Debates, Official Report. IV(11), pp. 915–56.

'Constructive Workers and their role in Free India'. n.d. *Shankarrao Deo Papers*, Subject File no. 10. New Delhi: NMML.

'Death of 25 Chained Inmates in Asylum Fire in Tamil Nadu v Union of India and others'. 2002. AIR (SC) 979.

'Dr. Upendra Baxi vs. State of Uttar Pradesh'. 1983 (2). SCC 308.

From resolutions passed at the conference of presidents and secretaries of PCCs at Allahabad, 22–24 February. 1947. AICC (1), File no. CPD 1 (Pt. II) of 1947 and File no. G 8 (KW 1) of 1947–48. New Delhi: NMML.

Government of India.1956. *Second Five Year Plan*. New Delhi: Planning Commission.

Government of India. 1995. *Annual Report; Department of Agriculture and Co-operation*. New Delhi: GOI Publication.

Government of West Bengal. 2004. *Human Development Report*. Development and Planning Department.

Govind Sahai's letter to the AICC. 1947. AICC (1), File no. PC 18 (Pt. III) of 1947–48. New Delhi: NMML. 16 October.

IDRC. 2010. 'Democratic Governance, Women's Rights and Gender Equality: Synthesis Report'.

'Indra Sawhney vs. Union of India'. 1992. SUPP 3 SCC 217.

Jawaharlal Nehru's article for Asia magazine. undated [c.1939]. Typescript, copy in *Indian Political Intelligence file, India Office Records*, L/PJ/12/94, f.9. London: British Library.

Jawaharlal Nehru's letter to John Matthai. 1950. *Patel Papers (Correspondence)*. Microfilm Reel no. 9. New Delhi: NAI. 27 June.

Jawaharlal Nehru's letter to Naga National Council. n.d. SWJN II, Vol. 2, p. 604.

Jawaharlal Nehru's letter to Rajendra Prasad. 1948. SWJN II, Vol. 5, pp. 113–23. 22 January.

Jawaharlal Nehru's letter to Vallabhbhai Patel. 1946. SWJN II, Vol. 1. pp. 62–65. 5 November.

Jawaharlal Nehru's message to the All-India Congress Socialist Conference at Meerut. 1936. SWJN, Vol. 7, pp. 60–61. 13 January.

Jawaharlal Nehru's note on the functions of the Prime Minister. 1947. *Patel Papers (Correspondence)*, Microfilm Reel no. 45. New Delhi: NAI. 6 January.

Jawaharlal Nehru's resolutions on Gandhi's Death. 1948. SWJN II, Vol. 5, pp. 37–38. 2 February.

Jawaharlal Nehru's secret note to the working committee. 1947. AICC (I), File no. 71 of 1946–47. New Delhi: NMML. 15 July.

Jawaharlal Nehru's speech at All-India Radio Broadcast. 1948. 'The light has gone out of our lives', SWJN II, Vol. 5, pp. 35–36. 30 January.

Jawaharlal Nehru's speech at Khusrupore. 1946. SWJN II, Vol. 1, p. 55. 4 November.

Jawaharlal Nehru's speech to the Associated Chambers of Commerce, Calcutta. 1947. SWJN II, Vol. 4, pp. 563–64. 15 December.

John Matthai's letter to Jawaharlal Nehru (enclosed with Nehru to Patel, 27 June 1950). 1950. *Patel Papers (Correspondence)*, Microfilm Reel no. 9. New Delhi: NAI. 17 June.

Jugal Kishore's letter to Sampurnanand. 1947. AICC (1), File no. G 6 (Pt. I) of 1947. New Delhi: NMML. 20 June.

'Justice L'Heureux-Dube in Egan v. Canada 1995 (2)'. 2001. S.C.R. 513 at 545 of Pothier.

'Khatri (I) and Others v. State of Bihar'. 1981 (1). SCC 623.

'Khatri (II) and Others v. State of Bihar and Others'. 1981. AIR (SC) 1068.

Kripalani's letter of resignation from the Congress presidency. 1947. AICC (I), File no. G 31 of 1946–47. New Delhi: NMML. 8 April.

Kripalani's letter to either Jawaharlal Nehru or Rajendra Prasad. n.d. AICC (1), File no. ED 7 (Pt. I) of 1947–48. New Delhi: NMML.

Krishna Chandra's letter to G.B. Pant. n.d. *Charan Singh Papers (Second Instalment)*, Subject File no. 262 of 1948–66. New Delhi: NMML.

Mohanlal Saksena's letter to Vallabhbhai Patel. 1950. *Patel Papers (Correspondence)*, 22 July, Microfilm Reel no. 13. New Delhi: NAI.

Mridula Sarabhai's letter to Rajendra Prasad. 1948. *Patel Papers (Correspondence)*, Microfilm Reel no. 4. New Delhi: NAI. 10 December.

Note on the role of the constructive programme. n.d. AICC (1), File no. CPD 2 & 6 of 1947. New Delhi: NMML.

P. Chakraverti's letter to the Secretary, DCC, Etawah. 1947. AICC File no. P 17 (Pt. I) of 1947–48. New Delhi: NMML. 11 December.

Rafi Ahmed Kidwai's press statement (enclosed with Muzaffar Hussain to Rajendra Prasad). 1948. AICC (1), File no. P 17 (Pt. I) of 1947–48. New Delhi: NMML. 28 June.

Rajendra Prasad's letter to Vallabhbhai Patel. 1948. *Patel Papers (Correspondence)*, Microfilm Reel no. 3. New Delhi: NAI. 22 September.

'Rakesh Chandra Narayan vs State of Bihar'. 1989. SUPP 1 SCC 644.

Ramadhar to Jugal Kishore. 1947. AICC (1), File no. CPD 8 of 1947. New Delhi: NMML. 25 August.

Ramadhar to Shankarrao Deo. 1947. AICC (1), File no. CPD 7 of 1947. New Delhi: NMML. 2 December.

Ramadhar to Shankarrao Deo. 1947. AICC (1), File no. CPD 8 of 1947. New Delhi: NMML. 22 August.

Rammanohar Lohia's note on Congress re-organisation. 1946. AICC (1), File no. G 6 (KW 1) of 1947. New Delhi: NMML.

Ramnarayan Singh's open letter to U.N. Dhebar. 1955. AICC (2) File no. G I (3) of 1955. New Delhi: NMML.

Report of Jawaharlal Nehru's talk with Z. A. Ahmad of the Communist Party of India. 1945. New Delhi: P. C. Joshi Archive, Jawaharlal Nehru University. June.

Report on the first meeting of the constructive programme committee held in New Delhi. 1947. AICC (1), File no. CPD 7 of 1947. New Delhi: NMML. 26 April.

Resolution passed at a meeting of the Banaras City Congress Committee. 1947. AICC (I), File no. 35 of 1946–47. New Delhi: NMML. 10 January.

Sadiq Ali's letter to Shankarrao Deo. 1947. AICC(I), G 18 (Pt. II) of 1947–48. New Delhi: NMML. 18 October.

Sampurnanand's letter to Jugal Kishore. 1947. AICC (1), File no. G 6 (Pt. I) of 1947, 6 June, New Delhi: NMML.

Satyanarain Sinha to all members of the Congress party in the Constituent Assembly (Legislative). 1949. *Patel Papers (Correspondence)*, Microfilm Reel no. 13, New Delhi: NAI. 8 March.

SDSA Team. 2008. *State of Democracy in South Asia: A Report*, CSDS. New Delhi: Oxford University Press.

Shankarrao Deo's note on Congress reorganisation (enclosed with note dated 15 January). 1950. *Patel Papers (Correspondence)*, Microfilm Reel no. 2. New Delhi: NAI.

'Sheela Barse vs. Union of India'. 1986 (3), vide order dated 15 April 1986. SCC 632.

Unsigned note. 1947. AICC (1), File no. 6. New Delhi: NMML.

Unsigned note on Congress re-organisation. n.d. AICC(l) File no. G 47 (Pt. I) of 1946. New Delhi: NMML.

Unsigned note on the party and the party system. n.d. AICC(2), Miscellaneous File no. 4008. New Delhi: NMML.

UPPCC Papers. Microfilm Reel no. 2. New Delhi: NMML.

UPPCC to AICC, General Secretary. 1952. AICC (2) File no. PG 40 of 1954. New Delhi: NMML. 22 December.

Vallabhbhai Patel's letter to Phool Singh. 1948. *Patel Papers (Correspondence)*, Microfilm Reel no. 48. New Delhi: NAI. 16 August.

'Veena Sethi vs State of Bihar'. 1983. AIR (SC) 339.

World Bank. 1989. *Poverty, Employment and Social Services*.

Books and Articles

Anonymous. 1934. 'Ourselves', *Congress Socialist*, p. 2. 29 September.

Agamben, Giorgio. (1995) 1998. *Homo Sacer: Sovereign Power and Bare Life*. Stanford: Stanford University Press.

Agnes, Flavia. 1999. *Law and Gender Inequality: The Politics of Women's Rights in India*. New Delhi: Oxford University Press.

Ahluwalia, M. 1977. 'Rural Poverty and Agricultural Performance in India', *Journal of Development Studies*, 13 (3): 298–323.

Ahluwalia, M. S. 2004. 'Understanding India's Reform Trajectory: Past Trends and Future Challenges', *India Review*, 3 (4): 269–77.

Ahuja, R. 1993. *Indian Social System*. New Delhi: Rawat Publications.

Anderson, Benedict. 1983. *Imagined Communities: Reflections on the Origins and Spread of Nationalism*. London: Verso.

Appadurai, Arjun. 1997. *Modernity at Large: Cultural Dimensions of Globalization*. New Delhi: Oxford University Press.

Aravamudan, Gita. 2007. *Disappearing Daughters: The Tragedy of Female Foeticide*. New Delhi: Penguin India.

Athreya, Venkatesh and Sheela Rani Chunkath. 2000. 'Tackling Female Infanticide: Social Mobilisation in Dharmapuri, 1997–99', *Economic and Political Weekly*, p. 4345. 2 December.

Austen, Granville. 1966. *The Indian Constitution: Cornerstone of a Nation*. New Delhi: Oxford University Press.

Bajpai, Kanti. 2000. 'Human Security: Concept and Measurement', Kroc Institute Occasional Paper, No. 19: OP: 1, p. 11. August.

Banerjee, Nirmala. 2002 and 2006. 'Between the Devil and the Deep Sea: Shrinking Options for Women in Contemporary India', in Karin Kapadia (ed.), *The Violence of Development: The Politics of Identity, Gender & Social Inequalities in India*, pp. 52–54, 57. New Delhi: Kali for Women/Zubaan.

Banerjee, Paula. 2003. 'Aliens in the Colonial World', in Ranabir Samaddar (ed.), *Refugees and the State — Practices of Asylum and Care in India, 1947–2000*, pp. 69–105. New Delhi: Sage Publications.

Bardhan, P. 2000. 'The Political Economy of Reform in India', in Z. Hasan (ed.), *Politics and the State in India*, pp.158–74. New Delhi: Sage Publications.

———. 2002. 'Decentralisation of Governance and Development', *Journal of Economic Perspectives*, 16 (4): 185–205.

———. 2005. 'Nature of Opposition to Economic Reforms in India', *Economic and Political Weekly*, XL (26): 4995–4998.

Bardhan P. and D. Mukherjee. 2004. 'Poverty Alleviation Efforts of Panchayats in West Bengal', *Economic and Political Weekly*, pp. 965–74. 28 February.

Baruah, Sanjib. 2004. *Between South and Southeast Asia: Northeast India and the Look East Policy*. Guwahati: CENESEAS.

Basu, Durgadas. 1955. *Commentary on the Constitution of India*. Kolkata: S. C. Sarkar and Sons.

Belsey, Timothy. S. Narayanan and K. Murthy. 2007. 'Panchayats in Four Southern Indian States', *Economic and Political Weekly*, pp. 45–57. 5 June.

Belsey, Timothy, Rohini Pande, and Vijayendra Rao. 2007. 'Political Economy of Panchayats in South India', *Economic and Political Weekly*. 24 February.

Beteille, A. 1991. 'Caste, Class and Power', in Dipankar Gupta (ed.), *Social Stratification*. New Delhi: Oxford University Press.

Bhaduri, A. 2007. 'Development or Development Terrorism?', *Economic and Political Weekly*, 42 (7): 552–53. 17–23 February.

Bhaduri, A. and D. Nayyar. 1996. *The Intelligent Person's Guide to Liberalization*. New Delhi: Penguin Books India.

Bhattacharyya, S. 2003. 'Caste, Class and Politics in West Bengal', *Economic and Political Weekly*, 38 (3). 18 January.

Borradori, Giovanna. 2003. *Philosophy in a Time of Terror — Dialogues with Jurgen Habermas and Jacques Derrida*. Chicago: University of Chicago Press.

Brosius, C. 2010. India's Middle Class: New Forms of Urban Leisure, Consumption and Prosperity. New Delhi: Routledge.

Brown, Wendy. 2006. *Regulating Aversion: Tolerance in the Age of Identity and Aversion*. Princeton and Oxford: Princeton University Press.

Chandhoke, N. 2005. '"Seeing" the State in India', *Economic and Political Weekly*, XL (11): 1033–1039.

Chatterjee, Partha. 1993. *The Nation and its Fragments: Colonial and Post-colonial Histories*. Princeton: Princeton University Press.

——. 1994. 'Development Planning and the Indian State', in Terence J. Byres (ed.), *The State and Development Planning in India*, pp. 51–72. New Delhi: Oxford University Press.

——. 1998. 'Development Planning and the Indian State', in idem (ed.), *State and Politics in India*, pp. 271–97. New Delhi: Oxford University Press.

——. 2000. 'Development Planning and the Indian State', in Z. Hasan (ed.), *Politics and the State in India*, pp. 115–42. New Delhi: Sage Publications.

——. 2008. 'Democracy and Economic Transformation in India', *Economic and Political Weekly*, 43 (16): 53–62. 19 April.

Chattopadhyay, Raghabendra. 1985. 'The Idea of Planning in India, 1930–1951', unpublished PhD dissertation. Canberra: Australian National University.

Chaudhuri, Pramit. 1978. *The Indian Economy: Poverty and Development*. New Delhi: Vikas.

Chaudhury, Anasua Basu Ray. 2000. *Energy Crisis and Subregional Cooperation in South Asia*. Colombo: Regional Centre for Strategic Studies.

Chhibber, P. and S. Eldersveld. 2000. 'Local Elites and Popular Support for Economic Reform in China and India', *Comparative Political Studies*, 33 (3): 350–73.

Chunkath, Sheela Rani and V. B. Athreya. 1997. 'Female Infanticide in Tamil Nadu: Some Evidence', *Economic and Political Weekly*, 32 (17). April. 3. http://www.cwds.ac.in/Library/collection/elib/sex_selection/ss_female_infanticide.pdf. Accessed 20 January 2010 and13 April 2001.

Connolly, William E. 1996. 'Suffering, Justice and the Politics of Becoming', *Culture, Medicine and Psychiatry*, 20: 251–77.

Das, Samir Kumar. 1988. 'On the Politics of Globalization: Managing Ethnicity in Northeastern India', in G. Das and R. Purkayastha (eds), *Liberalization and India's Northeast*. New Delhi: Commonwealth.

——. 2002. 'Extraordinary Partition and its Impact on Ethnic Militant Politics of Assam', in Girin Phukon (ed.), *Ethnicity and Polity in South Asia*. New Delhi: South Asian Publishers.

Das Gupta, Malabika. 2002. *The Economic Impact of Militancy on the Economy of the Jhumias of the Northeast: A Study of Tripura*, mimeo.

Dasgupta, Subhendu. 1996. *'Adhikarer tattwa nirman: Ekti khasra'* (Constructing a theory of rights: A draft), *Aneek*, 32 (8 & 9): 32–35. February–March.

Davey, B. 1975. The Economic Development of India: A Marxist Analysis. Nottingham: Spokesman Books.

De, Prabir and Buddhadeb Ghosh. 2003. *Infrastructure, Income and Regional Economic Development with Special Reference to Northeastern States: An Approach to Understand the Indo–Bangladesh Border Trade*, mimeo.

Derrida, Jacques. 2005. *Rogues — Two Essays on Reason*. Trans. Pascale-Anne Brault and Michael Naas. California: Stanford University Press.

Desai, A. R. (ed.). 2006. *Rural Sociology in India*. Mumbai: Popular Prakashan.

Deschouwer, K. 2006. 'Political Parties as Multi-Level Organizations', in R. S. Katz and W. Crotty (eds), *Handbook of Party Politics*. London: Sage Publications.

Deshpande, S. 2003. *Contemporary India: A Sociological View*. New Delhi: Penguin Books India.

deSouza, Peter Ronald, Suhas Palshikar, and Yogendra Yadav. 2008. 'Surveying South Asia', *Journal of Democracy*, 19 (1): 84–96. Baltimore, Maryland: The Johns Hopkins University Press. January.

Despres, Leo A. 1975. 'Toward a Theory of Ethnic Phenomenon', in Leo A. Despres (ed.), *Ethnicity and Resource Competition in Plural Societies*, p. 199. The Hague: Mouton Publishers.

Dhanagare, D. N. 1983. *Peasant Movements in India 1920–1950*. New Delhi: Oxford University Press.

Dhanda, Amita, 2000. *Legal Order and Mental Disorder*. New Delhi and Thousand Oaks: Sage Publications.

Draper, Hal. 1977. *Karl Marx's Theory of Revolution*, vol. 1. New York: Monthly Review Press.

Dreze, Jean and Reetika Khera. 2000. 'Crime, Gender, and Society in India: Insights from Homicide Data', *Population and Development Review*, 26 (2): 345–46. 2 June. http://www.jstor.org/stable/172520. Accessed 16 November 2009.

Elwin, Verrier. 1959. *A Philosophy for NEFA*. Shillong: North East Frontier Agency.

Engineer, A. A. 2004. 'Communal Darkness in Shining India', *Economic and Political Weekly*, 39 (9): 886.

Fernandes, L. 2007. *India's New Middle Class: Democratic Politics in an Era of Economic Reforms*. New Delhi: Oxford University Press.

Fernandes, L. and P. Heller. 2006. 'Hegemonic Aspirations: New Middle Class Politics and India's Democracy in Comparative Perspective', *Critical Asian Studies*, 38 (4): 495–522.

Floyd, Rita. 2007. 'Human Security and the Copenhagen School's Securitization Approach: Conceptualizing Human Security as a Securitizing Move', *Human Security Journal*, 5: 40. Winter.

Foucault, Michel. 1994. 'Governmentality', in James Faubion (ed.), *Essential Works of Michel Foucault, 1954–1984*, vol. 3, pp. 201–22. Trans. Robert Hurley. London: The Penguin Press.

Frankel, Francine. 1978. *India's Political Economy, 1947–1977: The Gradual Revolution*. Princeton: Princeton University Press.

Frankel, W. 1971. *India's Green Revolution: Economic Growth and Political Costs*. Berkeley: California University Press.

Geetha, V. 2007. *Patriarchy, Theorizing Feminism Series*. Kolkata: Stree.

Gellner, Ernest. 1983. *Nations and Nationalism*. Oxford: Blackwell.

———. 1983. 'Nations and Nationalism', in Eric Hobsbawm and Terence Ranger (eds), *The Invention of Tradition*.Cambridge: Cambridge University Press.

Gopal, S. (ed.). 1975 and 1984. *Selected Works of Jawaharlal Nehru*, Second Series. New Delhi: Nehru Memorial Fund.

Gramsci, A. 1971. *Prison Notebook*. London: Fontana.

Gramsci, A. 2004. *Selections from the Prison Notebooks*. Ed. and trans. Q. Hoare and G. Smith. New Delhi: Orient Longman.

Grapevine, Rebecca. 2007. 'The State and Home in Early Independent India: The Hindu Marriage Act', unpublished paper presented at the conference 'Beyond Independence'. London: Royal Holloway College, University of London. 11–12 April.

Grare, Frederic and Amitabh Mattoo (eds.). 2003. *India and ASEAN: The Politics of India's Look East Policy*. New Delhi: Manohar.

Hanstad, T., T. Haque and R. Neilson, R. 2008. 'Improving Land Access for India's Rural Poor', *Economic and Political Weekly*, 43 (10): 43–47. 8–14 March.

Hameed, Syeda S. 2005. 'Sexual Abuse in Revenge: Women as Targets of Communal Hatred', in Kalpana Kannabiran (ed.), *The Violence of Normal Times*, pp. 312–31. New Delhi: Women Unlimited.

Hardin, Russell. 1996. *Communities and Development: Autarkic Social Groups and the Economy*, mimeo.

Harrison, Selig. 1960. *India: The Most Dangerous Decades*. Madras: Oxford University Press.

Harriss, J. 2010. 'Class and Politics', in N. G. Jayal and P. B. Mehta (eds), *The Oxford Companion to Politics in India*, pp. 139–53. New Delhi: Oxford University Press.

Hasan, Z. 2010. 'Political Parties', in N. G. Jayal and P. B. Mehta (eds), *The Oxford Companion to Politics in India*. New Delhi: Oxford University Press.

Haq, Mahbub ul. 1994. *New Imperatives of Human Security, RGICS Paper No. 17*, p. 1. New Delhi: Rajiv Gandhi Institute for Contemporary Studies (RGICS), Rajiv Gandhi Foundation.

Heath, O. 2005. 'Party Systems, Political Cleavages and Electoral Volatility in India: State-wise Analysis 1998–1999', *Electoral Studies*, 24 (2): 177–99.

Heller, Patrick. 2000. 'Degrees of Democracy: Some Comparative Lessons from India', *World Politics*, 52, pp. 484–519. July.

Hobsbawm, Eric and Terence Ranger (eds). 1983. *The Invention of Tradition*. Cambridge: Cambridge University Press.

Hudson, Valerie M. and Andrea Den Boer. 2002. 'A Surplus of Men, a Deficit of Peace', *International Security*, 26 (4): 5, 11. Spring.

Hunter, Ian. 2010. 'The Man and the Citizen: the Pluralisation of Civil Personae in Early Modern German Natural Law', in Anna Yeatman and Magdalena Zolkos (eds), *State, Security and Subject Formation*, pp. 16–35. New York: Continuum.

Iralu, Kaka. 2002. 'Is Underdevelopment the Cause of Insurgency in Nagaland?', in C. Joshua Thomas and Gurudas Das (eds), *Dimensions of Development in Nagaland*, p. 19. New Delhi: Regency.

Issac, T. N. Thomas. 2000. *Local Democracy and Development*. New Delhi: Leftword Books.

Jaffrelot, C. 2003. *India's Silent Revolution: The Rise of Low Castes in North Indian Politics*. Delhi: Permanent Black.

Jalal, Ayesha. 1995. *Democracy and Authoritarianism in South Asia*. Cambridge: Cambridge University Press.

Jayal, N. G. 2001a. Democracy and the State: Welfare, Secularism and Development in Contemporary India. New Delhi: Oxford University Press.

———. 2001b. 'Reinventing the State: The Emergence of Alternative Models of Governance in India in the 1990s', in N. G. Jayal and S. Pai (eds), *Democratic Governance in India: Challenges of Poverty, Development, and Identity*, pp. 132–50. New Delhi: Sage Publications.

Jenkins, R. 1999. *Democratic Politics and Economic Reforms in India*. Cambridge: Cambridge University Press.

Joll, James. 1977. *Gramsci*. London: Fontana.

Joshi, P. C. 1970. 'Land Reforms in India and Pakistan', *Economic and Political Weekly*. December.

Junker, Detlef. 1996. 'Preface', in Hartmut Lehmann and Melvin Richter (eds), 'The Meaning of Historical Terms and Concepts: New Studies on *Begriffsgeschichte*', German Historical Institute Occasional Paper, No. 15, p. 6. Washington, DC.

Kannabiran, Kalpana. 2005. 'Introduction', in idem (ed.), *The Violence of Normal Times*, p. 3. New Delhi: Women Unlimited.

Kapadia, Karin. 2002/2006. 'Translocal Modernities and Transformations of Gender and Caste', in Karin Kapadia (ed.), *The Violence of Development: The Politics of Identity, Gender & Social Inequalities in India*. New Delhi: Kali for Women/Zubaan, pp. 142–82.

Kaviraj, S. 1989. 'A Critique of the Passive Revolution', *Economic and Political Weekly*, XXIII (45–47): 2429–2444.

Kazi, Seema. 2010. *Democratic Governance and Women's Rights in South Asia*. Ottawa: International Development Research Centre.

Keith, Lois. (1994) 1995. 'Tomorrow I'm Going to Rewrite the English Language', in idem (ed.), *Mustn't Grumble: Writing by Disabled Women*, p. 57. London: The Women's Press.

Khaitan, Tarunabh. 2008. 'Beyond Reasonableness — A Rigorous Standard of Review for Article 15 Infringement', *Journal of the Indian Law Institute*, 50 (2):177–208. April–June.

———. 2009. 'Reading Swaraj into Article 15: A New Deal for All Minorities', *NUJS Law Review*, 2 (3): 419–31. July–September.

Khilnani, S. 1997. *Idea of India*. New Delhi: Penguin Books India.

Kochanek, Stanley A. 1968. *The Congress Party of India: The Dynamics of One-party Democracy*. New Jersey: Princeton University Press.

———. 1987. 'Briefcase Politics in India', *Asian Survey*, XXVII (12): 1278–1301.

Kohli, Atul. 1989. 'Politics of Economic Liberalization in India', *World Development*, 17 (3): 305–28.

———. 2001. 'Political Change in a Democratic Developing Country', in Niraja Gopal Jayal (ed.), *Democracy in India*, p. 129. New Delhi: Oxford India Paperbacks.

———. 2006. 'Politics of Economic Growth in India, 1980–2005; Part 1: The 1980s and Part 11: The 1990s and Beyond', *Economic and Political Weekly* 41 (13 and 14): 1251–1259, 1361–1370.

———. 2009. 'What are You Calling a 'Historic Mandate?', edit page, *The Indian Express*. 19 May.

Koselleck, Reinhart. 1967. '*Richtlinien für das Lexicon politisch-sozialer Begriffe der Neuzeit*', in *Archiv für Begriffsgeschichte*, pp. 81–99. Bonn: Bouvier Verlag H. Grundmann

———. 1972. 'Introduction', in Otto Brunner, Werner Conze, and Reinhart Koselleck (eds), *Geschictliche Grundbegriffe: Historisches Lexicon zur politisch-sozialen Sprache in Deutschland*, vol. 1. Stuttgart: Klett.

———. 1979. '*Begriffsgeschichte und Sozialgeschichte*', in idem, *Vergangene Zukunft*, pp. 107–29. Frankfurt a.m: Suhrkamp.

———. 1985. '*Begriffsgeschichte* and Social History', in idem, *Futures Past*, pp. 73–91. Trans. Keith Tribe. Cambridge, MA: MIT Press.

Krishnamurthy, J. and G. Raveendran. 2008. *Measures of Labour Force Participation and Utilisation*. Delhi: National Commission for Enterprise in the Unorganised Sector.

Kumar, Ashutosh. 2008. 'Dissonance between Economic Reforms and Democracy', *Economic and Political Weekly*, 43 (1): 54–60.

———. 2009a. 'Rethinking State Politics in India: Regions within Regions', *Economic and Political Weekly*, 44 (19): 14–19.

———. 2009b. 'Disconnect Between Economic Reforms and Electoral Democracy: Explaining Why Indian Political Parties Do What They Do', *Journal of Asian and African Studies*, 44 (6): 719–39.

Kumar, R. 2006. 'Winds of Change across India and the Shaping of a New Polity', *Journal of South Asian Studies*, XXIX (1). April.

Kumar, S. 2004. 'Impact of Economic Reforms on Indian Electorate', *Economic and Political Weekly*, 39 (16): 1621–1630.

———. 2009. 'Patterns of Political Participation: Trends and Perspective', *Economic and Political Weekly*, 44 (39): 47–51.

Lenin, V. I. 1977. *Development of Capitalism in Russia*. Firebird Publications.

Lorenzen, David. 1999. 'Who Invented Hinduism?', *Comparative Studies in Society and History*, 41 (4): 630–59. October.

Low, D. A. 1997. *Britain and Indian Nationalism: The Imprint of Ambiguity, 1929–1942*. Cambridge: Cambridge University Press.

Madden, Frederick and D. K. Fieldhouse (eds). 1982. *Oxford and the Idea of Commonwealth*. London: Croon Helm.

Mainwaring, Scott and Timothy R. Scully. 2008. 'Latin America: Eight Lessons for Governance', *Journal of Democracy*, 19 (3): 116–20. July.

Malayiva, K. 1969. 'Agrarian India', in A. R. Desai (ed.), *Rural Sociology in India*. Bombay: Popular Prakashan.

Manela, Erez. 2007. *The Wilsonian Moment: Self-Determination and the International Origins of Anticolonial Nationalism*. Oxford: Oxford University Press.

Mao, Tse-Tung. 1965. *Chinese Revolution and Chinese Communist Party*. Foreign Languages Press.

Maxwell, Neville. 1970. *India's China War*. London: Cape.

Mayer, Arno. 1936. *An Autobiography*. London: Jonathan Cape.

———. (1959) 1963. *Wilson vs Lenin: Political Origins of the New Diplomacy 1917–1918*. New Haven: Yale University Press.

Menon, Ritu and Kamala Bhasin. 2001. 'Her Body and Her Being: Of Widows and Abducted Women in Post-Partition India', in Margaret Jolly and Kalpana Ram (eds), *Borders of Being: Citizenship, Fertility and Sexuality in Asia and the Pacific*, pp. 58–81. Ann Arbor: University of Michigan Press.

Mohapatra, B. 2010. 'Minorities and Politics', in N. G. Jayal and P. B. Mehta (eds), *The Oxford Companion to Politics in India*, pp. 219–37. New Delhi: Oxford University Press.

Mooij, J. (ed.). 2005. *The Politics of Economic Reforms in India*. New Delhi: Sage Publications.

Nair, Deepak. 2006. 'Economic Growth in Independent India: Lumbering Elephant or Running Tiger?', *Economic and Political Weekly*, 41 (15): 1451. 15–21 April.

Nanda, R. 1981. 'PUCL Bulletin'. November. http://www.pucl.org/from-archives/81nov/jails.htm. Accessed 17 August 2011.

Nossiter, T. J. 1982. *Communism in Kerala*. New Delhi: Oxford University Press.

Nayyar, D. 2001. 'Economic Development and Political Democracy: Interaction of Economics and Politics in Independent India', in N. G. Jayal (ed.), *Democracy in India*, pp. 362–96. New Delhi: Oxford University Press.

Nehru, Jawaharlal. 1946. *The Discovery of India*. London: Signet.

Nussbaum, Martha. 2003. 'Gender and Governance: An Introduction', in Martha Nussbaum, Amrita Basu, Yasmin Tambiah and Niraja Gopal Jayal (eds), *Essays on Gender and Governance*, pp. 6–10. Human Development Resource Centre, UNDP.

———. 2006. *Frontiers of Justice: Disability, Nationality, Species Membership*. New Delhi: Oxford University Press.

Oldenburg, Veena Talwar. 2002. *Dowry Murder: The Imperial Origins of a Cultural Crime*. Oxford: Oxford University Press.

Omvedt, Gail. 2004. *Ambedkar: Towards an Enlightened India*. New Delhi: Penguin Books India.

Oomman, T. K. 2007. 'Kerala's Social Sector under Neo-liberalism', *Economic and Political Weekly*, 43 (9). 7 March.

Palishkar, Suhas. 2004. 'Revisiting State Level Parties', *Economic and Political Weekly*, 39 (14), 1497–1508. 3–10 April.

———. 2009. 'Tentative Emergence of a New and Tentative Coalition?', *Economic and Political Weekly*, XLIV (21): 8–10.

Park, Richard L. 1949. 'Labor and Politics in India', *Far Eastern Survey*, pp. 181–87. 10 August.

Phillips, Anne. 2007. *Multiculturalism without Culture*. Princeton: Princeton University Press.

Rajagopalan, Swarna. 2005. 'Women and Security: In Search of a New Paradigm', in Farah Faizal and Swarna Rajagopalan (eds), *Women, Security, South Asia: A Clearing in the Thicket*, pp. 11–88, New Delhi: Sage Publications.

———. 2005. 'Research, Policy, Reality: Women, Security, South Asia', in *Sustainable Development: Bridging the Research/Policy Gaps in Southern Contexts, Vol. 2: Social Policy*, pp. 80–97. Oxford: Oxford University Press, Sustainable Development Policy Institute. http://www.swarnar.com/sdc03.pdf. Accessed 23 August 2011.

Rao, M. V. Ramana. 1959. *A Short History of the Indian National Congress*. New Delhi: S. Chand.

Rawal, V. 2008. 'Ownership Holdings of Land in Rural India: Putting the Record Straight', *Economic and Political Weekly*, 43 (10): 43–47. 8–14 March.

Rudolph, L. I. and S. Rudolph. 1987. *In Pursuit of Lakshmi: The Political Economy of the Indian State*. Chicago: University of Chicago Press.

Roy, Srirupa. 2007. *Beyond Belief: India and the Politics of Postcolonial Nationalism*. Durham: Duke University Press.

Russell, Bertrand. 1963. *Unarmed Victory*. Harmondsworth: Penguin.

Sachs, J. D., A. Varshney and N. Bajpayee (eds). 2000. *India in the Era of Economic Reforms*. New Delhi: Oxford University Press.

Saldanha, D. 1988. 'Antonio Gramsci and the Analysis of Class Consciousness', *Economic and Political Weekly*, XXIII (5): PE 12–16.

Samaddar, Ranabir. 2004. 'Colonial Constitutionalism', *Bayan: Constitutional Evolution*, II: 13–28. July.

Sanghvi, V. 2005. 'Two Indias', *Seminar*. 1 February.

Sanyal, K. K. 1988. 'Accumulation, Poverty and State in Third World', *Economic and Political Weekly*, XXIII (5): PE 27–30.

Schmitt, Carl. (1922) (1934) 1985. *Political Theology*. Chicago: University of Chicago Press.

Sen, Amartya. 1992. 'Missing Women', *British Medical Journal*, No. 304: 587–88.

———. 2003. 'Missing Women—Revisited: Reduction in Female Mortality has been Counterbalanced by Sex Selective Abortions', *British Medical Journal*, 327: 1297–1298. December.

Sen, Amiya P. (ed.). 2003. *Social and Religious Reform: The Hindus of British India*. New Delhi: Oxford University Press.

Sen, Suhit K. 1998. 'The Transitional State: Congress and Government in U.P., c.1946–'57', unpublished PhD dissertation. London: School of Oriental and African Studies, University of London.

Sengupta, Nitish and Arindam Banik. 1997. *Regional Trade and Investment in Developing Countries: The Case of SAARC*, mimeo.

Sharma, Arvind. 2002. 'On Hindu, Hindustan, Hinduism and Hindutva', *Numen*, 49: 1–36.

Shastri, Sandeep. 2001. 'Citizen in Political Institutions and Processes in India: A Study of the Impact of Regional, Social and Economic Factors', unpublished paper. Stellenbosch, South Africa: World Values Survey Conference. 17–21 November. http://www.worldvaluessurvey.org/wvs/articles/folder_published/conference_66. Accessed 20 August 2010.

Shastri, S., K. C. Suri, and Y. Yadav. 2009a. *Electoral Politics in Indian States: Lok Sabha Elections in 2004 and Beyond*. New Delhi: Oxford University Press.

———. 2009b. 'The Democracy Barometers: Surveying South Asia', *Journal of Democracy*, 19 (1).

Singh, K. S. (ed.). 1989. *Jawaharlal Nehru, Tribes and Tribal Policy*. Kolkata: Anthropological Survey of India.

Singh, M. P. 2001. 'India's National Front and United Front Coalition Governments: A Phase in Federalized Governance', *Asian Survey*, 41 (2): 328–50.

Sinha, A. 2005. *The Regional Roots of Development Politics in India: A Divided Leviathan*. Bloomington: Indiana University Press.

Smith, A. D. 1995. *Nations and Nationalism in a Global Era*. Cambidge: Polity Press.

———. 2004. 'History and National Destiny: Responses and Clarifications', *Nations and Nationalism* 10 (1–2): 195–209.

Som, Reba. 1994. 'Jawaharlal Nehru and the Hindu Code Bill: A Victory of Symbol over Substance?' *Modern Asian Studies*, 28 (1): 165–94.

Sridhar, V. 2004. 'The Neo-liberal Consensus', *Frontline*. 23 April.

Sridharan, E. 2004. 'The Growth and Sectoral Composition of India's Middle Class: Its Impact on the Politics of Economic Liberalization', *India Review*, 3 (4): 415–20.

———. 2006. 'Parties, the Party System and Collective Action for State Funding of Elections: A Comparative Perspective on Possible Options', in P. R. de Souza and E. Sridharan (eds), *India's Political Parties*, pp. 311–40. New Delhi: Sage Publications.

Srinivasan, Sharada. 2001. 'Gender Bias in Child Mortality', *Economic and Political Weekly*, p. 4768. 22 December.

Srinivasan, Sharada and Arjun S. Bedi. 2009. 'Girl Child Protection Scheme in Tamil Nadu: An Appraisal', *Economic and Political Weekly*, XLIV (48): 11–12. 28 November.

Stietencron, Heinrich von. 1989. 'Hinduism: On the Proper Use of a Descriptive Term', in Günther D. Sontheimer and Hermann Kulke (eds), *Hinduism Reconsidered*, pp. 11–27. New Delhi: Manohar.

Sundar N. 2005. 'Laws, Policies and Practices in Jharkhand', *Economic and Political Weekly*, 40 (41): 4439–4442. 8 October.

Suri, K. C. 2009. 'The Economy and Voting in the 15th Lok Sabha Elections', *Economic and Political Weekly*, 44 (39): 64–70.

Swaminathan, Padmini. 2002/2006. 'The Violence of Gender-biased Development: Going Beyond Social and Demographic Indicators', in Karin Kapadia (ed.), *The Violence of Development: The Politics of Identity, Gender & Social Inequalities in India*, pp. 69–141. New Delhi: Kali for Women/Zubaan.

Tambiah, Yasmin (ed.). 2002. *Women & Governance in South Asia: Re-imagining the State*. Colombo: International Centre for Ethnic Studies.

tenBroeck, Jacobus. 1966. 'The Right to Live in the World: The Disabled and the Law of Torts', *California Law Review*. http://heinonline.org. Accessed 3 April 2010.

Tharoor, Shashi. 2005. 'Who is this Middle Class', *The Hindu*. 22 May. Thorner, D. 1956. *The Agrarian Prospect of India*. Mumbai: Asia Publishing House.

Thorner, D. and A. Thorner. 1962. *Land and Labour in India*. London: Asia Publishing House.

Tully, James (ed.). 1988. *Meaning and Context: Quentin Skinner and His Critics*. Cambridge: Cambridge University Press.

Vaidyanathan, A. 1982. 'The Indian Economy since Independence (1947–70)', in Dharam Kumar (ed.), *Cambridge Economic History of India*, vol. II. Cambridge: Cambridge University Press.

van der Veer, Peter. 1994. *Religious Nationalism: Hindus and Muslims in India*. Berkeley: University of California Press.

Varma, P. 2000. *The Great Indian Middle Class*. New Delhi: Viking.

Varshney, A. 2000. 'Mass Politics or Elite Politics: India's Economic Reforms in Comparative Perspective', in J. D. Sachs, A. Varshney, and N. Bajpai (eds), *India in the Era of Economic Reforms*. New Delhi: Oxford University Press.

Varshney, A. 2007. 'India's Democratic Challenge', *Foreign Affairs*, 86 (2): 93–106.

Vasanthi, N. 2007. 'Disability and Labour Laws in India, *Supreme Court Journal*, 1: 40–46. Venkatesan, V. 1999. 'Party Finance: Chequered Relations', *Frontline*, 16 (16). 31 July–31 August. http://www.hindu.com/fline/fl1616/16160100.htm. Accessed on 20 August 2010.

Vyasuhu, V. 2004. 'Transformation in Governance since 1990s: Some Reflections', *Economic and Political Weekly*. 5 June.

Weber, Max. 1991. '*Politik als Beruf*', lecture, Munich University, 1918. 'Politics as a Vocation', in H. H. Gerth and C. Wright Mills (eds and trans.), *From Max Weber: Essays in Sociology* (new edn), pp. 77–128. London: Routledge.

Weber, Samuel. 2005. 'The Principle of Representation — Carl Schmitt's Roman Catholicism and Political Form', in idem, *Targets of Opportunity — On the Militarisation of Thinking*, p. 39. New York: Fordham University Press.

Yadav, Y. 1999. 'Electoral Politics in the Time of Change: India's Third Electoral System, 1989–99', *Economic and Political Weekly*, XXXIV (34–35): 2393–2399.

——. 2000. 'Understanding the Second Democratic Upsurge: Trends of Bahujan Participation in Electoral Politics in the 1990s', in F. Frankel, Z. Hasan, R. Bhargava, and B. Arora (eds), *Transforming India: Social and Political Dynamics of Democracy*, pp.121–45. New Delhi: Oxford University Press.

Yadav, Y. and S. Palshikar. 2009. 'Revisiting "Third Electoral System": Mapping Electoral Trends in India, 2004–2009', in S. Shastri, K. C. Suri, and Y. Yadav (eds), *Electoral Politics in Indian States: Lok Sabha Elections in 2004 and Beyond*, pp. 393–429. New Delhi: Oxford University Press.

Zachariah, Benjamin. 2004. *Nehru*. London: Routledge.

——. 2004. 'In Search of the "Indigenous": JC Kumarappa and the Philosophy of the Village Movement', in Michael Mann and Harald Fischer-Tine (eds), *Colonialism as Civilising Mission*, pp. 248–69. London: Anthem Press.

——. 2005. *Developing India: an Intellectual and Social History, c. 1930–1950*. New Delhi: Oxford University Press.

Zaidi and Zaidi, 1981. *Encyclopaedia of the Indian National Congress*, vol. xiii, *1946–50, India Wins Freedom*. New Delhi.

Website Sources

Anonymous. 2004. 'Positive Bias for Girls', *The Hindu*. 24 January. http://www.thehindu.com/2009/01/24/stories/2009012454430700.htm. Accessed 20 March 2010.

Australian Bureau of Statistics. 'Australian Population Clock'. http://www.abs.gov.au/. Accessed 1 September 2010.

Bakunin, Mikhail. 1874. 'Statism and Anarchy'. http://www.marxists.org/reference/archive/bakunin/works/1873/statism-anarchy.htm. Accessed 23 August 2011.

Bedi, Arjun. 2008. 'Bare Branches and Drifting Kites: Tackling Female Infanticide and Feticide in India', *ISS Public Lecture Series 2008*, No. 5, p. 26. The Hague, Netherlands. 16 October. http://campus.iss.nl/~bedi/inaugural_Bedi.pdf. Accessed 10 March 2010.

Benjamin, Judy A. and Lynn Murchison. 2004. 'Gender-Based Violence: Care & Protection of Children in Emergencies: A Field Guide', *Save the Children*, p. 3. http://www.savethechildren.org/publications/technical-resources/emergenciesprotection/Gender_Based_Violence_Final.pdf. Accessed 30 November 2011.

Bharatiya Janata Party website. http://www.bjp.org/. Accessed 23 August 2011.

Campaign against Sex Selective Abortion. 2007. 'Position Note on Cradle Baby Scheme', May. http://cassa.in/pdf/Position%20paper%20on%20% 20Cradle%20baby%20scheme%20English.doc. Accessed 4 January 2010.

Chaitanya Guide 3. 2005. 'Imrana's Gauntlet', August. http://www. chaitanyaconsult.in/chaitanya/guide/cg3gauntlet.htm. Accessed 23 August 2011.

Commission on Human Security. 2003. 'Human Security Now'. http://www. humansecurity-chs.org/finalreport/English/chapter1.pdf, p. 4. Accessed 3 January 2010.

Communist Party of India. www.cpindia.org/. Accessed 30 November 2011.

Communist Party of India (Marxist). www.cpim.org/. Accessed 23 August 2011.

George, Sabu M. 'Female Infanticide in Tamil Nadu, India: From Recognition to Denial?' http://www.hsph.harvard.edu/Organizations/healthnet/SAsia/ suchana/0225/george.html. Accessed 4 April 2001.

Gurung, Madhu. 1999. 'Female Foeticide', pp. 13–14. http://www.cwds. ac.in/Library/.../elib/foeticide/fo_female_foeticide.pdf. Accessed 25 September 2010.

Heyzer, Noeleen. 2002. 'Globalization and Democratic Governance: A Gender Perspective', *Background Paper for 4th Global Forum on Reinventing Government*. unpan1.un.org/intradoc/groups/public/documents/un/ unpan006228.pdf. Accessed 10 October 2010.

Info Change Women. 2003. 'New Report Shows Rise in Dowry Cases in India's Progressive States. 2 August. http://infochangeindia.org/200309062894/ Women/News/New-report-shows-rise-in-dowry-cases-in-India-s-progressive-states.html. Accessed 26 September 2010.

Inahara, Minae. 2009. 'This Body which is Not One: The Body, Femininity and Disability', *Body & Society*, 15 (1): 47–62. http://bod.sagepub.com/ cgi/content/abstract/15/1/47. Accessed 12 March 2010.

Jagori. 2009. 'Marching Together ... Resisting Dowry in India', p. 3. July. http://www.jagori.org/wp-content/uploads/2009/07/dowry_infopack. pdf. Accessed 22 August 2010 and 26 September 2010.

Jeeva, M. Gandhimathi and Phavalam. 1998. 'Female Infanticide: Philosophy, Perspective and Concern of SIRD', *Search Bulletin*, 13 (3). July–September. http://www.cwds.ac.in/Library/collection/elib/sex_selection/ ss_female_infanticide_philosophy.pdf. Accessed February 2010.

Kannan, Amutha. 2009. 'NCC Cadets Join Hands to Fight Female Infanticide', *The Hindu*. 31 August. http://www.hindu.com/edu/2009/08/31/stories/ 2009083150470200.htm. Accessed 13 October 2010.

Kannan, Ramya. 2003. 'SHG Launches Aggressive Campaign against Infanticide', *The Hindu*. 7 December. http://www.hindu.com/2003/12/07/ stories/2003120705190100.htm. Accessed 13 October 2010.

Lenin, V. I. 1918. 'The State and Revolution'. http://www.marxists.org/ archive/lenin/works/1917/staterev/. Accessed 23 August 2011.

———. 1920. 'Draft Theses on National and the Colonial Questions'. http:// marxists.org/archive/lenin/works/1920/jun/05.htm. Accessed 23 August 2011.

'Lok Sabha Elections 2009: Manifesto of the Indian National Congress'. http://www.aicc.org.in/new/manifesto.doc. Accessed 23 August 2011.

Mazumdar, Vina. 1994. 'Amniocentesis and Sex Selection, Centre for Women's Development Studies', Occasional Paper, pp. 12–14. http://www.cwds.ac.in/OCPaper/AmniocentesisVM.pdf. Accessed 26 September 2010.

Morrison, Andrew R. and Maria Beatriz Orlando. 2004. 'The Costs and Impacts of Gender-based Violence in Developing Countries: Methodological Considerations and New Evidence', Working Paper 36151, pp. 7, 28. World Bank. November. http://siteresources.worldbank.org/INTGENDER/Resources/costsandimpactsofgbv.pdf. Accessed 25 September 2010.

National Coalition against Domestic Violence. 2007. 'Factsheet on Domestic Violence'. http://www.ncadv.org/files/DomesticViolenceFactSheet%28National%29.pdf. Accessed 2 September 2010.

National Family Health Survey 3. 2006. 'Chapter 15: Domestic Violence', pp. 499, 512. http://www.nfhsindia.org/NFHS-3%20Data/VOL-1/Chapter%2015%20-%20Domestic%20Violence%20(468K).pdf. Accessed 24 September 2010.

Office of the Register General & Census Commissioner, India. 'Census of India, India at a Glance: Population'. http://www.censusindia.gov.in/Census_Data_2001/India_at_glance/popu1.aspx. Accessed 1 September 2010.

Oslo Governance Centre, UNDP. 2007. 'Human Rights and the MDGs: Making the Link', p. 11. http://www.hurilink.org/Primer-HR-MDGs.pdf. Accessed 3 April 2010.

'Population—Country Comparison', *Index Mundi*. http://www.indexmundi.com/g/r.aspx. Accessed 1 September 2010.

Rajagopalan, Swarna. 2004. 'Conceptualizing Security, Securing Women', 'National Seminar on Challenges to Peace and Security in South Asia: Emerging Trends'. Chennai: Department of Defence Studies, University of Madras. http://www.swarnar.com/securingwomen0204.pdf. Accessed 15 September 2010.

——. 2010. 'Violence against Women and Security', *InfoChange India*. November. http://infochangeindia.org/Governance/Security-for-All/Violence-against-women-and-security.html. Accessed 24 September 2010.

Sinha, A. 2005. 'Understanding the Rise and Transformation of Business Collective Action in India', *Business and Politics*, 7 (2): 1–35. http://www.bepress.com/bap. Accessed 30 November 2011.

Sivaraman, Mythily. 2001. 'Female Infanticide—Who Bears the Cross?', *People's Democracy*, XXV (25). 24 June. http://pd.cpim.org/2001/june24/june24_infanticide.htm. Accessed 7 January 2010.

Sridhar, Lalitha. 2004. 'Treating Infanticide as Homicide is Inhuman', *InfoChange News & Features*. August. http://infochangeindia.org/20040817165/Women/Features/-Treating-infanticide-as-homicide-is-inhuman.html. Accessed 7 January 2010.

Srinivas, M. N. 1957. 'Presidential Address at Indian Science Congress'. www.jstor.org. Accessed 30 November 2011.

Swaminathan, Mina, A. Mangai and S. Raja Samuel. 1998. 'Confronting Discrimination: Some Approaches to the Issue of Female Infanticide', *Search Bulletin*, 13 (3): 64–74. July–September. http://www.hsph.harvard.edu/Organizations/healthnet/SAsia/suchana/0110/swaminathan_etc.html. Accessed 13 April 2001.

Tamil Nadu Peoples' Forum for Social Development. 'Social Development in Tamil Nadu — Serious Concerns' — A Peoples' Memorandum to the Govt. of Tamil Nadu on the State Budget 2000–2001. http://www.swtn.org/publications/social_development_in_tamilnadu%e2%80%93serious_ concerns_2001.pdf. Accessed 30 November 2011.

Tamil Nadu State Government to the State Planning Commission. 2005. 'Human Development and Health', presentation by Health Secretary. 18–19 May. http://www.tn.gov.in/spc/workshop/6-HD%20and%20Health-SEC.PPT. Accessed 15 March 2010.

tenBroek, Jacobus. 1966. 'The Right to Live in the World: The Disabled and the Law of Torts', 54 Cal. L. Rev. 841. http://heinonline.org. Accessed 3 April 2010.

'The Human Rights Based Approach to Development Cooperation towards a Common Understanding Among the UN Agencies'. http://www.crin.org/docs/resources/publications/hrbap/HR_common_understanding.doc. Accessed 23 August 2011.

'The Human Rights-Based Approach'. http://www.unfpa.org/rights/approaches.htm. Accessed 30 November 2011.

UNDP. 1990. 'Defining and Measuring Human Development', *Human Development Report*, p. 10. http://hdr.undp.org/en/media/hdr_1990_en_chap1.pdf. Accessed 10 February 2010.

———. 1994. 'New Dimensions of Human Security', *Human Development Report*, pp. 22–24. http://hdr.undp.org/en/media/hdr_1994_en_chap2.pdf. Accessed 10 February 2010.

———. 1997. '"Preface," Reconceptualising Governance', Discussion Paper 2, p. x. New York: Management Development and Governance Division, Bureau for Policy and Programme Support. January. http://mirror.undp.org/magnet/Docs/!UN98-21.PDF/!RECONCE.PTU/!front.pdf. Accessed 10 October 2010.

———. 2002. 'Deepening Democracy in a Fragmented World', *Human Development Report*, pp. 51, 61. http://hdr.undp.org/en/media/HDR_2002_EN_Complete.pdf. Accessed 4 April 2010.

———. 2010. 'A Guide to UNDP Democratic Governance Practice', pp. 14–16. http://content.undp.org/go/cms-service/download/publication/?version=live&id=2551865. Accessed 10 October 2010.

UNICEF. 2005a. 'Early Marriage: A Harmful Traditional Practice', p. 22. http://www.unicef.org/publications/files/Early_Marriage_12.lo.pdf. Accessed 1 September 2010.

———. 2005b. 'Table 7: Child Marriage, Domestic Violence and Choice of Partner, Early Marriage: A Harmful Traditional Practice', p. 40. http://www.unicef.org/publications/files/Early_Marriage_12.lo.pdf. Accessed 1 September 2010.

UNICEF Innocenti Research Centre. 2000. 'Domestic Violence against Women and Girls', *Innocenti Digest*, no. 6: 12. June. http://www.unicefirc.org/publications/pdf/digest6e.pdf. Accessed 2 September 2010.

Vinoj Kumar, P. C. 2008. 'Where do Rejected Little Girls Go ...', *Tehelka Magazine*, 5 (12). 29 March. http://www.tehelka.com/story_main38.asp?filename = Ne290308where_rejected.asp. Accessed 4 January 2010.

Warrier, Shobha. 1999. 'Again a Girl! Are You Not Ashamed of Yourself?', 'The Rediff Special: A Special Report on Female Infanticide', Rediff.com. 8 March. http://www.rediff.com/news/1999/mar/08woman.htm. Accessed 4 April 2001.

———. 1999. 'The Girls Take an Oath that they Will Not be Involved in Female Infanticide either Directly or Indirectly', interview with Andal Damodaran, 'The Rediff Special: A Special Report on Female Infanticide', Rediff.com. 8 March. http://www.rediff.com/news/1999/mar/08woman2.htm. Accessed 4 April 2001.

World Bank. 1992. 'Governance and Development', p. 1. http://books.google.co.in/books?id = he3MVQqsqwC&printsec = frontcover&dq = World + Bank + (1992) + Governance + and + Development.&source = bl&ots = rUCYG Rwjvc&sig = 69AX0VGnryckTU7vArkU7VpRbE&hl = en&ei = bVqxTLPF LcXJcYSumYYH&sa = X&oi = book_result&ct = result&resnum = 8&ved = 0CC0Q6AEwBw#v = onepage&q = World%20Bank%20(1992)%20Governa nce%20and%20Development.&f = false. Accessed 10 October 2010.

World Values Survey on the World's Most Comprehensive Investigation of Political and Sociocultural Change. http://www.world-valuessurvey.org. Accessed 30 November 2011.

'Writ Petition No 1537 of 1984, Bombay'. www.cehat.org/humanrights/caselaws.pdf. Accessed 3 December 2008.

Yadav, Y. 2009. 'Why Manifestos Matter', *The Hindu*, Edit Page. 8 April. http://blogs.thehindu.com/elections2009/. Accessed 30 November 2011.

About the Editors

Ranabir Samaddar is founder of the Calcutta Research Group (CRG) and its journal, *Refugee Watch*, and subsequently the founder-director of the Peace Studies Programme at the South Asia Forum for Human Rights, Kathmandu. Known for his critical studies on contemporary issues of justice, human rights, and popular democracy in the context of post-colonial nationalism, trans-border migration, community history, and technological restructuring in South Asia, he has served on various commissions and study groups on issues such as partitions, critical dictionary on globalisation, patterns of forced displacement and the institutional practices of refugee care and protection in India, rights of the minorities and forms of autonomy, technological modernisation, and occupational health and safety. His recently published study of dialogues as part of war and peace politics, titled *The Politics of Dialogue* (2004), is a product of his four-year research on war and peace in South Asia. Prior to that he completed a three-volume study of Indian nationalism, the final one titled *A Biography of the Indian Nation, 1947–1997* (2001). Besides being the editor of three well-known volumes on issues of identity and rights in contemporary politics, *Refugees and the State* (2003), *Space, Territory, and the State* (2002), and *Reflections on Partition in the East* (1997), he is also the editor-in-chief of the *South Asian Peace Studies Series*. He is currently working on themes related to the materiality of politics.

Suhit K. Sen completed his doctoral dissertation in 1998 on the transition of India from a colonial to constitutional regime. He was a journalist for 10 years before returning to academics, first as Fellow at the Centre for Studies in Social Sciences, Kolkata and currently as Senior Researcher, Calcutta Research Group, Kolkata. He has published several articles in the *Economic and Political Weekly*.

Notes on Contributors

Kalpana Kannabiran is Chairperson of the Chityala Ailamma Centre for Interdisciplinary Research, set up by Asmita Resource Centre for Women.

Ratan Khasnabis is Professor, Department of Business Management, Calcutta University.

Ashutosh Kumar is Reader, Indian Politics, Department of Political Science, Punjab University, Chandigarh.

Swarna Rajagopalan is an independent Chennai-based scholar working as a writer and consultant. She is founder of Prajnya Initiatives.

Benjamin Zachariah is Reader, South Asian History, University of Sheffield.

Index